Prosperity, Depression and the New Deal THIRD EDITION

access to history

Prosperity, Depression and the New Deal THIRD EDITION

Peter Clements

Hodder Murray

A MEMBER OF THE HODDER HEADLINE GROUP

The Publishers would like to thank the following for permission to reproduce copyright illustrations: © Bettman/Corbis, pages 3, 14, 23, 67, 77, 88, 91, 96, 134, 150, 159, 162; © Corbis, page 34, 40, 61, 85, 103, 129, 199; Getty Images, page 39; Library of Congress, Prints and Photographs Division, FSA-OWI Collection, (LC-USF33-002972-M3), page 194; New York Daily News, page 178; Ohio Historical Society, page 9; Popperfoto, page 54; Tennessee Valley Authority, page 124; Westerville Public Library, page 30.

The Publishers would like to thank the following for permission to reproduce copyright material: Addison Wesley for an extract from *The American Nation* by J.A. Garraty (1991), used on page 64; AQA material is reproduced by permission of the Assessment and Qualification Alliance, used on page 187; Batsford Books for an extract from *USA the Twenties to Vietnam* by D. Snowman, used on page 61; Edexcel Limited for extracts used on pages 28–9, 112, 141, 207; Harper Collins for an extract from *A History of the American People* by P. Johnson (2000), used on page 63; Harper Collins for an extract from *The American Nation*, Vol. 2 by J.A. Garraty (1999), used on page 163; Heinemann for extracts from *The USA 1917–45* by D. and S. Willoughby (2000), used on page 28; Longman for an extract from *The Longman History of the USA* by H. Brogan (1999), used on page 112; W.W. Norton & Co for extracts from *The Anxious Decades* by M. Parish, used on pages 31, 81; Oxford, Cambridge and RSA (OCR) examinations for extracts used on pages 31, 32, 142, 171, 188, 209; Pantheon Books (Random House) for extracts from *Hard Times* by S. Terkel (1970), used on pages 80, 81; Penguin for an extract from *The Penguin History of the United States of America* by H. Brogan (1985), used on page 63; Perennial Classics for extracts from *Only Yesterday* by F.L. Allen (2000), used on pages 27, 80; Time-Life for an extract from *This Fabulous Century 1920–30*, Vol. 3 (1969), used on page 80.

Every effort has been made to trace all copyright holders, but if any have been inadvertently overlooked the Publishers will be pleased to make the necessary arrangements at the first opportunity.

Although every effort has been made to ensure that website addresses are correct at time of going to press, Hodder Murray cannot be held responsible for the content of any website mentioned in this book. It is sometimes possible to find a relocated web page by typing in the address of the home page for a website in the URL window of your browser.

Orders: please contact Bookpoint Ltd, 130 Milton Park, Abingdon, Oxon OX14 4SB. Telephone: (44) 01235 827720. Fax: (44) 01235 400454. Lines are open 9.00–5.00, Monday to Saturday, with a 24-hour message answering service. Visit our website at www.hoddereducation.co.uk

© Peter Clements 2005
Third edition published in 2005 by
Hodder Murray, an imprint of Hodder Education,
a member of the Hodder Headline Group
338 Euston Road
London NW1 3BH

Impression number   10 9 8 7 6 5 4 3
Year   2010 2009 2008 2007 2006

Cover photo shows poster by Vera Block, *Work Pays America* © Corbis
Typeset in Baskerville 10/12pt and produced by Gray Publishing, Tunbridge Wells
Printed in Malta

A catalogue record for this title is available from the British Library

ISBN-10: 0 340 88897 0
ISBN-13: 978 0 340 88897 1

Contents

Dedication

Keith Randell (1943–2002)

The *Access to History* series was conceived and developed by Keith, who created a series to 'cater for students as they are, not as we might wish them to be'. He leaves a living legacy of a series that for over 20 years has provided a trusted, stimulating and well-loved accompaniment to post-16 study. Our aim with these new editions is to continue to offer students the best possible support for their studies.

1

A Changing Nation

POINTS TO CONSIDER

This chapter is intended as an introduction to the study of the USA between 1917 and 1945. It is divided into three main sections:

• An historical background
• An outline of the political system of the USA
• An evaluation of why the role of government had grown in the years prior to the 1920s

You should read this chapter as an introduction and background to the period covered by the book.

Key dates
1917   Entry of USA into First World War
1918   Sedition Act

Introduction

In late October 1929, the New York Stock Exchange crashed. Thousands of people lost all the savings they had invested in stocks and shares. Thousands of businesses collapsed. This shocked many people because they believed the economy was doing very well at the time. It was the era of the 'Roaring Twenties', a period of unparalleled prosperity in American history. It was the age of jazz, movies, motor cars and fast living. Now a terrible economic depression had set in, with millions out of work, optimism gone, hope forlorn.

In 1932, Americans voted Franklin Delano Roosevelt to be their president. He offered new hope with a 'New Deal'. For the first time, the government would make itself responsible for people's welfare – it would create jobs, offer old-age pensions and social security. To many, Roosevelt was a saviour; others saw him as a dictator who increased the role of government to an unacceptable level.

This book covers the interwar period of American history. It will examine the 1920s to see if the decade really was one of fun and optimism, and consider whether the prosperity was real. It will discuss the causes and effects of the collapse of the stock market and the part this played in ushering in the Depression. Life during the Depression will be explored and the efforts made to restore prosperity. Finally, it will examine the New Deal in depth, what it was and what changes it brought about in the USA.

1 | Historical Background

The USA in the nineteenth century

Key question
How had the USA developed by 1920?

The history of the USA is relatively recent. Following their independence from Great Britain in 1783, Americans began to settle their new continent with amazing speed. By the mid-nineteenth century they had gained all the lands south of Canada and north of Mexico between the Atlantic and Pacific Oceans. This was achieved largely through purchase and warfare.

The vast land mass was 3,022,000 square miles in contrast with 94,525 square miles of the United Kingdom. It was settled so quickly that by 1890 the Census declared there was no longer any undeveloped territory available for settlement. Many of the people we shall meet in this book had spent at least the earliest part of their careers in the nineteenth century and still largely held on to its values.

The entire history of the USA until 1920 had happened in the space of 140 years. There was little time for the development of tradition as in Europe. The USA was a vast melting pot, where the individual was thought to be of supreme importance and a continent was there to be settled. The fact that it was settled so quickly and the country developed so rapidly led many people to believe in 'the American dream' – that with hard work and initiative one could achieve anything without expecting much help from the government.

The American people

The USA was a land rich in raw materials, fertile for crops and populated by an energetic, dynamic people who were, in the main, descended from immigrants. The nineteenth century had seen the biggest migration in history. Millions left the 'old world' of Europe and Asia and headed to America where they hoped to find work, land and freedom from persecution.

The USA was also originally made up of immigrants who had arrived not willingly, but often forcibly as slaves from Africa. The Civil War had torn the Union apart in the years 1861 to 1865. It had ended slavery but not the persecution of African-Americans. The North had grown wealthy from industrial development, while the South had remained predominantly rural. The West was populated in mythology by pioneers who had tamed a wilderness largely by their own efforts. It had developed as a region of fierce independence with little toleration of government interference.

Economic wealth

The USA had an economic structure in which people were free to make money with very little government interference. Industries grew wealthy partly because of three factors:

Westward the Course of Empire Takes its Way (1886).
This picture has helped create the myth of the way Americans moved West and settled the continent. Notice how one of the first buildings in the new town is a school. The picture also shows locomotives, covered wagons and the vast open spaces still to be settled.

- the relative abundance and cheapness of natural resources
- the availability of cheap, often immigrant labour
- the overwhelming demand in a continent developing so quickly.

Huge industrial concerns grew up in the great cities; but small-scale industry also thrived.

2 | The Political System

The USA has a **federal system of government**. This means there is both a federal (or central) government situated in Washington DC and also a series of state governments. The USA literally is a union of states, with each cherishing its own rights and customs. There were originally 13 states, but as the continent was settled, others were added. Today there are 50 and, in the period covered by this book, 48, with Alaska and Hawaii being subsequently added in 1959. Most states had voluntarily given up some of their own powers to the federal government in Washington. However, they jealously guarded those they kept and were wary of any excessive federal government interference.

The USA is a **republic**, with three arms of federal government: (1) the **Executive**, (2) the Legislature and (3) the Judiciary.

(1) The Executive

The president heads the Executive (or policy-making) branch. He is elected every four years through a complex voting system. Technically speaking, the electorate does not vote directly for the president. There is both a popular vote and electoral college vote in each state. Those who have been chosen to sit in the electoral college cast all their votes for the candidate who has won a majority in the popular vote in that state.

Key question
How is the USA governed?

Key terms

Federal system of government
Where there is both a central system of government and state governments – each state having its own powers that are not subject to interference from central government.

Republic
Country led by a president rather than a monarch.

Executive
The branch of government that makes policy.

The president is responsible for seeing that the laws are carried out. Traditionally he would ask Congress (the law-making body) to draft legislation he favoured. Only very rarely would the president draft laws himself. As we shall see, Roosevelt broke with this tradition during the New Deal years of the 1930s and increasingly produced his own legislation for the approval of Congress. The president has always appointed a Cabinet to help him govern. However, the number of presidential staff grew significantly during the New Deal years as the Executive took a far more active role in the running of the country. In 1939 the Executive Office of the President was created as a reflection of the huge growth of responsibilities accepted by the Executive (see pages 168–9).

(2) The Legislature

Congress is the **Legislature** in the USA. It has the job of framing the laws. It is divided into two houses: the House of Representatives and the Senate. Both houses need to agree a law before it is passed.

Legislature
The branch of government that passes laws.

Key term

The House of Representatives

This is composed of congressmen directly elected and representing the people of the USA. In particular it has the task of raising revenue.

The Senate

This is composed of 100 senators (during the period covered by this book, 96), two representing each state. The Senate has the power to agree or reject presidential appointments. It may, if necessary, impeach or seek to remove the president or any of his officers.

(3) The Judiciary

The Judiciary is the courts and judges. At the highest level, its job is to make sure that the president or Congress do not exceed the authority granted to them by the Constitution. If the Judiciary declare laws unconstitutional (i.e. illegal under the terms of the Constitution), they cannot be passed.

At the head of the Judiciary is the Supreme Court. It is made up of nine senior judges (called justices) appointed by the president. Their job is to ensure laws are actually legal and follow the principles of the constitution. Below the Supreme Court there is a network of federal courts spread throughout the country.

The Constitution

The Constitution was originally written by the 'Founding Fathers', the men who created the United States in the late eighteenth century. It clearly sets out the different roles of the different branches of government, in addition to defining the responsibilities of state governments and outlining individual rights. It was designed to set up a series of 'checks and balances' so that no one branch of government could become too powerful. Additions have been made over time by amendment, but basically the USA is still governed on the lines set out by the framers of the Constitution in the eighteenth century.

Growth of political parties

Key question
What are the main political parties in the USA and what did they stand for in the period covered by this book?

One thing the framers of the Constitution did not anticipate was the growth of political parties. The main parties in the USA over the course of the twentieth century have been the Republicans and Democrats.

In the period covered by this book, the Republicans tended to favour wealth, business and a reduced government role. The Democrats, on the other hand, tended to have a wider base of support and favoured more government involvement, for example in social issues. Democrats began to find favour increasingly with minority ethnic groups, the less well-off and urban dwellers. The Republicans, on the other hand, carried rural areas and small towns, particularly in the West. However, in the South, they were seen as the party who freed the slaves after the Civil War. During Roosevelt's period in office there was a significant realignment in political support, with African-Americans in particular turning to his party, the Democrats.

Limits on the president's power

When the majority in either or both houses in Congress is of a different party to the president, he can find it very difficult to govern effectively. He may have to administer laws he disagrees with. Often he cannot get Congress to pass laws he wants. The president does have the power to **veto** or say no to laws he disagrees with. However, if both houses agree by a two-thirds majority, they can override his veto.

Key terms

Veto
The president's refusal to pass laws he disagrees with.

Progressivism
Movement to expand the role of government in dealing with economic and social problems.

The Supreme Court, too, can smother the legislative programme of the administration by declaring laws unconstitutional. This became a huge problem for Roosevelt during the New Deal years. Many felt he was taking too much power from the other branches of government, and the Supreme Court was to declare much of the New Deal legislation unconstitutional.

The New Deal overall saw a huge growth in the business of all branches of government and an important issue considered in this book is how far the political system of the USA was changed as a result of it.

3 | The Growth of Government

Key question
How did progressivism and involvement in the First World War lead to the growth of government?

The New Deal apart, the first decades of the twentieth century saw a considerable growth in the role of federal government. This was due mainly to two developments: (1) **progressivism** and (2) the entry of the USA into the First World War.

(1) Progressivism

By the turn of the century many Americans were concerned with four major problems. These were:

- corruption in government
- social problems such as overcrowding in poor urban areas
- social ills such as drunkenness and immorality
- the power of big business to dominate the economy.

For example, large companies called corporations often combined together to form '**trusts**' that could control the market in their field. They did this by cutting costs of production, setting prices, fixing profits and ensuring others could not compete with them on equal terms.

The governments of Presidents T.R. Roosevelt, Taft and Wilson were known as 'progressive' because they tried to expand their role to address these problems with positive action. In fact, their achievements were relatively disappointing. Despite legislation, they failed in particular to block the power of the giant trusts.

Trusts
Large companies that got together to control manufacture, supplies and prices to ensure others could not compete, and therefore guarantee maximum profits for themselves.

Key term

(2) The entry of the USA into the First World War

The entry of the USA into the war in April 1917 had far-reaching effects on the role of federal government. For example, 33 per cent of the total cost of the war was raised by taxation – in 1918, the highest level of income tax was 77 per cent compared with seven per cent in 1913.

In spring 1918, Congress gave President Wilson almost dictatorial powers over the political and economic life of the nation. Over 500 agencies were set up to control and direct the war effort. In 1918 the Sedition Act made it illegal to criticise the USA. People who protested about its involvement in the war were sent to prison.

After the war was over, many Americans wanted to see the government dismantle these controls, cut taxes and also to stop getting involved in European affairs.

Entry of USA into the First World War: 1917

Sedition Act: 1918

Key dates

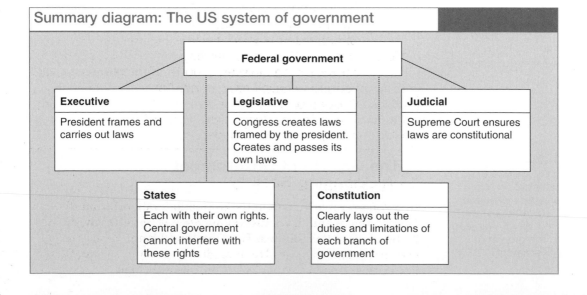

Summary diagram: The US system of government

- Federal government
  - Executive: President frames and carries out laws
  - Legislative: Congress creates laws framed by the president. Creates and passes its own laws
  - Judicial: Supreme Court ensures laws are constitutional
  - States: Each with their own rights. Central government cannot interfere with these rights
  - Constitution: Clearly lays out the duties and limitations of each branch of government

2 Problems and Tensions in the USA 1917–28

POINTS TO CONSIDER
The 1920s was a period of great changes in American life.
The chapter is divided into three main themes:

- Changes in society
- The presidency of Warren Harding 1920–3
- The tensions within society as a result of the changes
  that were taking place:
  - the movement to towns and cities
  - the problems caused by Prohibition
  - a religious and moral backlash in the face of 'sinful
    behaviour', particularly in cities
  - immigration laws and racism

Key dates

1917	Lever Act
1919	Eighteenth Amendment – introduction of Prohibition
1920	Nineteenth Amendment – gave women the vote
	Palmer Raids
1921	Presidency of Warren Harding
	Budget and Accounting Act
	Emergency Immigration Act
	Sheppard-Towner Act
1923	Death of President Harding
	Ku Klux Klan claimed 5,000,000 members
1924	Johnson-Reed Immigration Act
1925	Scopes or 'Monkey Trial'
1927	Execution of Sacco and Vanzetti
1933	Abolition of Prohibition

1 | A Changing Society

In 1927, an American, Charles Lindbergh, took off from Rooster
Field, Long Island in his tiny plane, *Spirit of St Louis*. Over
33 hours later he landed in Paris, the first man to fly non-stop
over the Atlantic Ocean. He immediately became an American
hero and seemed to symbolise the spirit of the age.

This appeared to be an era of unbounded optimism exemplified by the growth of the cinema; 'fads' such as sitting on top of flagpoles and the card game mah-jong; jazz and new and exciting dance crazes. Boundless opportunities seemed to be available. The USA led the world in terms of popular culture such as music, films and sport. It was a time of great change, of movement from the countryside to towns and cities, of women's liberation, of excitement and glamour. This decade was known as 'the Roaring Twenties'.

There was a darker side, however, to the outwardly carefree, fun-loving society of the 1920s. Issues existed that would show themselves in acts of racism and violence. This chapter examines this time of change and the tensions it generated. For example, giving women the right to vote was one such reform that provoked a range of responses.

Women's suffrage

In 1920, the Nineteenth Amendment gave women the right to vote in federal elections. Fifteen states, for example Wyoming in 1869, had already given women the right to vote in state elections. However, most states had not allowed women this right and before 1920 there had been a long-standing campaign to obtain it. Both the Democratic and Republican parties had already given their support in 1916.

From 1912 to 1920 Alice Paul organised **suffrage** parades in Washington. She had learned from suffragette tactics in Britain. The aim was both maximum publicity and disruption. In 1917 Paul and 96 other suffragists were arrested after picketing the White House and 'disrupting traffic'. They went on hunger strike in prison and were force-fed.

More states meanwhile gave women the vote – for example North Dakota, Ohio and Indiana in 1918. With widespread appreciation of the work women had undertaken during the war, President Wilson had himself come round to agree with women's suffrage.

A resolution to give women the vote was finally passed in both houses in 1918. The Nineteenth Amendment was passed to the cheers of women who sat knitting in the public galleries. The Amendment had to go back to the states for their agreement. Tennessee cast the final 'yes' vote for the necessary majority in August 1920.

Opposition came particularly from the alcohol and textiles trades. Suppliers of alcohol feared correctly that many women would support **Prohibition** (see pages 12–19). Employers in the textiles industries were afraid their largely female workforce would gain more influence over working conditions and pay if they were given the vote.

However, as we shall see in the next chapter, the right to vote did not make much difference to the lives of many women (pages 49–50). Although, on the surface, women seemed more assertive and 'liberated', their opportunities in society remained limited.

Key question
What effect did women's suffrage have on society?

Key date

Nineteenth Amendment passed, giving women the right to vote in federal elections: 1920

Key terms

Suffrage
The right to vote.

Prohibition
Banned the transportation, manufacture and sale of alcoholic beverages.

Indeed, the right to vote could be seen as an example of a major reform that did not, despite appearances, lead to the dramatic changes many people expected.

2 | The Presidency of Warren Harding

The 1920 presidential election campaign focused on the issues of isolationism in foreign affairs (see pages 173–6) and a reduced government role at home. The Republican nominee, Warren Harding, was a compromise candidate. He had won his party's nomination only when it was clear none of the front-runners had enough support to win. To avoid upsetting possible supporters, Harding himself had few policies – except the proposal to '**return to normalcy**'.

These were the political ideas of the nineteenth century, when, except in times of crisis, the Executive was generally weak. His Democrat opponent said much the same things on domestic matters. However, the Democratic Party had been hurt by its support for the League of Nations and the European peace treaties (see pages 174–5). In the event, Harding won the election by 16 million votes to nine million.

Harding and Coolidge

Harding and Calvin Coolidge, his vice-president, were men from small towns who had risen patiently and luckily up the political ladder. For example, Coolidge was a competent but uninspiring governor of Massachusetts who had attracted national fame at a lucky time for him (at the start of the nomination process) by dismissing striking policemen in Boston. By way of contrast,

Key question
What concerns did the 1920 presidential election campaign focus on?

Key term

'**Return to normalcy**'
Harding meant by this a return to minimal government with people being dependent on their own efforts and limited US involvement in foreign affairs.

Key question
What sort of men were President Harding and Vice-President Calvin Coolidge?

Harding knew how to make himself popular with the electorate. He once said, 'I cannot hope to be one of the great presidents but perhaps I may be remembered as one of the best loved'. Here we can see him charming the voters.

Harding, who bore a remarkable resemblance to George Washington, did actually look like what many people thought a president should look like – but he was very aware of his own limitations. 'My God', he once said, 'this is a hell of a place for a man like me'.

Strengths of Harding's presidency

Some historians have recently argued that Harding may have been a rather more effective president in some respects than his reputation suggests.

Harding made some very good appointments – Charles Evans Hughes as Secretary of State, Andrew Mellon as Treasury Secretary and Herbert Hoover as Secretary of Commerce. He had promised to cut government expenditure that had risen from $500 million in 1913 to $5000 million by 1920. In 1921, his government passed the Budget and Accounting Act by which departments had to present their budgets to the president for approval. By 1922, expenditure had fallen to $3373 million. This gave Mellon the opportunity to reduce taxes.

Harding also approved the Sheppard-Towner Maternity Aid Act, which gave **federal aid** to states to develop infant and maternity health programmes and has been seen by some historians as a precedent for later New Deal social legislation (see pages 152–4). As well as this, Harding pressurised US Steel to introduce a basic eight-hour working day.

Harding spoke out against racial segregation in Birmingham, Alabama, heartland of the racist South. However, some cynics have argued that he did this primarily to win the electoral support of northern African-Americans. Indeed, one historian has even claimed that Harding was inducted into the **Ku Klux Klan** in the White House. Certainly he did nothing to oppose the harsh immigration laws.

Weaknesses of Harding's presidency

Many historians still regard Harding as one of the weakest American presidents. He appointed to high office some very dubious characters who later went to prison for corruption.

The biggest scandal concerned Albert Fall, the Secretary of the Interior, whose salary of $12,000 was scarcely compatible with his lavish spending on his New Mexican ranch. It was discovered that Fall was given considerable bribes to offer valuable leases to oil companies to drill at Teapot Dome, Wyoming and Elk Hills, California. Both these sites were federal petrol reserves held in trust for the Navy. Fall had pressurised the Navy Secretary to transfer their administration to the Interior Department. He was fined $10,000 and went to jail for a year.

Harding's administration seemed to achieve comparatively little. But it must be remembered that Harding was, in fact, elected to do little – to reduce the role of federal government and to return the USA to 'normalcy'.

Key question
What were the main strengths and weaknesses of Harding's presidency?

Key terms

Federal aid
Help from the federal government for specific issues.

Ku Klux Klan
In the 1920s this was a racist group advocating white supremacy and adopting tactics of terror to intimidate other groups such as African-Americans and Jews. It was particularly prevalent in the southern and mid-western states.

Key dates

Budget and Accounting Act to make government spending more accountable: 1921

Sheppard-Towner Act: 1921

Assessment of Harding's presidency

Harding was undoubtedly well meaning. However, while he made some sound appointments, he also gave his cronies the chance to line their own pockets. He did try to make government more efficient – as, for example, with the Budget and Accounting Act – and approved programmes of federal aid. However it is difficult to find many other solid achievements in his administration.

Nevertheless, despite his advocating a return to 'normalcy', he was much more than a 'do-nothing' president. At the time, many within Congress were concerned about the level of Executive involvement in legislation. Harding called for an increased federal government role in the social and economic life of the nation. He addressed Congress no less than six times to put pressure on it to agree to issues he felt strongly about. He was no dynamic, reforming president but he had been elected to reduce, not expand, the role of federal government. The very fact that his government achieved as much as it did should be enough to make us reconsider the verdict that Harding was one of the weakest American presidents.

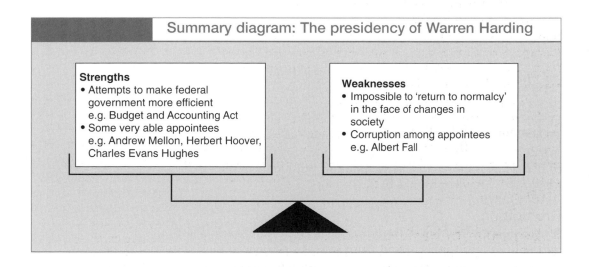

Summary diagram: The presidency of Warren Harding

Strengths
- Attempts to make federal government more efficient e.g. Budget and Accounting Act
- Some very able appointees e.g. Andrew Mellon, Herbert Hoover, Charles Evans Hughes

Weaknesses
- Impossible to 'return to normalcy' in the face of changes in society
- Corruption among appointees e.g. Albert Fall

Key question
What tensions were present in society?

White supremacy
The racist belief that white people are superior to those of other ethnic origins.

3 | Tensions in Society

It may be that, for all his good intentions, Warren Harding was simply not up to the job of president in the face of the huge changes taking place in American society. More people were moving to towns and cities where it was feared behaviour was often immoral. The government introduced Prohibition to try to ban the sale of alcohol. There was a religious reaction to the apparent godlessness of many Americans. The Ku Klux Klan stood for **white supremacy** in the face of immigration and greater tolerance of non-white cultures.

Harding had spoken of a 'return to normalcy'. However, despite the wishes of many Americans, 'normalcy' could not be restored – if it had ever existed in the first place. We often see the past through rose-tinted spectacles, and so while many hoped to return to the days of hardy, God-fearing pioneers, the reality of those times was very different from this image. In any case, even if this view of the past had been true, new conditions in society made such a return impossible.

Ironically, with a comparatively weak Executive at odds with Congress and with widespread corruption, Harding may indeed have recreated a fairly typical nineteenth-century administration. However, this was no longer adequate, if indeed it ever had been, to meet the needs of the USA. The USA was changing; it simply was not possible to turn back the clock. Harding's successor, Coolidge, tried to do the same thing, also without success. Neither understood the tensions that were developing within American society.

Movement to towns and cities

The 1920 census showed more people living in towns than the countryside for the first time in American history – 54 million out of 106 million Americans. However, urban areas were defined as those with a population of only 2500 plus. Moreover, of that 54 million, 16 million still lived in communities of fewer than 25,000 inhabitants. They clung to their rural values such as thrift, hard work and plain living.

Tensions in the 1920s were often, but not always, focused between those who lived in rural and small-town America and those who lived in cities, whose ways were seen as wild and sinful. From 1920 to 1930, numbers of those living in cities of more than 100,000 increased by a third. Many people viewed this growth of urban living as a real threat to what they saw as the American way of life. Their support for the Republican presidents of the 1920s was part of an effort to turn back the clock.

Prohibition

Prohibition illustrates well the contradictions in American society and politics during this period. Supported by those who looked to the government for 'moral regulation' – leading the way to ensure people led clean, wholesome lives – it involved the government interfering in private life to an unprecedented degree.

The Eighteenth Amendment banned the sale, transportation and manufacture of intoxicating liquor within the USA, and the separate Volstead Act defined 'intoxicating liquor' as any drink containing more than half a per cent of alcohol. Responsibility for enforcement was given to the Treasury. The first Prohibition Commissioner charged with implementing the Prohibition laws was John F. Kramer.

Prohibition was supported by a variety of interest groups.

The Eighteenth Amendment: 1919 | Key date

- Many women's groups saw alcohol as a means by which men oppressed them.
- Big business saw drunkenness as leading to danger and inefficiency in the workplace – particularly in large factories.

The Rockefeller Corporation and Heinz were two examples of large companies that supported Prohibition in the interests of greater workforce efficiency.
• Many religious groups believed alcohol was the work of the devil and was overwhelmingly responsible for sin and wrongdoing.

Supporters of Prohibition tended to be overwhelmingly Protestant, live in small towns in the South and West and, except in the South, vote Republican. Opponents were likely to be urban, of non-northern European ethnic origin, Roman Catholic and vote Democrat.

It may seem incredible to us that a nation as large and sophisticated as the USA could even attempt to ban something as commonly available as alcohol. Actually there was surprisingly little opposition to the measure. It had been in fact one of the main policies of the progressive movement (see page 6). There was a widespread belief that alcohol abuse led to social problems that could only be solved by its abolition. By 1917, 27 states had already passed Prohibition laws and there were 'dry' counties where alcohol wasn't allowed in several others. Two factors led to an increased popularity of Prohibition at this time: (1) the impact of war and (2) disorganisation of the opposition.

(1) The impact of war

The First World War gave several boosts to Prohibition. Grain used in the production of alcoholic drinks was needed for food. As a result, many people felt it patriotic to do without alcohol. In 1917 the Lever Act banned the use of grain in the manufacture of alcoholic drinks.

Many of the largest brewers, such as Ruppert, Pabst and Leiber, were of German origin. Their businesses had helped finance the National German–American Alliance that had supported German interests before the war. During the war, anti-German feeling led many not to buy alcohol from these companies.

Many people believed restrained behaviour in which people did not drink alcohol would be part of the 'brave new world' created after the war. It was felt that alcohol led young soldiers, who were away from home for the first time, into temptation and sinful ways – so best to remove it from their grasp.

(2) Disorganisation of the opposition

The forces against Prohibition were not well organised. There was a march and rally in New York City, a parade in Baltimore, and a resolution against taking away the working man's beer by the American Federation of Labor. Other than this, there was little protest.

Key date

Lever Act: 1917

Crime and gangsterism

There is no doubt that Prohibition led to a huge growth in crime and gangsterism. Mobsters controlled territories by force and established monopolies in the manufacture and sale of alcohol. These territories and monopolies were defended violently, as potentially hugely profitable enterprises were involved. John Torrio, for example, ran most of the illegal alcohol business in Chicago and retired in 1925 with savings of $30 million.

Gangsters could control politicians with ease. The Mayor of Chicago, 'Big Bill' Thompson, allowed gangsters to function unmolested in his city. In 1923 Thompson was defeated in the election, following the discovery that $1 million had gone missing from public funds. The new Chicago authorities tried to enforce Prohibition more effectively. Undaunted, the gangsters simply moved their headquarters to the suburb of Cicero Park until they could get their man elected again.

Al Capone, the most notorious of the gangsters and Torrio's chosen successor became something of a media star. He saw himself as embodying the spirit of free competition and enterprise in the USA. In an age when government interfered little in business, he seemed not to understand that what he was doing was wrong. Capone was a fervent Republican despite the fact that – or perhaps because – this was the party of Prohibition, and Prohibition provided him with his vast profits. When Capone finally went to jail in 1932 – for income tax evasion – it was estimated his gang had done some $70 million worth of business. Capone insisted he never forced anyone to enter his '**speakeasies**' or drink his liquor. He felt he was primarily a businessman who supplied what people wanted.

Capone was also a man of violence. Where Torrio had often negotiated with rivals, dividing up areas of the city between them, Capone preferred 'turf wars'. Indeed, it was the introduction of an honest police chief in Chicago who prosecuted gangsters and cut **bootleggers**' profits that led to war between the gangsters as they invaded each other's territory.

Capone built up an army of 700 gangsters who committed over 300 murders in Chicago. On 14 February 1929 five of his men, dressed as policemen 'arrested' seven of the rival 'Bugs Moran' gang and shot over 100 bullets into them. This became known as the 'St Valentine's Day Massacre'.

The failure of Prohibition

The Anti-Saloon League (an organisation which supported Prohibition) estimated a $5 million budget would be enough to enforce it successfully. In the event, Kramer was given $2 million.

Although Kramer insisted his department would ensure alcohol would be neither manufactured nor sold in the USA, Prohibition was to be a classic case of a law being passed that was impossible to enforce. There were seven main reasons for this:

Key question
What problems were caused by Prohibition?

Key terms

'**Speakeasies**'
Illegal clubs where alcohol was sold.

Bootleggers
People who made alcohol illegally to sell.

Key question
Why was Prohibition unsuccessful?

Profile: Al Capone 1899–1947

1899 – born in Brooklyn New York City
1913 – left school
1918 – married Mary 'Mae' Coughlin
1919 – moved to Chicago; went to work for Johnny Torrio
1922 – became Torrio's deputy and partner in 'speakeasies', gambling houses and brothels
1925 – became gang boss after Torrio retired
1926 – arrested for killing three men; spent only one night in jail because of lack of evidence against him
1928 – moved to Florida but kept control of Chicago business
1929 – St Valentine's Day Massacre
1932 – arrested for income tax evasion; imprisoned
1939 – released suffering from syphilis
1947 – died after a stroke

Early career

Capone left school and went to work for Frankie Yale, a New York criminal. While acting as a barman and bouncer in the Harvard Inn, a notorious dive owned by Yale, he got into a fight and received the scars that led some people to call him 'Scarface'. After he murdered two men, Yale sent him to Chicago until things cooled down.

Career in Chicago

Capone went to work for Johnny Torrio, a gang boss who was making a fortune out of Prohibition. Capone made himself indispensable and soon became Torrio's deputy and partner. Officially Capone gave his employment as a second-hand furniture dealer. In 1925, Torrio retired to Italy after being shot. Capone took control of all Torrio's business. Vicious 'turf wars' took place to gain control of more territory.

Capone was very skilled at having rivals killed. Hitmen would rent an apartment near to a victim's house and kill him when he ventured out. Capone was arrested for three murders in 1926 but was released because everyone was afraid to testify against him. Because of attempts on his own life he moved to Florida in 1928. The following year he had seven members of a rival gang killed in the St Valentine's Day Massacre. However, after a lengthy investigation, he was arrested for income tax evasion in 1932. He was sentenced to 11 years' imprisonment.

Later career

Capone served time in Atlanta and Alcatraz prisons. He was a model prisoner and was released early in 1939. However, he was already ill with syphilis. Unable to return to running his businesses, he lived quietly in Palm Island, Florida until his death from a stroke in 1947.

"Tonsilitis!"

Cartoons showing the difficulty of enforcing Prohibition. Americans could still acquire alcohol on prescription and it could be sold legally outside the three-mile limit.

The Volstead Market Day

(1) Geographical difficulties

The USA has 18,700 miles of coastline and land border. Those waters just outside the national limits became known, with good reason, as 'rum row'. Smuggling was so successful that in 1925, the officer in charge of Prohibition enforcement guessed that agents only intercepted about five per cent of alcohol coming into the country illegally. In 1924, they seized $40 million worth of alcohol so the actual volume of business has been estimated as $800 million.

(2) Bootleggers

Chemists could still sell alcohol on doctors' prescriptions. This was naturally open to widespread abuse. Many people known as 'bootleggers' went into business as producers and distributors of illegal alcohol. The 'King of the Bootleggers', George Remus, bought up various breweries on the eve of Prohibition for the manufacture of medicinal alcohol; he then arranged for an army of 3000 gangsters to highjack his products and divert them to the illegal **stills** of the big cities. In five years Remus made $5 million.

(3) Industrial alcohol

Industrial alcohol was easily diverted and re-distilled to turn it into an alcoholic drink. Illegal alcohol was often called '**moonshine**' because it was manufactured in remote areas by the light of the moon. However, it could equally be made in any old buildings. There was, of course, no quality control. The dangers for drinkers can easily be imagined and exotic cocktails were often invented to take away the unpleasant smell and taste of materials intended for industrial manufacture. There is a legend that one sceptical buyer took his bootleg whisky for analysis to a chemist – to be told that his horse had diabetes! Poisoning from wood alcohol (a simple alcohol made from wood spirit or methanol), although not common, did happen during this period. In one instance, 34 people died in New York City.

(4) Problems for Treasury Agents

At the most, 3000 Treasury Agents were employed to enforce Prohibition. They were paid an average salary of $2500 to shut down an illegal industry whose profits were estimated at $2 billion annually. It is no wonder that many were corrupt. One federal agent was said to have made $7 million selling illegal licences and pardons to bootleggers. While agents such as 'Izzy' Einstein and 'Moe' Smith became famous for the ingenuity with which they closed down illegal stills and 'speakeasies', it should be remembered that, between 1920 and 1930, about 10 per cent of Prohibition agents were fined for corruption. It is very likely that many more escaped prosecution.

(5) Popularity of 'speakeasies'

As the 1920s progressed, the mood of the nation changed. For many Americans, particularly those living in the cities, their main aim in life became having a good time. Illegal drinking in

Key terms

Still
Place where illegal alcohol is made.

Moonshine
Illegally manufactured alcoholic drinks.

gangster-run 'speakeasies' became popular venues for many fashionable city dwellers.

(6) Divisions among supporters

Against this, the 'dry' lobby, while very well organised to achieve Prohibition, was ill equipped to help enforce it. The Anti-Saloon League, for example, was bitterly divided. Some members sought stricter enforcement laws, believing the League should actually be given power over appointment of officers. Others who emphasised education programmes to deter people from drinking in the first place.

(7) Role of government

Some historians have argued that Congress did not do more to enforce Prohibition because it did not want to alienate rich and influential voters who enjoyed a drink. In addition, this was a period of a reduced role by federal government and most state governments were, at best, lukewarm in enforcement, particularly where cost was concerned. No one in government seemed to be prepared to say openly that Prohibition could not be enforced because Americans liked to drink alcohol. However, this was nevertheless apparent to many people.

End of Prohibition

In 1928, the Democratic presidential candidate, Al Smith, advocated the abolition of Prohibition. This was an about-turn because he had previously criticised the Republican government for not enforcing it effectively enough. Smith admitted to having served alcohol himself. He also appointed as National Chairman of the Democratic Party John J. Raskob, who was also leader of the Association Against the Prohibition Amendment.

The proposal to abolish Prohibition was too much for many of the Democratic supporters of Prohibition from the rural areas. It had the effect of splitting the party and helped Smith lose the 1928 election. It showed the tensions within a party that was an alliance of urban working classes, different ethnic groups and conservative forces from rural America, particularly in the South.

President Hoover, who did win the election, set up the Wickersham Commission to investigate Prohibition. When it reported after 19 months' deliberation, the findings were that the law could not be enforced – and yet the Commission as a whole favoured a continuation of Prohibition.

It was in fact President Roosevelt who finally abolished the measure in 1933. The Twentieth Amendment made it the responsibility of individual states to decide on the issue. It was an example of federal government cutting its own power rather than an abandonment of Prohibition in total.

Key date
Abolition of national Prohibition: 1933

Prohibition: for and against

By the end of the 1920s, many people questioned whether Prohibition had been worth it. It had certainly led to an explosion in crime. Between 1927 and 1930 alone, there were 227 gangland

Key question
What was successful and unsuccessful about Prohibition?

murders in Chicago with only two killers ever convicted. If Prohibition helped create organised crime, it did not die out with its repeal. The gangs found other areas of vast profit such as gambling, prostitution and, later, drugs. Some argue that had it not been for Prohibition such large criminal gangs would not have developed in the first place.

Moreover, illegal drinking made criminals of a good percentage of the population. Interestingly, it had been the working-class saloons that tended to be shut down; the 'speakeasies' that replaced them tended to sell spirits to a wealthy clientele. In this respect Prohibition worked to the detriment of the poor.

However, support for Prohibition remained in many rural areas. While it could take a stranger less than 20 minutes to find alcohol suppliers in big cities, they were very hard to find where the population did agree with Prohibition.

Supporters argued that alcohol consumption fell from an average of 2.6 gallons per person per year in the years before 1917 to one gallon by the 1930s. Arrests for drunkenness fell, as did deaths from alcoholism. There were fewer drunken drivers, therefore safer roads – indeed with the massive expansion of motor transport in the 1920s (see pages 39–43), this could be a significant factor in road safety. Also there were fewer accidents in the workplace, which was important when considering the increasing automation of industrial production with more complex and potentially dangerous machinery.

While many commentators regard Prohibition as a social catastrophe, it is important to remember that these less-quantifiable factors show that it did have some positive effects.

Summary diagram: Prohibition

Aim
To end manufacture and sale of alcohol for human consumption

↓

Supporters
- Women's groups
- Big business
- Religious groups

↓

Reasons for failure
- Geographical size made enforcement impossible
- 'Bootleggers'
- Easy to redistill industrial alcohol
- Lack of resources for enforcement
- Desires for pleasure among many Americans
- Disagreements among 'dry lobby'

↓

Effects
- Rapid growth in organised crime
- Millions of people became 'law breakers'

4 | Religion and Morality

Many people connected new ideas, particularly those associated with city life, with vice and immorality. There was widespread distrust of cinema, jazz music and its associated dances, particularly the Charleston and the Black Bottom. Women who wore short skirts, smoked in public and frequented 'speakeasies' were regarded as shameless.

There were a series of high-profile scandals, such as that which destroyed the career of 'Fatty' Arbuckle, a very popular comedy star. Arbuckle was accused of a sexual attack in which his victim died. Due in part to these scandals, the movie industry agreed in 1922 to self-censorship through an office run by Will Hays. This examined every movie made in Hollywood for any immoral content and also attempted to promote clean living among movie stars. There was concern with the growth of crime and fear that it might spread into rural and small-town areas.

Key question
How did religious and other moral groups respond to the supposed immorality of the period?

Religious fundamentalism

The concerns about effect of new ideas on morality led to something of a revival in religious belief and **religious fundamentalism**. Popular preachers (called evangelists), such as Billy Sunday, spoke of hellfire and damnation. They were quick to take advantage of both new marketing techniques, such as radio advertising, and old ones, such as mass rallies to win more and more people over to Christianity.

Church figures showed that while fewer people were going to worship, the churches they did go to were actually growing more popular. This was particularly the case in the cities, possibly as a reaction by God-fearing urbanites against the sinfulness of their neighbourhoods. Aimee Semple McPherson, for example, was an evangelist who ran the Angelus Temple in Los Angeles; it had a congregation of 5000 and contained a huge tank in which she could baptise 150 people at a time.

Religious fundamentalism
Involved, among other things, a belief in the literal truth of the Bible and a desire to live one's life according to its teachings.

Key term

The Scopes Trial

The real controversy over religion focused on the Scopes Trial of 1925. Fundamentalists had set up an Anti-Evolution League and six states, including Tennessee, had made it illegal for evolution to be taught in schools. Because evolution appeared to teach that man was descended from apes, this was also known as 'The Monkey Trial'.

John Scopes, a teacher in the small town of Dayton in Tennessee, was persuaded to put the law to the test. He taught evolution, was prosecuted and the ensuing trial became a media event. Prosecuting was the grand old figure of William Jennings Bryan, a former presidential candidate, while Clarence Darrow, one of America's leading liberal lawyers, agreed to lead the defence. During the trial Darrow ridiculed Bryan for his fundamentalist beliefs. The latter admitted to believing that Eve was literally created out of Adam's rib, that the whale swallowed Jonah and that the world was created in 4004 BC. While many

The Scopes Trial concerning the teaching of evolution: 1925

Key date

urbanites found this hilarious, the small-town jury nevertheless found Scopes guilty and he was fined $100.

This case highlighted the difference between small-town beliefs and those of many city dwellers. Many really thought evolution was a wicked doctrine and the story of creation in the Bible was literally true. Many sophisticated urbanites found these beliefs ludicrous.

However, it also led more tolerant Christians to insist there was no conflict necessarily between their beliefs and scientific knowledge, and their voice became louder as the years went on and became more influential. The trial could almost be seen as a battle between the beliefs of the nineteenth century and the twentieth. In the long term those of the twentieth century won, although religious fundamentalism is still important in modern US society.

Immigration laws

Key question
What laws were passed to limit immigration?

Key dates

Emergency Immigration Act: 1921

Johnson-Reed Immigration Act: 1924

In 1921 Congress passed an Emergency Immigration Law. This imposed an annual ceiling on immigration from any European country, limiting it to three per cent of the nationals from that country living in the USA in 1911.

In 1924 this was stiffened by the Johnson-Reed Immigration Act, which banned any immigration from Japan – other Asian groups having been barred earlier. It also set an absolute ceiling of immigration at 150,000 per year, allocated according to the native origins of the existing white population. This favoured those from north-western Europe, as this is was where most of the white population had originally come from. Interestingly, this law did not apply to Mexicans, whom Californian farmers traditionally used as a supply of cheap labour at harvest time.

Racism

Key question
How did racism show itself in the USA?

The USA prided itself on being a land born of immigrants. However, this did not prevent there being laws banning Asians from entry. The truth was that the USA basically welcomed white immigrants, preferably from north-western Europe rather than from non-white areas. The large-scale waves of immigration from southern and eastern Europe in the latter part of the nineteenth and early twentieth centuries led to racist concerns about the survival of the 'Anglo-Saxon' race.

Figures in 1920 showed that 58.5 per cent of the population had native white parents but there was nevertheless considerable racist concern that the 'Anglo-Saxons' were being swamped by 'inferior' races, who bred much more quickly. Racist tracts such as *The Passing of the Great Race* by Madison Grant, published in 1916, became best sellers. There were, in addition, dubious tests that seemed to suggest 'Anglo-Saxons' were superior to other races; these seemed to give support to the ideas promoted by Grant.

During the First World War, for example, the Army began to administer Stanford–Binet intelligence tests to new recruits to identify potential officers. However, most of the questions demanded good knowledge of American history and geography.

Recent immigrants from southern and eastern Europe tended not to have this. The result was that they came out seeming less intelligent than the northern Europeans who tended to have lived in the USA longer and were, therefore, more knowledgeable about its history and geography. Nevertheless, all this was fuel to the racist fire.

The 'Red Scare'

Key question
What was the 'Red Scare' and how did it lead to racist attitudes?

After the First World War, high inflation – in 1920 prices had doubled since 1913 – caused much industrial unrest. It was estimated that during 1919 four million workers went on strike. This was one in five of the labour force. Many people believed that strikers were led by Communists who sought revolution in the USA in the same way that it had been achieved in the USSR. Fears grew as a general strike brought the city of Seattle to a halt and in Boston the policemen were striking. In addition, 340,000 steel workers went on strike. The steel workers' leader, William Z. Foster, was believed to be a Communist.

Recent immigrants from eastern and southern Europe came, in particular, to be identified with Communism and attempts to overthrow the American system of government. There were, in addition, various assassination attempts on high-profile Americans, such as the billionaire John D. Rockefeller. In the period following the First World War and in the wake of the Russian Revolution there was a 'Red Scare' that saw 6000 arrests. These were known as the 'Palmer Raids', named after the then Attorney General, Mitchell Palmer, himself an intended target for assassination. Palmer had become very popular through his exposure of 'Communist activity' in the USA. He hoped he could use this as a springboard for Democratic nomination for the presidency in 1920.

In August 1919, Palmer had created the General Intelligence Division to investigate revolutionary activities. Under its head, J. Edgar Hoover, this became the forerunner of the Federal Bureau of Investigation (FBI) and Mitchell relied heavily on its information for his targets. However, most of those it detained had to be released within a few days due to a complete lack of evidence against them. The '**Palmer Raids**' of January 1920 netted no more than three pistols, while most of the 6000 arrested were long-standing US citizens of impeccable respectability.

Palmer announced there was to be a huge Communist demonstration in New York on 20 May 1920. When this failed to materialise he looked ridiculous and the 'Red Scare' died away – with it went his hopes of nomination for the presidency.

Sacco and Vanzetti

The case of Sacco and Vanzetti, on the other hand, would not go away. They were Italian immigrants, neither of whom spoke English well. When they were arrested, accused of carrying out an armed robbery near Boston in May 1920, they were found to be carrying guns. They also claimed to be **anarchists**. Although there was little concrete evidence against them, Sacco and

Key date
Palmer Raids: 1920

Key terms
Palmer Raids
Mass arrests of suspected revolutionaries.

Anarchists
People who believe in no government, no private ownership and the sharing out of wealth.

Key date

Execution of Sacco and Vanzetti: 1927

Vanzetti were found guilty and eventually executed in 1927 after years of legal appeals.

The case shocked many liberals in the cities, such as the humorist Dorothy Parker, who had vigorously protested the innocence of the two. Even though someone else confessed to the crimes for which they had been found guilty, the sentence remained. There were widespread protests in cities throughout the USA at their execution.

In rural America, there were many who supported the executions. They were ready to believe that cities were filled with 'foreigners' who would not adopt American ways and who were determined to overthrow the American way of life.

The Ku Klux Klan

Key question

What was the Ku Klux Klan and how did it add to racist attitudes?

Racism was widespread, particularly in small towns and rural areas, against African-Americans and other non-white groups. The Ku Klux Klan had flourished in the South in the years following the Civil War, where it had terrorised African-Americans and stopped them from taking part in the political process. It was reborn in 1915 as an organisation to promote white supremacy and gained considerable support in the Midwest as well as the South. Using modern business and salesmanship techniques coupled with more brutal methods, such as telling members to play on whatever prejudices were most common in their particular area, it had attracted 100,000 followers by 1921.

Two of its leaders, Edgar Clark and Elizabeth Tyler, were professional fundraisers and publicity agents. They divided the country into eight 'domains', each under a 'Grand Goblin'. Domains were subdivided into 'realms', each under a 'Grand Dragon', with a bewildering array of minor posts under him –

The Ku Klux Klan showed its strength by a 40,000 strong parade in Washington in 1925.

such as Kludds and Kleagles. Recruits were charged $10, most of which went to local Klan officials, and were paid on a commission basis for signing up further new members.

The robes, which cost $3.28 to make and sold for $6.50, were manufactured by a Klan-owned clothing company, and all printed material was published at vast profit by the Searchlight Publishing Company, again owned by the Klan. It even moved into land sales through the Clark Realtor Company. All in all, the Klan made a large amount of money out of its members.

The Klan was opposed not just to African-Americans, but also to Jews, Catholics and foreigners. It attacked new ideas such as evolution and working on the Sabbath. It also opposed any borrowing from non-'Anglo-Saxon' cultures, for example the popularity of jazz music, which it saw as being based in African-American culture.

Influence of the Ku Klux Klan

Undoubtedly, the Klan met a need among many Americans. It gave them a sense of importance, belonging and power. With its secretive language, hoods and robes, burning crosses and violence, it added purpose and glamour to the humdrum lives of the farmers, artisans and shopkeepers who were the mainstay of its membership. It also appealed to the bullying and sadistic instincts in many. Victims could be tarred and feathered, branded and even killed. Plain living, Prohibition and church attendance could now be upheld by terror.

However, despite its apparent success, the Klan appealed to those who lacked confidence in the future. It was made up of people who were afraid of changes that they neither understood nor had control over. Hiram Wesley Evans, a Texas dentist, became Imperial Wizard of the Klan on the death of Clark in 1924. He said the Klan was made up of 'plain people, very weak in matters of culture but representing the old pioneer stock, the blend of the Nordic races which had given the world its civilisation'. He meant by this whites who saw themselves as the descendants of the people who had settled and civilised the USA and now felt threatened by the emergence of other ethnic and social groups such as Jews, immigrants from southern and eastern Europe, Catholics and, of course, African-Americans.

The Klan had very little influence in big cities. It was overwhelmingly a movement of small towns and rural areas. There is little doubt that while not all would go to its extremes in terms of violence, many in these areas broadly supported its ideas – and just like the gangsters, the Klan had control of influential politicians. It has been alleged, for example, that in 1924 it helped elect governors in Maine, Ohio, Colorado and Louisiana. At one point both Georgia senators were Klansmen. Certainly it helped destroy the campaign of Al Smith – a Catholic New Yorker – to be nominated for president in 1924. It fought energetically against him again in 1928. Evans claimed there were 5,000,000 members of the Klan in 1923.

Ku Klux Klan claimed 5,000,000 members: 1923

Key date

Key question
Why did support for
the Klan collapse?

The collapse of the Ku Klux Klan

The Klan rapidly collapsed as a mass organisation. In Indiana, David Stevenson had built the Klan into a powerful political machine. His downfall was sudden, following the suicide of a woman he had raped. He was convicted of second-degree murder. Stevenson's wickedness helped kill off large-scale support of the Klan. The organisation was also hurt by revelations of financial mismanagement in Pennsylvania.

By 1929, its membership had fallen to 200,000. Evans tried to turn the Klan into more of a social club by emphasising outdoor activities such as camping expeditions, as opposed to its political role and attraction to violence. This angered the extremists who felt it had gone soft. By 1930 the power and influence of the Klan was broken on the national stage, although its terrorism continued at local levels.

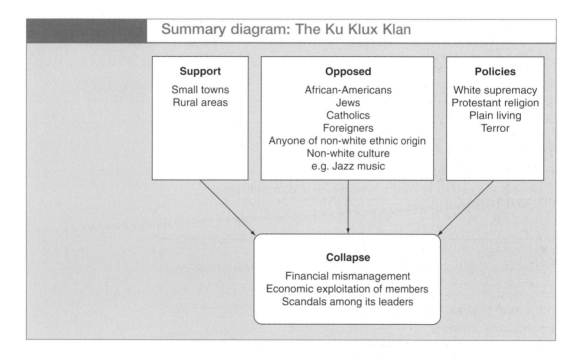

Summary diagram: The Ku Klux Klan

Support
Small towns
Rural areas

Opposed
African-Americans
Jews
Catholics
Foreigners
Anyone of non-white ethnic origin
Non-white culture
e.g. Jazz music

Policies
White supremacy
Protestant religion
Plain living
Terror

Collapse
Financial mismanagement
Economic exploitation of members
Scandals among its leaders

Key question
How do factors such
as the movement to
towns, Prohibition,
the 'Red Scare',
religion and morality,
immigration and the
Ku Klux Klan illustrate
the tensions in the
USA in the 1920s?

5 | The Old Versus the New

Many historians have seen these developments – Prohibition, fundamentalist religion and racism – as last-ditch attempts by people in small-town and rural America to turn back the tide of the twentieth century. They wanted to keep the USA white, Anglo-Saxon and Protestant (WASP). They feared immigrants would shift the racial balance, introduce foreign ideas such as Communism, and overthrow the existing order. Even Roman Catholicism was distrusted, as it was seen by many as a threat to American religious practices. Many people believed the use of alcohol had led to sinfulness and sexual licence in cities, which they saw as hotbeds of vice. They feared African-Americans and the influence of their culture on the young. Above all, they feared change. They believed in a largely imagined past of hard work, high moral standards of behaviour and unquestioning belief in the literal truth of the Bible.

As with all mythologies, the period to which these people yearned to return had never existed – for all its achievements, the history of the USA had often been turbulent, violent and racist. However, if the 1920s were a volatile decade, many of the problems came to be concealed by a veneer of optimism, excitement and unparalleled prosperity.

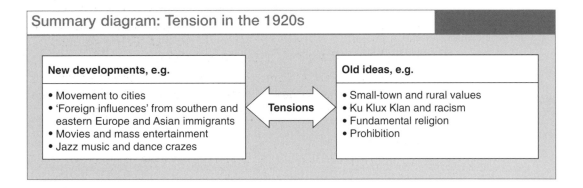

Summary diagram: Tension in the 1920s

New developments, e.g.
- Movement to cities
- 'Foreign influences' from southern and eastern Europe and Asian immigrants
- Movies and mass entertainment
- Jazz music and dance crazes

Tensions

Old ideas, e.g.
- Small-town and rural values
- Ku Klux Klan and racism
- Fundamental religion
- Prohibition

Study Guide: AS Questions

In the style of AQA

Examine the extent to which Prohibition was unsuccessful between 1919 and 1929.

> **Study tips**
>
> The cross-references are intended to take you straight to the material that will help you answer the question.
>
> You need to strike a balance in your answer. Prohibition was not wholly unsuccessful.
>
> - You could examine a variety of reasons why Prohibition was unsuccessful, such as lack of resources, geographical size of the USA and the difficulty in patrolling the coastline (pages 15–18).
> - You could also consider how and why both gangsters and ordinary people broke the law (pages 14–15).
> - However, don't forget the positive effects of Prohibition for example support in rural areas, less drunken driving (page 19).
> - The best answers will also place Prohibition within the wider context of 1920s society, for example pleasure-seeking, movement to cities, the reduced role of federal government (pages 11–12 and 25–6).

In the style of Edexcel

Study Sources 1–5 below and on page 28 and answer the questions that follow.

Source 1

From: the Saturday Evening Post, *a US newspaper, 3 July 1926.*

It's the new and better thing that stirs the people's heart. On Broadway a new play triumphs: and for months great crowds queue to watch it.

In Miami there appears a chic new fashion: and the country immediately takes it to its heart. In Chicago, a new invention revolutionises an industry; and the nation pays eager tribute. Out of Los Angeles comes words of a remarkable discovery, and people everywhere thrill to the achievement.

THIS IS AMERICA! Ever seeking to improve upon the past. Those who would appeal to America, and win and hold America's favour, must keep pace with America's desire for progress.

Source 2

A photograph of two young women in the USA in 1925.

Source 3

From: Frederick Lewis Allen, Only Yesterday, *1931.*

As the profits from beer and 'alky cooking' [illicit distilling] rolled in, young Capone acquired more skill – particularly in the management of politics and politicians. By the middle of the

1920s he had gained complete control of the Chicago suburb of Cicero, had installed his own mayor in office, had posted his agents in the wide-open gambling resorts and in each of the 161 bars, and had established his personal headquarters in the Hawthorne Hotel. He was taking in millions now. But his conquest of power did not come without bloodshed. As the rival gangs – the O'Banions, the Gennas, the Aiellos – disputed his growing domination, Chicago was afflicted with such an epidemic of killings as no modern city had ever before seen, and a new technique of wholesale murder was developed.

Source 4

From: Abner Bender, a policeman in Chicago remembers the 1920s. He was writing after the end of Prohibition.

The saloon keepers would always welcome you. You couldn't pay for anything. The bottle was there and you were supposed to drink.

We were just ordinary policemen, but if you did anything by way of enforcement, your bosses would move you somewhere else. It was a conspiracy and the higher ups were being taken care of. I was assigned to 12th Street and I backed into a doorway to see what was going on. A fella dashed up to me, handed me an envelope and said 'This is for you.' I took it and he was gone. I opened it and there was $75 in it.

The payoff was such a common thing. Believe me, I never went seeking it. It just came as a matter of course. I tried to do my job, but it was laughable.

Source 5

From: Doug and Susan Willoughby, The USA 1917–45, *2000.*

It can be argued that if any single factor were responsible for the social and moral 'revolution' of the 1920s in the USA it would have to be Prohibition. Evasion of the Volstead Act was imaginative and varied. It was also blatant, violent and corrupt. The Act appears to be an outrageous imposition of federal legislation that attacked individual liberty and freedom. However, in reality Prohibition was a response to a huge groundswell of public opinion. Moreover, for everyone who evaded the law, there were at least the same number, if not more, who actually supported it throughout the period it remained on the statute books. The failure of Prohibition was because it was over-ambitious rather than fundamentally unjust.

(a) **Study Source 1**
   What does Source 1 reveal about attitudes in US society in the 1920s? (6 marks)

(b) **Use your own knowledge**
   Use your own knowledge to explain why so much attention was paid to the trial of John T. Scopes in Dayton, Tennessee, in 1925. (10 marks)

(c) **Study Sources 3 and 4**

How far does Source 4 support what Source 3 says about the effects of Prohibition? (10 marks)

(d) **Study Sources 2 and 4**

How useful are Sources 2 and 4 to an historian studying US society in the 1920s? (10 marks)

(e) **Study Sources 3 and 5 and use your own knowledge**

Do you agree with the view, expressed in Source 5, that Prohibition failed 'because it was over-ambitious rather than fundamentally unjust'?

Explain your answer, using these two sources and your own knowledge. (24 marks)

Source: Edexcel, May 2002

Exam tips

The cross-references are intended to take you straight to the material that will help you answer the questions.

1. In Question **(a)** you need to infer from the source. You could, for example, mention the air of optimism. Beware applying your own knowledge and note that the question asks about attitudes rather than simply about society as a whole.

2. In Question **(b)** you are marked on your knowledge of why the trial attracted so much publicity rather than the trial itself. The higher level answers will put into the context of issues of religion and morality in the 1920s (pages 20–1).

3. Question **(c)** asks you to cross-reference the two sources in order to answer the question 'How far?'. This requires a judgement based on using the sources as evidence rather than simply telling the examiner in your own words what they say. First make sure you understand what Source 4 is saying about the effects of Prohibition and then consider how far Source 3 supports it. Remember that Source 4 is evidence given by a police officer who might be expected to be honest.

4. Question **(d)** asks you about usefulness rather than reliability. What are the advantages and disadvantages of this photograph and this memory as evidence? It is important to keep to the sources in question and not generalise about photographs and memories as a whole.

5. Question **(e)** requires a much longer answer than the others and the higher levels will require a judgement. You need to use the sources critically as well as your own knowledge. Ensure you write analysis in terms of the statement rather than a description of Prohibition. You could, for example, consider issues such as the difficulties in enforcing Prohibition and the levels of support for it. You may discuss the levels of organisation among those determined to break the law and the relative disorganisation of its supporters. Don't forget to come to a conclusion in terms of the statement based on your analysis (pages 15–19).

Study Guide: Advanced Level Questions
In the style of OCR

Source A
From: a contemporary poster produced in 1919 by the Anti-Saloon League against the Liquor trade, calling for the introduction of national Prohibition. The caption read 'Our religion demands that every child should have a fair chance for citizenship in the Kingdom of heaven. Our patriotism demands a saloonless country and a stainless flag' (P. Baker, General Superintendent, Anti-Saloon League of America)

The OVERSHADOWING CURSE

THE LEGALIZED SALOON

HAS SHE A FAIR CHANCE?

Source B

From: M. Parish, Anxious Decades, *published in 1992, an historian who highlights economic reasons behind the introduction of national Prohibition.*

Many saw liquor as a contributory cause of unemployment. For leaders of the new corporate elite, being sober in the workplace had become an urgent issue as technology and business organisations grew more complex. A drunken shoemaker alone at his bench or a tipsy farmer behind a horse drawn plough did not present the same danger to other employees or profits as the intoxicated worker on the assembly line. War finally tipped the balance decisively in favour of the Women's Christian Temperance Union. How could a government that called for maximum agricultural production justify the wasteful use of grain for intoxicants? After less than three day's debate the 18th Amendment, banning the sale or transportation of intoxicants throughout the United States swept through Congress. By early 1919 the required 36 states had ratified it. Later that year Congress passed the Volstead Act, which defined as 'intoxicating' any liquor having as much as 0.5% alcohol. It gave enforcement responsibilities to the Department of the treasury. On the statute books at least, America was dry.

Compare the views expressed in Sources A and B on the reasons for attempting National Prohibition (15 marks)

Source: OCR, June 2002

Exam tips

In answering these type of questions avoid paraphrasing the passages. The question is one of comparison. As such, answers will focus on similarities and differences in the passages.

- Source A suggests moral, social and religious factors were behind the drive for Prohibition, while Source B implies it was more to do with the introduction of new industrial techniques. Source B then focuses more on economic motives. Source A also makes a call to patriotism in its denunciation of alcohol.
- The difference in interpretation is to do in part with motivation. Source A is produced by a body trying to achieve Prohibition at the time, while Source B takes a more objective view from the distance of time and with hindsight.
- However, Source B also mentions the Women's Christian Temperance Union, another moral group, so there are some similarities with its analysis and the messages of Source A.
- Both passages agree the reasons for prohibition were practical rather than philosophical ones.

In the style of OCR

Discuss the extent to which national Prohibition met the aims of its supporters during the period 1920 to 1933. (45 marks)

Source: OCR, January 2003

Exam tips

The cross-reference is intended to take you straight to the material that will help you answer the question.

The main two areas to consider are who supported Prohibition and how far it met their aims.

- You should avoid generalised discussion of why Prohibition failed. The question is about its shortcomings and successes in relation to what people hoped from it. You need to bring in references to the historical debate about Prohibition within your argument. However you need to evaluate this debate rather than simply write uncritically about what historians have said.
- You could discuss how it was difficult to enforce, how it led to lawlessness and how it appeared not to lead to greater moral behaviour in the cities within the context of what people expected from it (pages 15–19).
- However many did continue to support and obey Prohibition in towns cities as well as in the countryside. Try not to be too scathing in your judgements.
- Remember to make your judgement in terms of 'the extent'.
- The best answers will strike an informed balance based on a convincing and informed judgement.

3 Prosperity?

POINTS TO CONSIDER
On the surface the USA enjoyed great prosperity in the 1920s. This chapter examines the apparent prosperity in terms of four themes:

- The presidency of Calvin Coolidge
- The boom years
- Reasons for prosperity: why was the USA apparently so prosperous in the 1920s?
- Problems in the economy: how real and widespread was this apparent prosperity?

Key dates

1921	Emergency Tariff Act
1922	Fordney-McCumber Act
	Creation of Debt Funding Commission
1923	Beginning of the Presidency of Calvin Coolidge
	Agricultural Credit Act
1924	McNary-Haugen Bill first debated
	Dawes Plan
1926	End of the Florida Land Boom
1929	Young Plan

1 | The Presidency of Calvin Coolidge

Key question
What sort of president was Calvin Coolidge?

On 2 August 1923 Warren Harding died. His vice-president, Calvin Coolidge, was visiting his family in his home state of Vermont at the time. Coolidge was duly sworn in as the thirtieth president by his father, a local lawyer, in the kitchen of the family homestead in the tiny hamlet of Plymouth Notch. This action was in fact unnecessary. John Coolidge had not the authority to swear in a new president, and in any event his son automatically succeeded Harding as Chief Executive. However, the gesture did set the tone for Coolidge's presidency. He liked to be thought of as a man of, and from, the people – particularly those of small-town America whose values included hard work, thrift, looking after their own and not expecting the government to bail them out in times of trouble.

Calvin Coolidge presided over the largest boom period in US history. Many Americans did not want their government to do much. They believed that they had never been so well off and that the prosperity they enjoyed was permanent. Calvin Coolidge, they felt, had done a fine job as their president.

Coolidge's attitude to government

Coolidge was essentially a man of the nineteenth century whose views were outdated when he came to office. The USA was undergoing dramatic social and economic changes that he quite failed to understand. His way of governing was effectively that of the previous century, when governments traditionally interfered as little as possible in people's lives. It has been argued that Coolidge suffered a deep depression after the tragic death of his son Calvin Junior in 1924 and this affected his decision-making and willingness to act. However, there is little evidence to support this, or indeed that Coolidge has been more active as president before this tragedy.

Historians have generally criticised Coolidge for his low work rate and reluctance to get involved in issues. They have generally seen him as one of the weakest of American presidents. However, this is not how many viewed him at the time. 'Silent Cal' made more speeches and saw more people than any other president before him. He courted publicity and liked to be photographed in outlandish costumes such as Native American head-dress. But his face always seemed to bear the same dry expression, as though he was bemused by, and slightly superior to, all that was going on around him. His frequent distasteful facial expression was likened to someone who was 'weaned on a pickle'.

Despite all this, Coolidge was a popular president. He represented all those Americans, particularly from '**Middle America**', who wanted to enjoy the prosperity unfettered by government regulation, but who still sought to maintain high moral standards in society. There is little doubt that had Coolidge chosen to run for a second full term as president in 1928, he would easily have been re-elected. He gave off an aura of confidence. He was always calm and unflappable. Most people felt there could not be much wrong with the USA with such a dependable pilot at the helm.

Middle America
Phrase used to describe the vast majority of Americans who just want to get on with their lives without government interference. It also implies decent living and high moral standards. There is some implicit suggestion that the phrase refers primarily to Americans who live away from large cities in small semi-rural communities.

Key term

Profile: Calvin Coolidge 1872–1933

1872 – born in the village of Plymouth, Vermont, son of a farmer
1891 – qualified as a lawyer in the town of Northampton, Vermont
1910 – became Republican town mayor of Northampton
1912 – elected state senator of Vermont
1916 – elected Lieutenant Governor of Massachusetts
1919 – elected governor of Massachusetts
1920 – chosen to become Warren Harding's running mate in the presidential elections
1921 – became Harding's vice-president
1923 – became president on Harding's death
1924 – won the presidential election
1928 – decided not to run for a second term as president
1933 – died in Northampton, Vermont

Childhood and early career

Coolidge came from an old established family in rural Vermont. His father ran the local store. As a boy, Coolidge helped out on the family farm and went to a one-room school-house in the tiny village of Plymouth. His mother became bedridden shortly after his birth and passed away when he was 12 years old. His sister died from a burst appendix when he was in his teens. His father, whom Coolidge admired and respected intensely, was very hardworking and said little. Coolidge sought to copy him in saying little, if not in working hard. He had a slow work rate and tired easily. All his life he loved the countryside and disliked cities. He particularly disliked sophisticated city people.

Young Calvin went away to school at Ludlow and his father brought him home for the weekends in a horse-driven wagon. He went to college at Amherst and later qualified as a lawyer. He practised at Portsmouth because it had the nearest courthouse to where he was born. He entered local politics and rose steadily until he became State Governor of Massachusetts. In the meantime, in 1905 he married Grace Goodhue, a charming woman who came to love him dearly although he often appeared to treat her with indifference. It is said that shortly after their marriage he presented her with a bag of 50 socks to be darned.

Coolidge as governor and vice-president

Coolidge was an unspectacular governor of Massachusetts until he won national renown with his handling of the police strike (see page 9). This was enough to make him Warren Harding's running mate and vice-president. In this office he did very little.

Coolidge as president

Coolidge was honest and decent. He had a strong sense of personal morality. Unlike his predecessor, there were no scandals attached to him. Quiet and shy, 'Silent Cal' established an indolent routine in the White House. He enjoyed a nap most afternoons and it was always early to bed in the evening. Official functions were known to end prematurely if they were due to go on past his usual bedtime.

Coolidge was rarely burdened with affairs of state. He tired easily and his work rate was slow. He once said, 'If you see ten troubles coming down the road, you can be sure that nine will run into the ditch and you will only have to battle with one'. Critics said he failed even to do that. Coolidge certainly believed that a good government should do as little as possible. It should at best help things to run themselves.

In his first address to Congress as president in 1923 Coolidge did acknowledge that the USA had problems. He condemned lynching, child labour and argued the need for a minimum wage for women. He recognised the difficulties that farmers faced. However, the substance of his message was concerned with tax reductions and economy in government. As president, he was determined to do less, not more, than his predecessors.

Coolidge in later life

Coolidge retired to Northampton where he wrote his memoirs. He died four years later.

2 | The Boom Years

In popular mythology, the 1920s in the USA saw a period of unparalleled economic prosperity that ended suddenly in October 1929 with the collapse of the New York Stock Exchange. This picture is far too simple. There certainly was a boom period and the New York Stock Exchange did indeed collapse. However, these two events are not necessarily connected; the relationship between them is complex.

Key question
How prosperous was the USA in the 1920s?

The extent of prosperity

There was in the 1920s a real feeling of prosperity and optimism among many groups in the USA. It had emerged from the First World War as the most prosperous country on Earth. Many believed that the USA would set an example to the world with its emphasis on technological developments, economic efficiency and minimal government interference in business. The figures for prosperity appear to speak for themselves.

Following a brief postwar **recession** in 1920 and 1921, average unemployment never rose above 3.7 per cent in the years 1922–9. Inflation never rose higher than one per cent. Employees were working fewer hours – an average of 44 per week in 1929 compared with 47 in 1920. They were paid more. The real wages of industrial workers rose by 14 per cent between 1914 and 1929, and on average they were two or three times higher than those in Europe. There was huge economic growth. Production of industrial goods rose by 50 per cent between 1922 and 1929. **Gross national product (GNP)** stood at $73 billion in 1920 and $104 billion in 1929. Consumption of electricity doubled and in 1929 alone $852 million worth of radios were sold.

Many Americans had more time for leisure and more money to spend on it. Electrical labour-saving devices, such as vacuum cleaners and washing machines, were introduced and became affordable by more and more people. Motor cars eased travel both to and from work and for leisure pursuits. It was the golden age of cinema – by 1929, 80 million tickets were sold weekly for the movies. Sport attracted vast crowds of paying spectators. When Gene Tunney defended his heavyweight boxing title against Jack Dempsey in September 1927, the attendance was 107,943 and receipts were a record $2,658,660.

Key terms

Recession
Downturn in the economy.

Gross national product (GNP)
The amount earned over the country as a whole.

Problems with evidence

Caution is needed when using figures, such as those quoted above, and the specific examples that support them. They might give us an overall picture but they cannot tell us about individual circumstances. For example, the unemployment figure above does not tell us whether the low figure was applied to all sectors of the economy or whether some industries suffered high or seasonal unemployment. Were many employees just part-time? What could they buy with their wages? Was the overall prosperity spread throughout the nation or was it principally located in specific parts of the country? Did it apply to all ethnic groups?

How did women fare? To answer questions such as these requires the more specific evidence that will be considered later in this chapter.

In the next section the apparent economic successes of the decade and the reasons behind them will be discussed, specific evidence looked at and the problems surrounding the topic considered. This approach should enable an informed judgement to be made about whether the period of the 1920s was, in fact, one of real prosperity.

3 | Reasons for Prosperity

The prosperity of the 1920s was based on several factors such as favourable government policies that included high tariffs, tax reductions and a benevolent foreign policy, technical advances, improvements in business organisation, easy credit and advantageous foreign markets. In this section these factors will be considered in turn.

Government policies

According to Calvin Coolidge, 'The chief business of the American people is business'. It was the policy of his government to let business operate, as far as possible, free of regulation. Both he and his Treasury Secretary, Andrew Mellon, believed firmly in the **free market**. Mellon, a Pittsburgh banker and industrialist, was one of the richest men in the USA. He believed that wealth filtered down naturally to all classes in society and that therefore the best way to ensure increased living standards for all was to allow the rich to continue to make money to invest in industrial development.

There appeared to be much sense to this argument. Industrial expansion meant more job opportunities, which in turn meant more employment, more wage earners, more consumption, more industrial expansion and so on. During the 1920s this policy seemed to work and Mellon had few contemporary critics.

The basic government policy was *laissez-faire*. However, the picture was not quite as simple as that, and the government did intervene to support business with benevolent policies in four main ways.

(1) High tariffs

The Fordney-McCumber Act, passed in 1922, raised tariffs to cover the difference between domestic and foreign production costs. In almost every case it became cheaper for American consumers to buy goods produced within the USA than abroad. The tariff level made foreign goods more expensive than goods produced in the USA even when they could be produced in their home countries more cheaply. In effect, this meant that for some products import duties were so high that domestic producers were given an almost guaranteed market. Throughout the 1920s the general level of tariffs was upwards. The level of foreign trade was obviously reduced by this, while domestic demand for goods

Key question
How did government policies contribute to prosperity?

Key terms

Free market
A system that allows the economy to run itself with minimal government interference.

Laissez-faire
An approach where the government deliberately avoids getting involved in economic planning, thus allowing free trade to operate.

Key date
Fordney-McCumber Act: 1922

remained high. However, as we shall see in a later section (pages 46–7), the power and influence of USA businesses meant they still exported goods abroad while importing less. American industry stood to make huge profits from the high-tariff policy. It also meant of course that Americans bought comparatively few foreign goods.

(2) Tax reductions

The government reduced federal taxes significantly in 1924, 1926 and 1928 (see Table 3.1). These reductions mainly benefited the wealthy. During his eight years of office, Mellon handed out tax reductions totalling $3.5 billion to large-scale industrialists and corporations. Despite this, Coolidge's government actually operated on a surplus; in 1925, this was $677 million and in 1927, $607 million. The avowed aim of the government was to reduce the national debt, and it seemed on course to do so. However, federal tax cuts meant little to people who were too poor to pay taxes in the first place.

Table 3.1: Highest tax levels

1920	65%
1928	25%

(3) Fewer regulations

Economies in government meant fewer regulations and fewer personnel to enforce them. The **Federal Trade Commission**, for example, was increasingly unable and unwilling to operate effectively. This trend meant that businesses were often left unhindered to carry on their affairs as they saw fit. Laws concerning sharp business practice, such as **price fixing**, were often ignored. Where the government did prosecute, the offenders usually won on appeal.

This lack of regulation could be an important contributor to a company's profits. Many people welcomed less government. However, it should also be remembered that there was, for example, no organisation with the authority to stop child labour in the textile mills of the South, where a 56-hour week was common and wages rarely rose to more than 18 cents an hour.

Federal Trade Commission
Body charged to ensure businesses were operating fairly.

Price fixing
Where companies agreed to fix prices between them, thereby preventing fair competition.

Key terms

(4) Foreign policies

Coolidge avoided intervention in foreign affairs wherever possible. This was in part due to budget cutting and a recognition that Americans didn't want to see troops getting caught up in foreign disputes. Outstanding disputes with Mexico over the rights of American businesses to own land there, for example, were solved by diplomacy. This policy of conciliation helped American investment abroad by removing any ill feeling towards the USA.

This lenient approach to foreign policy also meant that investors often favoured profit over more ethical concerns. An example here was their willingness to invest in Japan, which was becoming increasingly aggressive towards other countries such as China, rather than stimulating American–Chinese trade links which would have enabled China to modernise. Investors were, for example, investing in the Japanese-built South Manchuria Railroad. This went through sovereign Chinese territory and gave the Japanese the excuse to maintain a military presence in Manchuria to defend the railroad – a military presence that would be used in 1931 to invade and take over Manchuria. American investors were more interested in the profits that accrued from this investment than listening to protests from the State Department, which looked after foreign affairs. It was far less profitable to invest in China than Japan, and as a result China remained weak and open to attack.

Technical advances

During this period great technical advances in industrial production made possible huge increases both in the quantity and in the variety of products on sale. While this is true of many different types of commodity, the motor vehicle industry and electrical consumer goods are particularly striking examples, which is why they are considered below.

Key question
How was the motor industry developed and what was the impact of its growth?

Key term

Mass production
Making large numbers of the same item using machinery and conveyor belts.

Motor vehicle industry

The motor vehicle industry grew dramatically in the 1920s. By the end of the decade there were 23 million cars on the road and the industry was the biggest in the USA. It was the largest market for commodities, such as steel and rubber, and one of the most desirable products among consumers. Asked about workers' aspirations, one official said that 65 per cent are working to pay for cars.

Henry Ford revolutionised the motor vehicle industry. He had begun to use methods of **mass production** long before the 1920s and his famous 'Model T' car had first appeared in 1908. Previously, cars had been only for the wealthy, but Ford wanted ordinary Americans to be able to afford one.

Ford's first assembly line in 1913.

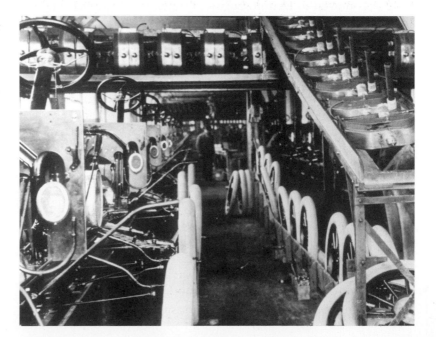

When he introduced his moving line assembly in 1914, the cost of the Model T came down from $950 to $500. By 1920 Ford was producing 1,250,000 cars per year, or one every 60 seconds. By 1925, when the price had fallen to $290, his factory could produce one every 10 seconds. Petrol meanwhile cost between 20 and 25 cents a gallon at a time when average wages in manufacturing industries were in the region of 50 cents an hour.

By this time, Ford was facing increasing competition from General Motors and Chrysler. These 'Big Three' firms dominated the American motor industry and it was very difficult for independent companies to survive unless they produced specialist vehicles for the wealthy. In 1930, 26.5 million cars were on American roads.

Despite the demand, the supply always exceeded it, and in this industry as in many others it was increasingly obvious that demand had to be actively encouraged. Henry Ford was slow to learn this lesson. His Model T was renowned for durability and trustworthiness. However, there was no variety: only black ones were ever produced. The car came without frills. It was certainly adaptable; farmers could even attach a plough to it. However, his rivals, in their models, emphasised variety, comfort and style.

When, in 1927, Ford noticeably began to lose his share of the market, he closed down his factory, laying off 60,000 workers. During this layoff, the factory was retooled for the new Model A vehicle. If the market was to remain buoyant, car design had to stay ahead of the market and customers had to want to buy the new model rather than keep the old one.

Profile: Henry Ford 1863–1947

1863	– born in Greenfield Township, Michigan
1879	– moved to Detroit, began to learn about engineering
1888	– married Clara Bryant, moved back to Greenfield Township
1893	– son, Edsel Ford born
1896	– built first automobile, the quadricycle
1903	– organised Henry Ford Company, with himself as chief engineer
1908	– first Model T Ford appeared
1913	– introduced first mass production line at factory at Highland Park, Michigan
1917	– began a giant factory at Dearborn, Michigan.
1919	– handed over presidency of company to Edsel but in reality kept control himself
1921	– Ford Motor Company claimed 55% of the motor industry's total output
1926	– began to expand into aviation and developed the Trimotor aeroplane
1927	– shut down automobile production for five months while factory re-tooled for Model A
1933	– resisted efforts to bring unions into his factory

1937 – Battle of the Overpass between Ford security staff and union organisers; Ford was forced by the courts to accept unions
1943 – Edsel Ford died
1945 – Ford handed over presidency of the company to grandson Henry Ford II
1947 – Ford died

Early life
Henry Ford was born into a farming family and was educated in a one-room schoolhouse. Bored with rural life, he walked to Detroit in 1879 in search of work. He learnt engineering and began to experiment with automobiles. His first completed car was the Quadricycle, with a carriage frame mounted on four bicycle wheels.

Ford Motor Company
Ford began his own company in 1903 and built the Model T in 1908. This was hugely successful and by 1913 he had begun to mass-produce them. In 1917, the company moved to a giant factory at Dearborn, Michigan. Ford was shocked when rival companies began to get an increased share of the market in the later 1920s and shut down his plant for five months to re-tool for the new Model A Ford.

Ford also introduced a minimum wage of $5.00 per day and acted as a benevolent dictator to his workforce. His factories were very clean, with excellent safety records and nutrition experts ensured every employee's lunchbox contained 800 calories. He would not accept unions, however, and used strong-arm men to stop any union activity. He employed a man of violence, with connections to the Mafia, Harry Bennett, to take care of labour relations, and particularly in the 1930s, Ford employees often went in fear of Bennett and his henchmen. In one Communist demonstration in 1932, Bennett's 'Service Department' shot four protestors dead. Eventually, Ford was forced by the courts to accept unions. Apparently because of all the turmoil, his wife Clara threatened to leave him if he didn't give in to them.

Later life
Ford's son Edsel died in 1943 and Ford handed over the running of the Company to his grandson Henry Ford II in 1945. By this time the elder Ford was a sad figure. In the interwar period, he had produced a newspaper, the *Dearborn Independent*, which had attacked Jews and Catholics. These views did him no favours, particularly in the light of what was happening to Jews in the Second World War. Ford died in 1947.

Key question
What were the effects of the growth in car ownership?

The effects of the growth in car ownership
The growth of the motor industry had major social and economic effects. Henry Ford, with his limited imagination, had seen the car as strengthening what he believed to be traditional American values. The family would bond together through outings, the

breadwinners could go further afield to seek work, and so on. He did not foresee its use by courting couples nor did he realise family outings might take the place of church attendance. He had no idea that road deaths would stand at 20,000 per year by the later 1920s, or indeed that the industrial organisation would stimulate the trade unionism which he loathed and forcefully kept out of his own factory.

In economic terms, by 1929, the motor industry employed seven per cent of all workers and paid them nine per cent of all wages. By far the largest industry in the USA, it also stimulated many others as may be seen by studying Figure 3.1. This shows the percentages of the total production of various items in the USA that were used by the car industry alone. The temporary closure of Ford was indeed a contributory factor to the recession of 1927. Not only were his workforce laid off, but the loss of business by companies providing components to Ford created real problems in the economy.

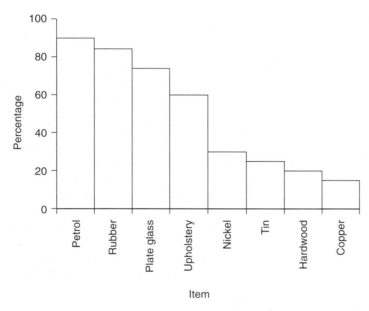

Figure 3.1: Use of products by the car industry

Road building
Breaking with the policy of *laissez-faire*, the federal government expended a great deal of energy on road building in the 1920s. Until 1921 this had largely been the responsibility of the states and many had made little progress since the previous century. Of three million miles of road in 1920, the vast majority were intended solely for the horse. Only about one per cent of roads were suitable to take the pounding of motor vehicles. The horse was by far the main form of road transport and the quantity of its dung on the highways was felt to be a national health hazard.

The Federal Highway Act of 1921 gave responsibility for road building to central government and highways were being constructed at the rate of 10,000 miles per year by 1929. But this was not enough. New roads could not keep pace with the growth of traffic. Congestion was common, particularly in the approaches to large urban centres. In 1936 the Chief Designer in the Bureau of Public Roads reported that between 25 and 50 per cent of modern roads built over the previous 20 years were unfit for use because of the amount of traffic that was quite simply wearing them out.

Motor vehicles also created the growth of new service industries such as garages, motels, petrol stations, and used car salerooms. They gradually changed the landscape alongside the highways of the USA.

Improved transportation also afforded new opportunities for industry. For example, goods could be much more easily moved from factories to their markets. The number of truck registrations increased from less than one million in 1919 to 3.5 million by 1929, when 15 billion gallons of petrol were used and 4.5 million new cars were sold.

Electrical consumer goods

Key question
What was the impact of the growth in electrical goods?

The development of new technologies such as mass production led to the large-scale development of labour-saving devices, for example vacuum cleaners and washing machines. This is because they were much cheaper to produce. In 1912, 2.4 million items of electrical goods were sold; in 1929 the figure was 160 million.

However, this trend should not be exaggerated. Much of rural America was still without electricity in the 1920s. Even where electrical power was available, many items we take for granted today were not widely in use. In 1925, for example, Clarence Birdseye patented his freezing process but in 1928 there were only 20,000 refrigerators in the whole country. While there was an industrial capacity to produce millions of electrical goods, by the end of the decade nearly everyone who could afford them or who had access to electricity had them. This meant there was serious overproduction. As we shall see later in this chapter (pages 52–3), this was to lead to problems in the economy by the late 1920s.

New business methods

This was a period that saw the growth of huge corporations, of scientific methods of management and of advertising, which through the exploitation of the new mass media, gained an influence previously unimagined. The effect was to make business more efficient and well run, which in turn helped profits.

Growth of huge corporations

Key question
What were the effects of the growth in large corporations?

Most large corporations, such as Firestone who produced rubber, were manufacturing businesses. They could invest in and exploit the plentiful raw materials of the USA on a vast scale. By 1929 the largest 200 corporations possessed 20 per cent of the nation's wealth and 40 per cent of the wealth generated by business activities. Mergers in manufacturing and mining enterprises trebled to over 1200 during the decade leading to even larger business concerns.

Large corporations could dominate an industry in various ways.

- They could operate a **cartel** to fix prices. Although this was technically illegal, the government tended to turn a blind eye. They could, as in the case of the petroleum companies, control the entire industrial process. This involved the exploitation of the raw materials, the manufacture of the product, its distribution to wholesale and retail outlets, and its sale to the consumer.
- Some organisations, for example US Steel, were so huge that they could dictate output and price levels throughout the industry. They could create **holding companies**. For example, Samuel Insull built up a vast empire based on electrical supply. Eventually he controlled 111 different companies with as many as 24 layers between him and the company actually distributing the electricity. The chain became so complex that even he lost an overall understanding of it. Many businessmen turned up on the boards of directors of numerous companies. The result was that firms supposedly competing with each other were in effect one and the same, with the power to fix output and prices.

It is important to remember that government policies made these developments possible and that they acted against the interests of small businesses. However, at the time many people saw businessmen as heroes who had made possible the great boom period they were enjoying.

Management science

The increased size of businesses meant that they were more complex to manage. This led to the development of different management roles performed by different people in administration. Entrepreneurs like Henry Ford who tried to control all management operations became increasingly old fashioned. Specialisms developed in production, design, marketing, accounts and finance in ways that had been unheard of in the previous century.

One particularly noticeable aspect of these developments was the growth of business schools – in 1928 there were 89 of them, with 67,000 students. The fact that **management science** became a respectable occupation for members of the upper middle classes was also an indication that it was becoming increasingly difficult to start one's own company. To rise up the ladder of an established giant offered greater career opportunities than to compete with them.

Many new 'scientific' management theories were put into operation, particularly the '**time and motion**' work of Frederick W. Taylor and his followers. These dated from the latter years of the nineteenth century. Levels of production undoubtedly increased, but in extreme cases all initiative was removed from the labour force, which tended to become simply extensions of the machine – this development was satirised memorably in Charlie Chaplin's 1936 film, *Modern Times*. However, it should be

Key terms

Cartel
Group of companies agreeing to fix output and prices, to reduce competition and maximise their profits.

Holding companies
Where one huge company would obtain a controlling interest in smaller companies to control the market.

Key question
How did management science affect business?

Key terms

Management science
The application of technological principles to running a company.

Time and motion
A system in which production techniques are allocated set times for completion and production targets laid down on this basis.

remembered that these developments applied almost exclusively to large business concerns. Outside the big cities most manufacturers still worked in small workshops.

Advertising and salesmanship

Key question
How was advertising used to create demand for goods?

The new mass media, principally cinema and radio, brought about a revolution in advertising.

Cinema

By 1928 there were 17,000 cinemas in the USA. Few areas were out of the reach of the 'movies'. A 10-cent ticket could buy admission to a fantasy world far beyond the previous experience of the vast majority of the audience. The darkened auditorium enabled people to forget their troubles for a few hours and to enter into a world of beauty and glamour where seemingly no one had to work or pay the mortgage.

With millions of cinema-goers aching to copy the appearances and lifestyles of the stars, the potential for advertising was enormous. The big producers were not slow to exploit this, and the time between the features was soon filled with commercials.

Radio

The radio business effectively began when the KDKA station in Pittsburgh announced the results of the 1920 presidential election. As other stations started to broadcast, a demand for radio sets was created. These began to be mass produced in 1920.

By 1929 there were 618 radio stations throughout the USA, some of them broadcasting from coast to coast. The vast majority of them were controlled by two companies, the National Broadcasting Company and Columbia Broadcasting System. The potential audience was vast. An estimated 50 million people listened to live commentary on the 1927 Dempsey–Tunney fight referred to on page 36. In 1922 the radio station WEAF in New York began the most important trend when it broadcast the first sponsored programme, advertising the delights of Jackson Heights, a housing development.

As more advertisers began to sponsor programmes, radio networks began to poll listeners to see what sort of programmes they wanted. With more and more programmes catering to mass appeal, which was based firmly in the areas of light music and humour, there was considerable criticism from those who felt radio should be educational and enlightening. However, these critics were firmly in the minority. By the end of the decade, radio costs were generally covered by advertising and many programmes were firmly linked in people's minds with the name of the sponsor.

The constant need to create demand

The growth in industrial production needed a continuous market. It was no longer enough, as Ford had done with his Model T, to sell a durable unchanging product that might last the purchaser for life. Now, to fuel the boom, it was necessary for people to buy new things frequently. They had to be convinced that they could not do without the latest model of an electrical appliance or the new design in clothing.

This necessitated far-reaching developments in advertising and salesmanship. Indeed, with most products virtually the same in quality, these often became the deciding factors in the market. A successful advertising campaign might well be the only difference between huge profit and huge loss. Possibly the most important aspect of a campaign was to find some way to differentiate between one's product and that of one's competitors – to promote a unique selling point.

One of the pioneers of high-pressure salesmanship was Bruce Barton who tried to show that consumer society and the accumulation of wealth was in no way incompatible with Christian teaching. In a series of books such as *A Young Man's Jesus* (1924) and *The Man Nobody Knew* (1926), Barton even tried to show that Christ himself was a high-pressure salesman. He wrote, 'He would be a great advertiser today, as, I am sure he was the great advertiser of his own day. Take any of the parables, no matter which – you will find it exemplifies all the principles on which advertising text books are written'.

For many consumers advertising techniques worked. Not only did they associate products with a slogan, but they also believed they could not manage without the product being advertised. *The Kansas City Journal-Post* was hardly exaggerating when it wrote, 'Advertising and mass production are the twin cylinders that keep the motor of modern business in motion'.

Easy credit

The massive consumer boom was financed largely by easy credit facilities. By 1929 almost $7 billion worth of goods were sold on credit; this included 75 per cent of cars and half of major household appliances. One study showed that men earning $35 a week were paying the same amount per month for the family car.

Unfortunately, while the ready availability of credit enabled consumers to buy goods they otherwise could not have afforded, it often led to problems if the borrowers took on debts they could not repay. Companies, as well as individuals, used easy-credit facilities to finance many of their operations. It seemed that almost everyone was in debt but there was little concern over this. It was assumed that everyone's credit must be good. Banks and loan companies seemed to be falling over backwards to lend money, often with few questions asked.

Influence in foreign economies

Reference has already been made to high tariffs that protected US markets. However, the government also encouraged businessmen to develop extensive interests abroad particularly in terms of raw materials that fuelled technological developments. Business corporations bought oil concessions in many countries including Canada, Venezuela, Iraq and the Dutch East Indies. The Firestone Corporation developed a rubber industry in Liberia, while the Guggenheims invested in South America for

Key question
How did the availability of easy credit affect the economic boom?

Key question
How was the boom affected by foreign resources and markets?

nitrates, copper and lead. The United Fruit Company had a larger budget in Costa Rico than the government of that country. Often US investment saw the development of public health schemes and schools in developing countries to provide and maintain a healthy and adequately educated workforce.

The US also exported vast amounts of manufactured products. The US dominated Canadian markets; indeed, US automobile firms effectively destroyed the native Canadian industry, which simply could not compete with them. Similarly, the Canadian electrical industry was dominated by US firms both in terms of supply of power and manufacture of products.

Of particular interest is the economic relationship between the USA and Soviet Russia. While Coolidge's government refused to recognise the Soviet state, American businessmen were nevertheless encouraged to develop commercial ties. The First Five Year Plan for Soviet economic growth was so dependent on its success for exports from the USA that the Soviet Amtorg Trading Company set up offices in New York City. By 1928, 25 per cent of all foreign investment in Soviet Russia emanated from the USA and, astonishingly, 33 per cent of all exported Ford tractors went to Soviet Russia; indeed, by 1927, 85 per cent of all tractors in Soviet Russia were manufactured by Ford.

In all, private investment by the USA in foreign countries rose from $7000 million in 1919 to $17,200 million by 1930. As we will see in Chapters 4 and 5, this international reliance on American investment would have devastating effects on the global economy when the Great Depression arrived.

Prosperity: appearance and reality

It seemed in the 1920s that with almost full employment, low inflation, high tariffs keeping foreign goods out of the USA, benevolent government policies and a consumer boom, the prosperity would go on forever. The period was a time of great optimism. It wore a happy face. However, one did not have to delve very far beneath the surface to discover real problems within the system.

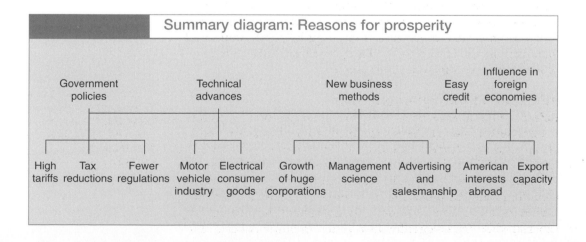

Summary diagram: Reasons for prosperity

4 | Problems in the Economy

While it appeared on the surface that the economy was booming, there were many warning signs that things were not so healthy. These included:

Key question
What were the warning signs that the economy was doing less well than most people believed?

- uneven distribution of wealth
- rural poverty
- the instability of 'get-rich-quick' schemes
- problems with the banking system
- the cycle of international debt.

In this section these will be dealt with in turn.

Uneven distribution of wealth

Industry and income were all distributed unevenly within the USA, which meant that some regions were much more prosperous than others. In addition, employment could be unstable with much unemployment and short-time working. Different sections of society were better off than others; many women, for example, did not share in the prosperity, nor did ethnic groups such as native and African-Americans.

Distribution of income

Income was distributed very unevenly throughout the country. The North East and Far West enjoyed the highest **per capita incomes**; in 1929 these were $921 and $881, respectively. In comparison, the figure for the South East was $365. To paint an even gloomier picture, within the region of the South East, in South Carolina, while the per capita income for the non-agricultural sectors of the economy averaged $412, that of farmers was only $129.

Key question
How was income and industry distributed within the USA?

Per capita income
Income per head of the population.

Key term

In 1929 the Brookings Institute, a research organisation, found that income distribution was actually becoming more unequal. Its survey discovered that 60 per cent of American families had annual incomes of less than $2000. Two sociologists Robert S. Lynd and Helen Lynd conducted major surveys about how people lived in the town of Muncie, Indiana, which they identified as 'Middletown'. As part of their investigations, they sampled 100 families and discovered that 75 per cent earned less than the amount the Federal Bureau of Labor recommended as the minimum income needed to support an acceptable standard of living.

Distribution of industry

The old industries of the USA had been centred in the North East and Midwest, especially in the states of Illinois, Michigan and Pennsylvania. They had grown originally on the basis of nineteenth-century technology, powered by coal and steam. Old industries were generally experiencing hard times. Coal, for example, suffered from competition from newly discovered energy sources, notably oil. The introduction of synthetic fibres lessened the demand for cotton. Moreover, changes, particularly in young women's fashions, such as shorter skirts, reduced the quantity of material required. The textile mills of the South employed cheap labour, including children, and many northern mills, whose workforce enjoyed higher wages and shorter hours of work, simply could not compete in a shrinking market. Railways faced competition from motor transport – although it must be said that, because of the expansion of the economy, rail-freight traffic increased 10 per cent during the decade. Farmers fared particularly badly during this period.

The new industries, such as the motor vehicle and electrical industries, were also drawn to the regions of the North East and Midwest. This was due to the availability of minerals such as coal, the well-established transport network, a mobile, often immigrant labour force, and proximity to centres of large population, such as Boston, Philadelphia and New York. As a result, other regions of the USA, notably the West and the South, had only sparse industrial development, with comparatively small towns still acting as commercial centres for wide rural areas. In other words, things had not altered in much of the USA since the previous century, and for much of the country the major occupation was still agriculture

Stability of employment

Key question
How stable was employment in the USA?

Employment was often unstable owing to fluctuating demand for goods. Robert and Helen Lynd found that, during the first 9 months of 1924, of 165 families they surveyed, 72 per cent of the workers had been unemployed at some stage. Of these 43 per cent had been jobless for over a month. This was at a time when there was very little welfare or unemployment benefit and most relief was supplied by charitable organisations.

Women

Key question
What opportunities were open to women?

Women did not on the whole enjoy improved career opportunities during this period. By 1930, for example, there were only 150 women dentists and less than 100 female accountants in the whole of the USA. In 1928, the League of Women Voters reported that while 145 women held seats in state legislatures, there were only two women among the 435 delegates in the House of Representatives.

There were more jobs for women as clerical workers and salespeople, but overall they tended to remain in comparatively low-paid and often menial jobs; 700,000 women were domestic servants. There were few female industrialists or managing directors. The number of women receiving a college education actually fell by five per cent during the decade. Even when women worked in the same job as men, they normally received less money. Despite the image of fun-loving young women known as 'flappers', women were generally expected to concentrate on marriage and homemaking. It is largely a myth that the 1920s saw more opportunities for women to get to the top in terms of employment opportunities.

Legislation did little to help women, although the Sheppard–Towner Act of 1921 (see page 10) did fund healthcare for pregnant women and gave women some control over the clinics it set up. However some feminists feared this measure simply reinforced the stereotypical view of women's main role as having lots of children and drew attention away from the need for birth control. Legislation to protect women in the workplace such as the banning of night shift work was similarly attacked. This was because it often meant women simply lost their jobs when they were no longer allowed to work such shifts. Therefore they became more economically dependent on men. Despite the efforts of the Women's Party set up by former Suffragist Alice Paul, women never voted as a block and women's movements remained fragmented throughout this period.

Native and African-Americans

As groups, Native Americans and African-Americans did not share in the prosperity. Native Americans often eked out a miserable existence on infertile reservations. African-Americans made up 10 per cent of the total population, but 85 per cent still lived in the South, itself the poorest region in the USA. There was considerable migration north in search of better opportunities, particularly to the large cities, but here too African-Americans faced discrimination in housing and employment. Often they were concentrated in 'ghetto' areas such as Harlem in New York, whose African-American population had swelled from 50,000 in 1914 to 165,000 in 1930. Here overcrowding and poor living conditions added to their problems in the mainstream economy.

A study showed that in Pittsburgh that African-Americans were kept unskilled through lack of employment opportunities and forced to operate in the casual labour market. This left them more exposed to joblessness and fears of destitution than before they had begun their migration north. The Ku Klux Klan still terrorised much of the Midwest and South, although the number of lynchings was falling. Comparatively few African-Americans were allowed to share in any prosperity; 14 per cent of farmers were African-Americans.

Rural poverty

The Census showed in 1920 that for the first time the USA was essentially an urban nation. The total population was 106,466,000; of these 31,614,000 lived on the land, but the rest lived in towns. The growth of urbanisation was particularly significant because farming had been extremely influential in American life and culture. Not only did farmers produce the food to feed the population, but they had also given the USA much of its perceived national character – hard work, self-reliance, and the ability to overcome adversity through one's own efforts. The farmers were traditionally regarded as the people who had tamed and civilised a wilderness. As the majority of Americans had traditionally lived in rural areas, the **farm lobby** had been very powerful in influencing the government. However, it now felt that

Key question
What opportunities were open to African-Americans and Native Americans?

Key question
What were economic conditions like in farming communities?

Farm lobby
Politicians and interest groups who put forward the farmers' case to the federal government and Congress.

Key term

its influence was under threat from other groups such as those representing urban interests.

Economic problems facing farmers

The years preceding the 1920s had been relatively good ones for farmers. During the war years prices had risen to over 25 per cent, and more land had been taken into cultivation. However, after the war falling demand led to falling prices. For example, wheat fell from $2.5 to $1 per bushel.

There were several reasons for this:

- Prohibition cut the demand for grain previously used in the manufacture of alcohol. In addition, higher living standards meant Americans ate more meat and comparatively fewer cereals.
- The growth of synthetic fibres lessened the market for natural ones, such as cotton.
- At the same time, technical advances meant that more crops could be produced on the same or even a reduced acreage. During the 1920s, 13 million acres were taken out of production. Farm population fell by five per cent yet production increased by nine per cent.
- Greater use of tractors meant fewer horses were necessary and this in turn meant less demand for animal food.
- Ironically, because many farmers became more efficient through mechanisation and new techniques, such as the use of improved fertilisers and better animal husbandry, they simply produced too much.

Key term

Share-croppers
Farmers who rented land and were paid by the landowners a percentage of what they produced.

As a result of these factors, possibly as many as 66 per cent of farms operated at a loss. Wage labourers, tenant farmers and **share-croppers** – in the South, these were mainly African-Americans – fared particularly badly. Some farmers grew rich by selling their land for housing and industrial development, but most appeared not to share in any prosperity in the 1920s.

Key question
What role did the government play in problems facing farmers?

Role of the government

Many farmers blamed the government for their plight. During the war, it had urged them to produce more but now it did little to compensate them for their losses. Many farmers were particularly angered by the fact that tariffs protected industry but not agriculture.

Government policy was to encourage farms to co-operate together to market their produce. To this end the Agricultural Credits Act of 1923 funded 12 Intermediate Credit Banks to offer loans to co-operatives. However, the measure was of little benefit to small farmers. The last thing they needed was more debt. But large agricultural businesses could afford to take loans to market their produce more effectively, thus squeezing the small farmers even more.

Key dates

Emergency Tariff Act: 1921
Fordney-McCumber Act: 1922
Agricultural Credits Act: 1923

Two measures of the early 1920s did, in theory, protect farmers from foreign competition: the 1921 Emergency Tariff Act and the 1922 Fordney-McCumber Act placed high tariffs on food imports.

However, because foreigners retaliated by placing similar tariffs on American foodstuffs, farmers could not export their surpluses.

Although the farm lobby refused to accept this, the reality was that if the USA was to continue to develop as an industrial nation, it was essential that manpower and resources were shifted from agriculture. But economic realities are little comfort to those badly affected by them – people who may have to leave their homes, their families and uproot themselves to try to find work in towns. However, agriculture would have to change – and change it did.

Overproduction

The biggest problem for farmers was overproduction. Too much food meant prices were too low. Farmers were reluctant to underproduce voluntarily because they could not trust their neighbours to do the same. Ideally they sought guaranteed prices, with the state possibly selling their surpluses abroad for whatever price it could get. American farmers produced so much that there were surpluses despite the rising population. However, prices had fallen to below those of 1914. Farmers considered this the 'parity' price, by which they meant the price that enabled them to break even on the costs of production.

In 1924 the McNary-Haugen bill was proposed in Congress. By its terms an Agricultural Export Corporation would be set up to buy commodities on the American market to sell abroad. It would pay farmers at the 1914 prices and sell the produce abroad at the prevailing world prices. Farmers who agreed to join the scheme would pay an **equalisation fee**. However, it was hoped by artificially reducing the amount of produce on the home market, prices would rise above 1914 levels, thus making it profitable for farmers to pay the fee and join the scheme.

In its final form, the bill transferred the equalisation fee from the farmers to the transportation and processing companies who handled the produce after it had been bought from the farmers. The bill passed twice through Congress, only to be vetoed by Coolidge, in a rare burst of energy, on each occasion. The president opposed the measure for three reasons:

- because it failed to address the overall question of overproduction
- because he felt that 'dumping' American food abroad would sour foreign relations by making American exports cheaper than foodstuffs produced in those countries, thus damaging their own agricultural sectors
- because he thought it would create the bureaucratic nightmare of attempting to co-ordinate the work of thousands of businesses.

In any event the bill was based on two very shaky assumptions: that higher prices would not stimulate additional domestic production; and that foreign markets would actually remain open to American surpluses.

Key date

McNary-Haugen Bill: 1924

Key term

Equalisation fee
The fee farmers would pay to join the proposed McNary-Haugen scheme. It was based on the difference between the price the Agricultural Export Corporation paid farmers for their produce and the price they could be sold for on the world markets.

Although there was much sense in his arguments, Coolidge did little to relieve farmers from their distress. More and more saw their mortgages foreclosed and lost the land their families had farmed for generations. Many farmers naturally became very bitter.

'Agricultural businesses'

The days of the small-scale, self-reliant farmer had already largely passed. In order to survive in the long term, farmers needed to make a profit. The 1920s saw the growth of '**agricultural businesses**' – large-scale, well-financed cereal cultivation, ranching and fruit production enterprises – using the techniques of mass production. They required comparatively little labour, except possibly in the case of fruit gathering at harvest time.

It was mainly the small-scale farmers who went bankrupt. These often asked the state for help, as they thought of big business and the banks as being in league against them.

'Get-rich-quick' schemes

While many people saw easy credit as a strength in the economy, there were also considerable drawbacks. 'Get-rich-quick' was the aim of many Americans in the 1920s; they invested in hugely speculative ventures and inevitably many lost their money. Moreover, this situation provided golden opportunities for confidence tricksters and crooks. In the early 1920s, for example, Charles Ponzi, a former vegetable seller, conned thousands of gullible people into investing in his ventures. He promised a 50 per cent profit within 90 days. Few, of course, ever saw a cent of their money again. When sentencing him to prison, the judge criticised his victims for their greed. Ponzi had not forced people to part with their money.

The period saw other more large-scale speculations, notably during the Florida Land Boom and on the Stock Exchange in the latter part of the decade.

The Florida Land Boom

While on bail awaiting trial, Ponzi found employment selling land in Florida. This was a venture well-suited to his talents. Until this time, Florida was a relatively undeveloped state with a small population. In 1910, Miami was by far the biggest city but with a population of only 54,000. Then wealthy industrialists such as Henry M. Flagler of Standard Oil built elegant hotels in the state for the rich to enjoy holidays there. With the coming of the motor car, Florida's all-year-round sunshine became accessible to the nation's middle classes and massive interest grew in the state as a paradise for vacations and retirement.

This led to a land boom. Between 1920 and 1925, the population of the state increased from 968,000 to 1.2 million. There were large-scale coastal developments. Parcels of land began to be sold to wealthy northerners on the basis of glossy brochures and salesmen's patter. People began to invest their money in unseen developments hoping to sell and make a quick

---

Key term

Agricultural businesses
Large-scale farms using machinery and techniques of mass production.

Key question
What problems were caused by 'get-rich-quick' schemes?

Building taking place on the Miami sea-front during the Florida Land Boom.

profit. Often they paid on credit, with a 10 per cent deposit known as a 'binder'. Success stories abounded to fuel the boom. It was said that someone who had bought a parcel of land for $25 in 1900 had sold it for $150,000 25 years later.

The land boom could be sustained only as long as there were more buyers than sellers. But demand tailed off in 1926. There were scandals of land advertised as within easy access of the sea that was really many miles inland or in the middle of swamps. One company, Manhattan Estates, advertised land as being three-quarters of a mile from the 'prosperous and fast growing' town of Nettie, a place that did not exist. Then nature played its part, with hurricanes in 1926 killing 400 people and leaving 50,000 homeless. With thousands of people bankrupted, the Florida land boom collapsed, leaving a coastline strewn with half-finished and storm-battered developments. With a Mediterranean fruit fly epidemic devastating the state's citrus industry in the 1930s, recovery did not begin until the Second World War when Florida became a major military training centre.

Stock market speculation

It seemed that few people were prepared to learn the lessons of Florida. As one way to get rich quickly closed so another seemed to open up. In the period from 1927 to 1929 many Americans went 'Wall Street crazy'. Easy credit meant many were able to invest in stocks and shares. They could be bought **'on the margin'**, on credit with loans from their broker.

'On the margin' Buying stocks and shares on credit.

Key term

Increasingly, people purchased stocks and shares not to invest in a company but as a speculation. If the price rose shares were sold, so making a quick and easy profit. For a time this seemed to work. Share prices seemed constantly to rise, some spectacularly so. According to the Wall Street Index, stock in the Radio Corporation of America rose from 85 to 420 points in the course of 1928. There were stories of ordinary people making immense profits.

Of course, in reality relatively few ordinary people ever dealt in shares; the figure was probably never higher than 1.5 million.

What was more significant was that large concerns were investing their profits in the stock of others. For example, Bethlehem Steel Corporation and Electric Bond and Share each had invested $157 million in the market by late 1929. If prices should fall, these firms might lose their investments and go bankrupt.

The banking system

Key question
How did the banking system lead to problems in the economy?

The banking system of the USA was out of date by the 1920s even though the central banking system had only been created in 1913. Twelve regulatory reserve banks were headed by the **Federal Reserve Board** – usually known as 'the Fed' – with seven members appointed by the president. The system, it was felt, allowed banks to regulate themselves without the government having to interfere. However, there was a significant potential problem. The Reserve Banks represented the interests of the bankers and so could not be completely relied on to act in the best interests of the nation if there was a conflict of interests. As we shall see (page 95) the Reserve Banks limited the amount of money in circulation during the Great Depression. This meant high interest rates for the banks as less money was available for borrowing. However, critics argued that more money in circulation would encourage more economic activity, which might help cure the Depression.

Key term

Federal Reserve Board
A centralised system that allowed banks to run their own affairs with only limited government interference.

While national banks had to join the centralised system, local state banks did not. Most ordinary people's money, particularly in rural and semi-rural areas, was invested in the latter. In the 1920s there were almost 30,000 banks in the USA. Most were very small and therefore unable to cope with financial problems. If they collapsed their depositors would probably lose virtually all their savings.

The Federal Reserve Board wanted to keep the market buoyant so it favoured low-interest rates. This fuelled the easy credit discussed above. The Fed also wanted to see a flow of gold from the USA to Europe, so Europeans could afford to pay back their debts.

The cycle of international debt

Key question
What was the cycle of international debt and how did it lead to problems in the US economy?

The cycle of international debt was at the heart of the economic problems of the USA. America's priority was for Europeans to repay the loans they had taken out to finance the First World War. When the problem of European countries' ability to repay came up, Coolidge is reported to have said, 'They hired the money, didn't they?'. Although the quotation is possibly fictitious, it did accurately express the sentiment of many Americans that the countries should repay their loans. However, most European countries, still suffering from depressed economic conditions arising from the war, could not afford to repay their loans.

In February 1922 Congress created the Debt Funding Commission. It suggested that the maximum deadline for repayment should be 1947 at an interest rate of 4.25 per cent. However, the simple truth was that Europeans just could not afford to repay the loans. The prohibitive tariffs made matters worse. European countries could not export their manufactured goods to the USA in great quantities; therefore they found it impossible to earn the money to repay the loans.

However, an agreement was made with Britain in January 1923 for her to repay her $4600 million debt within 62 years at an interest rate of 3.3 per cent. Following this agreements were made within the next five years with 15 countries under which interest rates were to be scaled down and more generous repayment time limits allowed.

Key dates

Creation of the Debt Funding Commission: 1922

Dawes Plan: 1924

Young Plan: 1929

The problems caused by Germany

Repayment of debts was only part of the problem. Germany had, by the terms of the Treaty of Versailles, been forced to pay **reparations** of $33,000 million to the victorious nations of Europe. Under the **Dawes** and **Young Plans**, the USA lent it the money to do so. With this money, the European victors repaid the USA what they could of the loans. The USA was thus effectively paying itself back with its own money. Indeed, the $250 million it lent to Germany under the Dawes Plan corresponded to the amount Germany actually paid the Allies in reparations, which in turn corresponded with the amount the USA received from the Allies in debt repayments.

This situation became even more confused through the Dawes and Young Plans further scaling down German reparations. With Germany paying the European victors less, this meant that they in turn could repay less of their own debts to the USA. All in all, no one gained from an incredibly complex situation that, according to one commentator, would have made more sense if 'the US had taken the money out of one Treasury building and put it in another'.

The banks hoped the movement of American funds to Europe would help the victors repay the loans. American investors did increasingly put their money in European ventures. However, this investment took place particularly in Germany where $3900 million was invested after the Dawes Plan. Wall Street brokers earned fat commissions for putting investors in touch with businesses requiring investment. Massive over-investment took place. Once again it was often a case of investors hoping to make a quick profit without going too carefully into the actual details of the transaction. As a result, there were absurd examples such as the Bavarian village that asked for $125,000 to build a swimming pool, and received $3 million.

However, with reparations reduced, investment in Germany hardly helped the European victors repay their American loans. Its main effect was to make the tangle of international debt even more complex.

Key terms

Reparations
Under the postwar settlements Germany had been required to pay compensation of $33,000 million to the victorious countries.

Dawes Plan 1924
Offered Germany scaled-down reparations and provided it with a loan of $250 million to help stabilise its currency.

Young Plan 1929
Offered further scaled-down reparations.

Was the boom slowing down?

The boom was dependent on continuing domestic consumption. High tariffs and generally depressed economies in Europe meant that American producers could sell comparatively little abroad.

Key question
What were the signs that the economic boom of the 1920s slowing down?

There were, by the late 1920s, three indicators that the boom was slowing down.

(1) Problems in small businesses

The decade, as we have seen, witnessed the growth of huge corporations with considerable marketing power. As a result, smaller businesses often faced hard times. During the course of the 1920s, for every four businesses that succeeded, three failed. The number of motor vehicle companies, for example, fell from 108 in 1920 to 44 by the end of the decade. The government was no more prepared to help out failing industrial concerns than it was the farmers.

(2) The construction industry

Economic historians tend to agree that the state of the construction industry is generally a good indicator of the overall health of the economy. The mid-1920s saw a great boom in construction, particularly in housing, office building and highways. However, after 1926 demand began to tail off. This led to a fall in demand for building materials, skills such as plumbing and building materials transportation. This, in turn, led to higher unemployment in construction-related businesses and had serious knock-on effects on concerns dependent on their custom.

(3) Falling domestic demand

By the late 1920s, production was outstripping demand. The domestic market was becoming flooded with goods that could not be sold. More and more people were in no position to spend on non-essential items. In April 1929, for example, it was estimated that 10 per cent of Philadelphia's labour force was unemployed even though the national unemployment statistics remained low. Irving Fisher, a Yale economist, estimated that in 1929 as many as 80 per cent of the American people were living close to subsistence – even when they were in work.

Labor unions

Key term

Labor union American term for trades unions, set up to look after the interests of their members.

Workers could not on the whole look to **labor unions** for help. The government did nothing to protect them, and indeed the Supreme Court had blocked attempts by unions to ban child labour and impose a minimum wage for women as being unconstitutional. Many employers operated 'yellow dog' clauses by which their employees were not allowed to join a union. During the 1920s union membership declined overall by one million.

Interestingly, the employers in the new industries tended to be most anti-union, which explains why during this period unions failed to get more than a toehold in these. The older industries tended, as we have seen (pages 48–9), to be in trouble during the decade. The government successfully sought injunctions against union activities earlier in the 1920s and by the close of the decade, employees generally were more anxious to keep their jobs than embark on union agitation.

With growth in the new industries beginning to slow, full-time employment fell and the economy entered into a downward spiral. A fall in income led to a fall in demand, which in turn led to a fall in production that added to unemployment and underemployment (short-time working). However, the fact that the economy was experiencing problems was concealed by superficial optimism and the frenzy of stock market speculation.

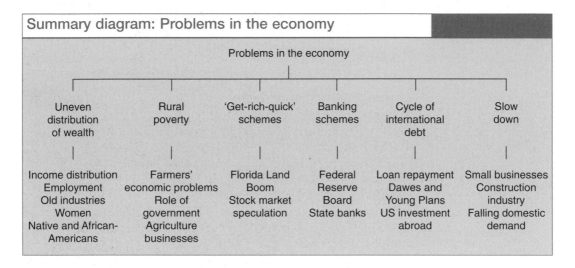

Summary diagram: Problems in the economy

5 | The Strength of the Economy

Key question
How strong was the American economy in the 1920s?

It is easy with hindsight to see the problems in the American economy. At the time, however, detailed understanding of how a developed economy works was far less sophisticated than it is today. While there was concern among experts, some even forecasting accurately the coming collapse, they had little influence. Many historians would agree with Hugh Brogan who wrote in 1985 that, 'At every stage the story displays the devastating consequences of a bland unawareness of economic and political essentials'. Arthur Schlesinger Jr and J.K. Galbraith are influential historians who have been particularly scathing about the role of the government.

Others, however, particularly economic historians, have been less critical. The American economy seemed to be doing well especially when compared to others, notably those in Europe. After all, the figures denoting growth seem to speak for themselves. It is also important to note that the capitalist system survived the coming financial collapse almost intact. Many of the manufacturing and marketing companies of the 1920s have continued to operate to the present day, as have the banking and investment houses.

While many Americans felt confidence and optimism for the future, within a year the USA was in the grip of the deepest depression in its history. In the following chapter we will consider the Wall Street Crash and its relationship with the onset of this economic catastrophe.

Summary diagram: Prosperity?

Year	1922	1923	1924	1925	1926	1927	1928
Political	Fordney-McCumber Act	Dawes Plan	McNary-Haugen bill Tax cuts		Tax cuts		Coolidge retired
Social/economic				Florida Land Boom	Collapse of Florida Land Boom Peak of construction boom	Speculation on Stock Exchange Ford closure until introduction of Model A	

Government

High tariffs
Tax cuts — Industrial expansion ← Mass production
Less government — Growth of advertising
Consumer boom

Little help for farmers — Agricultural depression ← Rural poverty
Small farms go out of business
Rural unrest

Policies of *laissez-faire* — Unregulated economy ← Great extremes of wealth and poverty
Unchecked speculation
Little government help for needy members of society

Study Guide: AS Questions

Many economic questions look at the 1920s in the context of the Wall Street Crash and these will be considered at the end of Chapter 4.

In the style of AQA

How widespread was the prosperity of the 1920s in the USA?

Study tips

The cross-references are intended to take you straight to the material that will help you to answer the question.

Here you need to consider different economic areas such as farming (pages 50–53) and manufacturing (pages 39–43) and different regions, particularly in terms of the rural/urban divide (pages 48–9) before coming to an informed judgement in your conclusion.

In your planning, in order to consider more deeply the issue of how strong the American economy was during this period, you might find it helpful to construct a chart:

Strengths	Weaknesses	Both strengths and weaknesses	Unsure

The columns should include factors you consider appropriate to each. When you have completed the chart, you can expand your notes by explaining why you have placed the factors where you have done. You should then be able to make an informed judgement on the strength of the American economy in the 1920s.

In the style of Edexcel

Study Sources 1–5 below and on pages 61–2 and then answer the questions that follow.

Source 1

From: an interview given by a small town banker in 1925.

The ambition to own an automobile does not confine itself to the upper classes and those with substantial incomes, but reaches down to 'white collar workers' – the clerks and salaried men on limited incomes. In my own bank fifty per cent of the force own cars and drive to work in them. I do not believe the middle classes are getting ahead as they once were. What formerly went into the bank now goes into the motor car. The thought in the minds of many workers is not how much they can save, but how long it will be before they can have a motor.

Source 2

From: a speech by Calvin Coolidge given in 1928.

In the domestic field there is tranquillity and contentment, harmonious relationships between management and the wage earner, freedom from industrial strife, and the highest record of years of prosperity. The country can regard the present with satisfaction and anticipate the future with optimism.

Source 3

From: a letter by Bernard Baruch written in 1925. Baruch made millions dealing in stocks and shares. Allegedly he realised the market had reached its peak when even a beggar offered him stock market tips.

Now let me make a prediction to you. Business has undoubtedly reached its zenith [peak], and what we see in motors, steel and railroad statements, is evidence of what has gone by and not what is before us. There has been a simulation of business by high power salesmanship on the partial payment plan (buying on credit) of homes, radios, automobiles etc. Whereas it is wise to buy things on the partial payment plan that will result in time in increased economies and better living, at the same time it can be overdone. I am afraid it has now been overdone.

Source 4

Poverty in the 1920s

Source 5

From: Daniel Snowman, USA the Twenties to Vietnam, *in 1968.*

In the long term however the bonanza of the 1920s could not last – and it was likely to come to an end partly because of the existence of the very pockets of poverty upon which it had earlier been built. Manufacturers continued to produce goods (including large quantities of new luxury goods) at an unprecedented rate, but the extent to which they could seek foreign markets was severely limited by the economic isolationism of the decade. Many of them were therefore forced to try to sell most of their products in the glutted domestic market. As the decade progressed, the home market showed signs of reaching saturation point... Since wages were low and unemployment not infrequent, a sizeable body of potential consumers was simply not equipped to join in the spending spree.

(a) **Study Source 1**
What does Source 1 reveal about attitudes to car ownership in the USA in the 1920s? (6 marks)

(b) **Use your own knowledge**
Use your own knowledge to explain why the agricultural sector did not share in the prosperity of the 1920s.
(10 marks)

(c) **Study Sources 2 and 3**
How far does Source 3 support the argument put forward in Source 2? (10 marks)

(d) **Study Sources 3 and 4**
How useful are these two sources to the historian enquiring into prosperity in the USA in the 1920s? (10 marks)

(e) **Study Sources 2 and 5 and use your own knowledge**
How far do you agree with the statement in Source 2, that in terms of the economy, 'The country can regard the present with satisfaction'?

Explain your answer using Sources 2 and 5 and your own knowledge. (24 marks)

Exam tips

The cross-references are intended to take you straight to the material that will help you to answer the questions.

1. Question **(a)** suggests that car ownership was very important to the middle classes. Note that it suggests they might be wiser to save their money than go for the instant gratification of car ownership.

2. Question **(b)** requires your own knowledge to discuss why the agricultural sector appeared not to be doing well. It is crucial to keep to the question why rather than just describe factors (pages 50–3).

3. Question **(c)** invites you to cross-reference the two sources in terms of how far Source 3 supports Source 2. To cross-reference you need to compare what each source is saying and come to a judgement supported by evidence from the sources to show how far Source 3 supports Source 2 – in what ways do they agree, and in what ways disagree?

They do not have to agree, in which case you could argue that Source 3 does not give Source 2 much support. While it recognises the USA appears prosperous at present, it feels there will be a downturn and the domestic market is saturated with goods. Source 2, on the other hand, is wholly optimistic both about the present and the future.

4. Question **(d)** is concerned with how useful a historian would find these sources. You need to consider issues such as how typical they might be in the opinions they express, how objective, how well they are supported by evidence. Note that a letter may offer a private view that is not intended for publication. We don't know how typical the photograph is of conditions, although it would certainly suggest that families like the one depicted could not share in any consumer boom.

5. Question **(e)** invites you to consider the two sources and your own knowledge to make a judgement about how correct Coolidge was in suggesting Americans could look to the future with optimism. You need to consider both the apparent economic successes such as technical advances and new business methods (pages 39–46) and the signs that the economy was slowing such as the problems with small businesses, the construction industry and falling domestic demand to show how demand was falling (pages 56–8).

Study Guide: Advanced Level Questions

In the style of OCR
Study the following four passages, A, B, C and D on 1920s prosperity and answer both sub-questions that follow.

Passage A
From: a speech by Herbert Hoover, Republican candidate for the presidency in 1928.

We have in the 1920s decreased the fear of poverty, fear of unemployment, the fear of old age. Prosperity is no idle expression. It is a job for every worker, it is the safety and safeguard of every business and every home. We are nearer today to the ideal of the abolition of poverty and fear from the lives of men and women than ever before in any land.

Passage B
From: Paul Johnson, A History of the American People, *new edition published in 2000, an historian who argues that there was real prosperity in the USA in the 1920s.*

The prosperity of the Coolidge era was huge, real, widespread but not ubiquitous and unprecedented. It was not permanent – what prosperity ever is? But it is foolish and unhistorical to judge it insubstantial because we now know what followed later. At the time it was as solid as houses built, meals eaten, automobiles driven, cash spent and property acquired. Prosperity was more widely distributed in the America of the 1920s than had been possible in any community of this size before, and it involved the acquisition, by tens of millions of ordinary families, of an economic security that been denied them throughout all previous history.

Passage C

From Hugh Brogan, The Penguin History of the United States of America, *first published in 1985, an historian who tries to find warning signs beneath the apparent prosperity of the 1920s.*

Already the forces which were to destroy Coolidge prosperity were at work. Indeed, the first signs of trouble came as early as 1926, when the sale of new housing began to slacken. This had various causes, among them the collapse of a land boom in Florida, where thousands of sun hungry Northerners had been hoaxed into buying pieces of swamp, miles from the sea, in the belief that they were getting valuable property near the beach... A more serious cause of the housing slowdown was the fact that the market was becoming saturated, like the market for farm products. Of course there were still tens of millions of Americans who needed better housing than they were ever likely to get, but they had no money. By 1926, those who had money had usually already acquired their houses or mortgages; and though new buyers came on to the market every year, they were not numerous enough to sustain the boom.

Passage D

From: John A Garraty, The American Nation, *1991, in which the historian summarises the problems behind the apparent prosperity of the 1920s.*

While most economic indicators reflected an unprecedented prosperity, the boom time rested on unstable foundations. The problem was mainly one of maladministration of resources. Productive capacity raced ahead of buying power. Too large a share of the profits were going into too few pockets. The 27,000 families with the highest annual incomes in 1929 received as much money as the 11 million with annual incomes of under $1500, the minimum sum required at that time to maintain a family decently. High earnings and low taxes permitted huge sums to pile up in the hands of individuals who did not invest the money productively.

(i) Compare the views expressed in Passages A and B as interpretations of the prosperity of the 1920s. (15 marks)
(ii) Using these four passages and your own knowledge, discuss the claim that the collapse of prosperity was evident as early as 1926. (30 marks)

Exam tips

The cross-references are intended to take you straight to the material that will help you answer the questions.

(i)   In comparing passages as interpretations you need to look at issues such as who is the author, when the source dates from, what biases the author might be expected to have and how much evidence is being offered in support. The emphasis is on evaluation of the passage rather than attempting to analyse what they say.

  • Passage A is from an optimistic speech from a Republican candidate for the presidency. We would expect him to be confident as he is to a certain extent asking to be elected because his predecessors' policies had been so successful. He did not have the benefit of hindsight and could not see that the prosperity might be coming to an end. Even if he did know this he would be expected to keep quiet about it in an address intended for those he wanted to vote for him.

  • Passage B has been written many years later, and while on the surface it would seem to support the view that the prosperity was real at the time, there are nevertheless provisos that it was not permanent. However, we should be not be coloured in our view of 1920s prosperity by the Depression that followed it.

  • Overall then, while the two passages may appear similar in what they say, there are differences that you should discuss. Try to evaluate the passages in relation to each other rather than discussing them separately.

(ii) The examiner is looking at the quality of your argument rather than the conclusion you reach. You will be assessed on the depth and breadth of your answer and how well you marry your own knowledge with information contained in the four passages.

  • Passage A is a political speech suggesting the prosperity is real and there is no mention of any problems.

  • Passage B, while acknowledging the prosperity didn't last, nevertheless insists it was real at the time.

  • Passages C and D go beyond this to look at underlying weaknesses. While Passage C focuses on the building industry as an indicator of economic conditions, Passage D takes a more general view about production outstripping demand.

  • You could supplement these factors with discussion taken from pages 48–56 looking at problems in the economy. You could consider issues such as uneven distribution of income, problems in agriculture, 'get-rich-quick schemes, the cycle of international debt and whether or not the boom was slowing down.

  Again it is important to consider the passages in relation to each other rather than separately. You also need to bring in the historical debate as to when the signs of a downturn in the economy were apparent. You need to cross-reference both the sources and your own substantiated judgements in order to arrive at a balanced answer.

4 The Collapse of the Wall Street Stock Market October 1929

POINTS TO CONSIDER
In October 1929 the Wall Street stock market crashed. This chapter has three aims:

- To give an account of the Wall Street Crash
- To examine the causes of the Crash
- To consider its effects, particularly in relation to the onset of the Great Depression

Key date
1929   October 24–9 'Wall Street Crash' – collapse of the stock market

1 | The Wall Street Crash

Key question
What chain of events led to the Wall Street Crash?

In October 1929 the New York Stock Exchange crashed. It handled about 61 per cent of stocks and shares transactions in the USA. Crashes in other stock exchanges throughout the country soon followed. While the collapse in Wall Street had been forecast by many financial experts, their warnings had gone largely unheeded. The event was to affect millions of people, most of whom did not own stocks and shares. The Wall Street Crash is perhaps the most famous event in the period covered by this book; and it is the purpose of this chapter first to describe what actually happened and then to examine its causes and significance.

The stampede to sell

On Thursday 24 October 1929 a massive amount of selling began in the New York Stock Exchange. This forced prices down and led to more selling still as **brokers** feared they would be left with worthless stock. By 11 am, a mad panic had set in. US Steel, which had opened that morning at 205.5 points, was down to 193.5, General Electric had fallen from 315 points to 283 and Radio Corporation of America had collapsed from 68.75 points to 44.5. No one appeared to understand what was going on.

Broker
Person who buys and sells stocks and shares.

Key term

Key term

Ticker
Ticker-tape on which stocks and shares transactions were recorded.

People are afraid of the unknown, of things they cannot control – and what was going on here was certainly out of control. On one wall of the Stock Exchange was a large board recording transactions; this was called the **ticker**. Unfortunately, as the volume of sales mushroomed, it could no longer keep pace with them and began to fall badly behind. At 10-minute intervals, a separate bond ticker in the corner would punch out a list of selected up-to-date prices. As brokers hushed to hear these read out, they realised with horror that stocks bought possibly just moments earlier were now worth considerably less than they had agreed to pay for them.

As more and more brokers rushed to sell, the scenes became so wild that the police had to be called in to restore order. As news of the panic spread, an excited crowd gathered outside the building. It was even said that some coach-tour companies diverted their vehicles to take New York sightseers to witness the goings-on. A workman repairing a high building was believed to be a broker contemplating suicide. He was possibly inadvertently responsible for the myth that bankrupted brokers were throwing themselves from the rooftops. Comparatively few brokers did, in fact, go bankrupt. It was largely their clients' wealth that was being lost.

Efforts to protect the market

A meeting of six important bankers was going on in the offices of J.P. Morgan Ltd at 23 Wall Street. Each of them agreed to put up $40 million to shore up the market by buying stocks and shares. Thomas W. Lamont, senior partner at J.P. Morgan Ltd, held a press conference. 'There has been a little distress on the stock market', he said, with a masterly sense of understatement. He went on to explain that this was due entirely to a technical

Panic on Wall Street 'Black Thursday' 29 October 1929. Notice the policemen on horseback to control the crowds.

difficulty, and the situation was 'susceptible to betterment' – by which he meant things would improve.

Meanwhile, the vice-president of the Stock Exchange, Richard Whitney, a floor broker for J.P. Morgan Ltd, was buying stock above current prices in lots of 10,000 in an attempt to restore confidence in the market. The bankers having come to the rescue, confidence returned and the situation improved. At the close of the day the **New York Times Index**, based on an aggregate of 25 leading industrial stocks, was only 12 points down.

The ticker, however, did not record the final transactions until eight minutes past seven in the evening – dealing closed at 3 pm – and clerks worked long into the night on the accounts resulting from all this business.

Altogether nearly 13 million shares had changed hands. By comparison, a normal day's transactions would be about 3 million. Stock-market employees, letting off steam after such a frenzied day, caused the police to be called to Wall Street again.

For the next few days calm was restored in the market. Everyone who had weathered the storm breathed a sigh of relief. A Boston investment trust placed an advertisement in the *Wall Street Journal*: 'S-T-E-A-D-Y Everybody! Calm thinking is in order. Heed the words of America's greatest bankers'.

On Sunday, churchgoers heard that a divine warning had been sent concerning the dangers of financial greed and speculation. However there was little evidence that many would heed the warning. Most newspapers appeared confident that the stock market was healthy and the days ahead would see a rush to buy at the new lower prices.

> **Key term**
>
> **New York Times Index**
> An indicator of how well stocks and shares are doing based on the 25 leading stocks.

The Crash

In the event, while the volume of trading on Monday was less than that of the previous Thursday, the fall in prices was far more severe. The New York Times Index showed a drop of 49 points on the day's trading and no Richard Whitney had appeared with orders to buy. After the close of business, bankers held a two-hour meeting at J.P. Morgan Ltd. Those expecting them to come to the rescue again were to be sadly disappointed. It was not their business, the bankers explained, to protect stock-market prices, but simply to ensure the market was orderly.

Next day, confidence collapsed completely. This was Tuesday 29 October, the day that the stock market on Wall Street crashed. Altogether, 16,410,030 shares were sold and the New York Times Index fell a further 43 points. In the chaos of frenzied selling, there was talk of closing the Exchange at noon, but it was felt this would simply increase the panic. However, the Exchange did remain closed the next day and only opened one afternoon, on Thursday, during the remainder of the week. Prices continued to fall, and despite occasional rallies the overall trend was downward. In a few weeks, as much as $30 billion had been lost. This represented a sum almost as great as that which the USA had spent on its involvement in the First World War. Figure 4.1 gives some indication of the level of losses.

Company	Share price on 3.9.1929	Share price on 3.11.1929
American Can	187.86	86.00
Ananconda Copper	131.50	70.00
General Motors	72.75	36.00
Montgomery Ward	137.86	49.25
Radio	101.00	28.00
Woolworth	100.37	52.25
Electric Share and Bond	186.75	50.25

Figure 4.1: The fall in share prices. Source: Frederick Allen, *Only Yesterday*, Harper & Row, 1931.

Key question
How extensive was the Wall Street Crash?

Extent of the Wall Street Crash

It is worth remembering that even after October 1929 prices still stood higher than they had done at any time during the previous year. What had been wiped out were the spectacular gains of the first nine months of 1929. After the Crash, experts did not believe that lasting damage had been done. On 26 October, for example, the Harvard Economic Society felt that the fall in prices would be temporary and would not cause any economic depression. Prices did not really plunge until 1932, when it was clear that the Great Depression dating from the early 1930s was going to continue into the long term and recovery was not, as President Hoover had continued to insist, just around the corner. On 8 June 1932, for example, the New York Times Index closed at 58.46. By contrast it had stood at 164.43 in November 1929, less than a month after the Wall Street Crash

It is often popularly believed that the Wall Street Crash led to the Great Depression. However, many historians have argued that it was simply one sign of a depression already well on the way. Moreover, stock markets had crashed before and have done since without any ensuing economic depression. In order to analyse the part played in this history by the Wall Street Crash, it is necessary first to identify its causes and then to examine its impact within the context of an economy whose growth was, as we have seen in Chapter 3, already slowing.

Key question
What factors caused the huge growth in the stock market after 1927?

2 | Causes of the Wall Street Crash

Historians have identified several causes of the Wall Street Crash.

The nature of the bull market

The stock market contained the seeds of its own collapse. To understand these we need to examine how the market operated in the years up to the Wall Street Crash. A 'bullish' market is characterised by a large volume of buying and selling. Reference has already been made in Chapter 3 to the nature of the stock market between 1927 and 1929, which earned it the nickname 'Great Bull Market'.

The New York Times Index averages (which reflected the volume of trading) rose considerably from 1924 to 1929 (see Table 4.1). Brokers spoke excitedly of breaking the ceiling of five million transactions in one day. But even they had underestimated. On 23 November 1928, shortly after the electoral victory of President Hoover, seven million transactions took place. The cost of a seat for a broker on the New York Stock Exchange rose to $580,000. America, it seemed, went 'Wall Street Crazy'. There were scores of anecdotes to encourage further speculation. Examples include the nurse who became rich on the stock-market tips of grateful patients and the broker's valet who made $250,000. Bernard Baruch, who had made a fortune on the stock market, reported that one day he was given tips on what stocks to buy by a beggar. Presumably he chose not to heed the advice.

The amount of trading on the market grew, particularly after Hoover's victory in the 1928 presidential election when optimism about American prosperity, fuelled by statements of confidence coming from the government, seemed unshakeable. In summer 1929, for example, loans to stock-market investors climbed towards the figure of $6 billion compared to $3.5 billion at the end of 1927. Prices of popular stocks rose dramatically.

There are many causes of the **bull market**, not least, as we have seen, the desire of people to 'get rich quick' (see pages 53–5). There were, however, several other factors to consider.

Reduction of interest rates

Historians agree that the trigger was the decision by the Federal Reserve Board to lower **rediscount rates** in August 1927 from four per cent to 3.5 per cent. This step was actually taken to encourage American trade abroad, but in fact the main effect of lower interest rates was to encourage borrowing at home.

Confidence in the economy

Financiers, it should be remembered, were very confident in the strength of the economy. Those with surplus funds naturally wanted to use them to make even more money. The Stock Exchange offered just such an opportunity. Wall Street stock-broking firms encouraged people to invest in shares by opening more and more offices – in 1919 there were 500 but in October 1928 there were 1192.

Buying shares 'on the margin'

An estimated 50,000 people bought their shares 'on the margin' (see page 54). This meant they put down only a fraction of the price, borrowing the rest from the broker who in turn borrowed largely from the banks to pay for the shares.

Table 4.1: New York Times Index averages

Date	Average
May 1924	106
Dec. 1925	181
Dec. 1927	245
Sept. 1929	542

Key terms

Bull market
Stock market where there is lots of confidence and lots of buying and selling.

Rediscount rates
The interest rates at which banks borrow money from the Federal Reserve banks.

With prices rising constantly, few paused to consider what might happen if they fell. Purchasers would in fact be left still having to pay the original price for assets that were worth less than the amount that they had agreed to pay for them. Many people no doubt saw buying 'on the margin' in the same way as they saw hire-purchase arrangements – as a way of buying now and paying later. They believed that by this method they could pay their debts out of the profits that their shares were expected to make. It seemed a foolproof way of growing rich.

Media encouragement
Stock-market investment was further encouraged by the popular press. For example, an article entitled 'Everyone Ought to be Rich' appeared in the *Ladies' Home Journal*. The author showed that if readers saved $15 per month and invested this in stock and then allowed dividends to grow, they would, at the end of 21 years, have at least $80,000. This would give them interest payments of $400 per month. How could anyone fail? Could investors afford to miss out?

Brokers' selling techniques
Brokers' selling techniques were very persuasive. Potential buyers were advised to consider the wealth of someone today who had bought 100 shares in General Motors in 1919; they were warned that prices would never be as low as this again. With endorsements of the strength and soundness of the market from the president as well as from influential businessmen, many people were prepared to invest more than they could afford.

Types of people who bought shares
J.K. Galbraith, an eminent economic historian has identified three types of purchasers of shares:

• Those who believed in the strength of the enterprise in which they invested. This group normally expected their dividends to come from the profits of the concern; often they would keep their shares for a considerable period of time, take an interest in the company, attend share-holders' meetings and the like. In a stable market, they would tend to be the biggest group of purchasers of shares.

However, this was not the case in the bull market of the late 1920s. Many people were buying shares in businesses not in the expectation that they might make a profit, but simply that the value of its stock would increase. This would give them the opportunity to sell at a quick profit. Radio Corporation of America, for example, saw its share prices rise from 94.5 points to 504 in 18 months without ever having paid a single dividend.

This very fact alone helps demonstrate that it was a speculative market rather than one based on real economic growth. There was no indication that Radio Corporation of America was a reliable and prosperous company other than the demand for its shares. Share purchase followed what was in vogue at the time. Buying stock in aeronautical companies became popular after the exploits of aviators such as Charles Lindbergh, the first man to fly solo across the Atlantic.

- Those who sought to 'get rich quick'. They were, perhaps, the majority of players in the 'Great Bull Market'. They are sometimes described as the innocents who did not understand the workings of the market, although they thought they did. Generally, they expected prices to keep rising. They would sell specific stock at what they believed were the best times to maximise their profits – before they expected prices in that specific stock to fall. Characteristically, this group bought stock purely as speculation. They had no thought of investing in an actual concern but bought and sold simply on the expected movement of prices. Not unnaturally, this was the group that tended to lose heavily in the Wall Street Crash.

- Those who were 'streetwise' and took full advantage of the boom, intending to get out before the inevitable collapse. These tended to be the large-scale financiers and bankers. Typically, many of these attempted to inflate prices artificially. William Durant, for example, operated the famous '**bull pool**'; he and his colleagues bought and sold shares back and forth to each other, giving the impression of great market interest in a particular issue. Once unwary outsiders began to buy, sending the prices still higher, they would sell, making a huge profit. This selling would cause prices to fall and the outsiders would be left with much depreciated stock. There was little regulation of activities such as 'insider dealing' and it was easy to take advantage of others' naivety.

Key term

Bull pool
Method by which unscrupulous brokers bought and sold stock to and from each other to keep prices high.

Instability in the market

In fact, the market was not characterised by an unbroken rise in prices. There were falls – in March, June and December 1928, and in March 1929 for example. However, the market had always recovered, casting doubts on those financial experts who warned that prices were dangerously high. Roger Babson seems to have been remarkably farsighted when, in September 1929, he warned that existing prosperity rested precariously on a 'state of mind' and not on economic facts. He went on to predict a crash that would lead to massive unemployment and economic depression.

However, Babson and others were criticised as being overpessimistic, threatening to undermine the economic well being of the nation. Both President Coolidge and President Hoover had given periodic reassuring noises. However, Coolidge had been alerted as early as 1927 by William R. Zipley of Harvard University to the fact that there were serious problems with the Stock Exchange. Coolidge did not believe it was the job of government to involve itself in the stock market. Hoover tried to blame Governor Roosevelt of New York for the Crash, saying it was his responsibility to regulate Wall Street and he had failed to do this. At the time, few listened to any attempt to shift the blame by Hoover. However, Roosevelt had not shown any public concern

Key question
How stable was the stock market?

about the volume of Stock Exchange trading. Others said that the governor of New York should have done more to control the market.

The truth was that most experts seemed confident that the market was strong and the vast majority of people had little reason to doubt them. For example, on 17 October 1929 Professor Irving Fisher stated that prices had reached 'what looks to be a permanently high plateau'.

We can see with hindsight that the market was so unstable that its eventual collapse was highly likely. However this should not blind us to the optimism and faith in the strength of the market that people felt at the time. It is worth remembering, too, that experts at the time often had an antiquated understanding of the way markets worked and had failed to see how these had become outmoded by twentieth-century developments, such as the expansion of credit.

Key question
What part did the banking system play in the Wall Street Crash?

The banking system

One of the most frequent criticisms of the 'Great Bull Market' was that there was no effective control over its activities. The government, as we have seen, pursued policies of *laissez-faire* that tended to favour big business, and the regulatory powers of the central banking system were severely limited.

The Federal Reserve Board could intervene in the market in three principal ways.

(1) Sale of government securities

The Federal Reserve Board could authorise the sale of government securities on the market, hoping purchasers might prefer these safe investments to those which paid higher dividends but were riskier in terms of price fluctuations. In the event, instead of doing this, the Board actually bought government securities from the banks that owned them. This meant, of course, that after selling them, the banks now had more funds to lend for possibly risky investments. The Board did this for sound reasons. Economic growth was slowing and it believed that if banks had more money to lend this would stimulate the economy. However, the major effect was to stimulate borrowing and stock-market speculation.

(2) Raise interest rates

Raise the rediscount rate to discourage further borrowing. As we have seen on page 70, the Federal Reserve Board unwittingly helped create the bull market by reducing the rediscount rate from four per cent to 3.5 per cent in spring 1927. Concerned at the vast spread of credit, it did finally raise the rediscount rate to five per cent in December 1928. However, this had little effect on a market running out of control.

Indeed, the Board overruled a proposal by the New York Reserve Bank to raise the rediscount rate further to six per cent. A rise at this level would in any event have been quite inadequate to deter borrowing at a time when brokers' loans were finding plenty of takers at twice that level of interest. To make matters worse, non-banking concerns such as Bethlehem Steel and Chrysler were also lending monies to brokers that could otherwise have been invested in their own development.

In this situation, the Federal Reserve Board seemed quite powerless. It did raise the rediscount rate to six per cent in August 1929 but, as expected, this had no noticeable effect on checking speculation. The Board was worried that if the rediscount rate was increased too much, a crash might result. Probably many senior bankers did privately realise just how delicate the market actually was and so were very wary of meddling too much with it lest they might set off a panic and possible collapse.

Moreover, the bankers who made up the Federal Reserve system had what they considered to be sound reasons for not raising interest rates.

- First, being private bankers, they tended to put their financial concerns before those of the national interest. They had no wish to harm banks (and themselves) by making them pay more for funds by raising interest rates.
- Second, it should be remembered that a major aim of bankers was to promote foreign trade. They judged that higher interest rates were likely to make American goods too expensive for foreign buyers in already depressed foreign markets.

The simple fact was that, while it may well have been in the interests of the country to control credit through higher interest rates, the picture was much more complex than that. Other considerations dictated that higher interest rates would not be a satisfactory option for bankers. The stock market, meanwhile, continued to operate unchecked.

(3) Moral leadership

The Federal Reserve Board could offer moral leadership. On 2 February 1929, for example, it said that it would not support banks who lent money for risky ventures.

The immediate result of this was a fall in stock prices and an increase in the interest rate on brokers' loans to as high as 20 per cent. The meetings of the Federal Reserve Board were held in secret; this certainly made the market uneasy. This again demonstrated how delicate the situation actually was.

In the event, Charles A. Mitchell, President of New York's National City Bank and a director of the New York Federal Reserve Bank, announced on 26 March that if money became tight as a result of higher rediscount rates, his bank would pump a further $25 million into the brokers' loan market. This was later called 'the single most irresponsible decision of 1929'.

Mitchell was attacked in Congress for sabotaging the policy of the Federal Reserve Board. The accusation was certainly true. The market recovered and prices soared until the crash. The Federal Reserve Board was shown to have been an irrelevance to the market, its powers wholly inadequate to supervise what was going on. However, it is also true that the Board could have asked Congress for more powers, for example over the control of credit, but it did not.

Wider powers

It is unlikely that the Board would have been granted further powers had they been requested. There are five possible reasons for this:

Key question
What reasons worked against the banks being given more powers to regulate the economy?

- The mood of the country was generally against regulation in any aspect of economic life.
- The Federal Reserve Board was made up of bankers who operated principally in the interests of their own banks and, if these clashed with the national interest, their own interests invariably came first (see pages 55 and 74).
- The bull market was associated in the public eye with prosperity. It had not collapsed. To the average layman, it seemed to be in a very healthy state, and there would have been no great support for its regulation.
- The main policy of the Federal Reserve System was to encourage the movement of funds to Europe through increased trade. This necessitated low interest rates so investors could afford to borrow funds to invest in Europe. This policy was particularly associated with one of the leading American bankers of this period, Benjamin Strong, Governor of the New York Federal Reserve Bank.

Strong died in 1928. Some historians have argued that, had he lived, he would have had the skills and influence to curb speculation without risking a market crash. However, although Strong was privately concerned about the level of speculation and borrowing, there is no evidence to suggest that he would have done anything more than anyone else to stop it. Raising the rediscount rate would have threatened the USA's trading policies by making their goods even more expensive for foreigners to buy.

Loss of confidence

Key question
How far did loss of confidence contribute to the Wall Street Crash?

It has been emphasised that the market structure was maintained largely by the confidence that people had in it. Historians point to various reasons why that confidence collapsed in October 1929, rather than at any other time:

- The British financial empire built up by Clarence Hatry collapsed at this time. Hatry had been involved in various dubious ventures before making a fortune in the development of vending and automatic photography machines. However, he was caught issuing fraudulent stock to raise badly needed revenue to keep his enterprises solvent. Hatry's business collapsed and he went to jail. This showed that enterprises financed by debt, as his was, were vulnerable. Investors in the USA began to look with concern at some of the businesses in which they had stock.

- Rumours spread that many of the biggest players on the stock market, such as Bernard Baruch and Joseph Kennedy, both of whom had made huge fortunes on the stock market, were selling their stock.
- There were rumours that the Federal Reserve Board was about to tighten credit facilities by making it more difficult for people to borrow.

In this atmosphere of increasing uncertainty, lenders began to call in credit. For example, over the weekend between 25 and 28 October 1929 banks began to demand repayment from the brokers to whom they had lent money. The brokers in turn began to put the squeeze on their clients, who had to sell stock in order to repay their loans. This increased selling brought down prices.

Pressure for repayment meant that credit was evaporating. One lady, presented by her broker with a bill for $100,000, was alleged to have demanded 'How could I lose $100,000. I never had $100,000'. While this anecdote may well not be true, it shows the naivety of many of those buying and selling shares, who either did not realise or chose to ignore the fact that prices could indeed plummet as well as soar. Certainly the Crash saw pawnbrokers turning away people seeking loans on their jewellery to repay their stock-market debts. In the event, it tended to be the 'innocents' who were ruined by the Wall Street Crash – although this is not to suggest that other, more professional financial interests did not also suffer.

However, the truth is that the market, supported by so little real wealth, could have collapsed at any time. There is little really noteworthy about the actual timing.

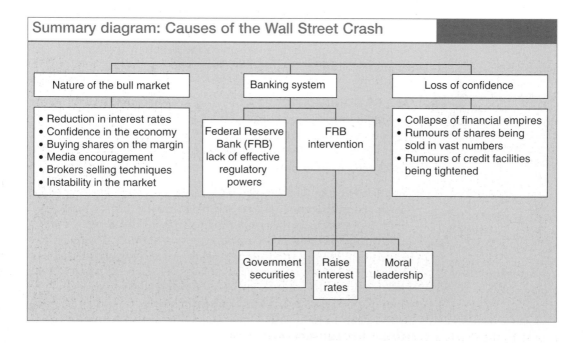

Summary diagram: Causes of the Wall Street Crash

Nature of the bull market
- Reduction in interest rates
- Confidence in the economy
- Buying shares on the margin
- Media encouragement
- Brokers selling techniques
- Instability in the market

Banking system

Federal Reserve Bank (FRB) lack of effective regulatory powers

FRB intervention

Loss of confidence
- Collapse of financial empires
- Rumours of shares being sold in vast numbers
- Rumours of credit facilities being tightened

Government securities

Raise interest rates

Moral leadership

3 | Effects of the Wall Street Crash

Key question
What was the relationship between the Wall Street Crash and the onset of the Great Depression?

Although the myth is persuasive, the Crash did not actually cause the Depression. This was widely recognised at the time and has been largely accepted by historians ever since. American business was too big and too diversified to be influenced to a significant extent by the stock market. There is little doubt that by the time of the Crash, the Depression was well on the way for the reasons discussed in Chapter 3.

As well as overspeculation, living on credit and get-rich-quick schemes, there were the great inequalities of wealth and prosperity; problems with international trade; depression in staple industries, such as agriculture; overproduction and falling domestic demand, which had already resulted in serious problems in the building and, to a certain extent, in the car industries. The Crash was essentially a financial issue, while the Depression had much deeper causes of which financial concern was only one.

However, although there is little doubt that the Crash was more of an effect than a cause of the Depression, we have to recognise that effects can worsen the problems they have resulted from. In this respect the Crash was an important trigger in worsening the Depression. Certainly too, the nature of the bull market added to the frailty of the economy.

Effects of the Crash on the economy

Key question
How far did the Wall Street Crash affect the US economy?

There is some disagreement about the relative significance of the effects of the Wall Street Crash on the economy, although most commentators are in broad agreement about what they actually were.

Collapse of businesses

Individuals and business concerns lost billions. Thousands were bankrupted and even those who remained solvent were often

Ruined by the Crash, a businessman needs some ready cash.

hard hit. Clarence Mitchell's bank lost half its assets; the President of Union Cigar plunged to his death from the ledge of a New York hotel when stock in his company fell from $113.50 to $4 in a single day. Even the Rockefellers lost over $50 million in a vain effort to shore up the market.

The point is, of course, that people who had lost heavily could no longer afford to consume or invest further. So much of the prosperity of the 1920s had been based on continuing demand for **consumer durables**, and these tend not to be replaced when times are hard. Therefore, the industries that supplied these products in the USA found demand slipping further. The power of advertising, for example, had little influence on a people who increasingly had nothing to spend. All this was eventually to lead to a massive level of company cutbacks and often bankruptcy. As workforces were laid off, there was even less money within the economy for spending. This led in turn to a further slowing of the economy as it ground its inexorable way into a depression.

Consumer durables Goods that can last a long time, e.g. motor cars, electrical appliances.

Key term

Collapse of credit

The stock-market crash led to the collapse of credit. Loans were called in and new ones refused. Although stock might now have little value, it was nevertheless accepted by banks as repayments from brokers who couldn't otherwise repay their debts. With their own assets thereby reduced, banks were even less likely to make further loans. This led to a credit squeeze and to an accompanying fall in demand and business activity. No one, it seemed, was prepared to take a financial risk.

Effects of the Crash on confidence in the USA

The Crash signified an end of confidence. To many people, Wall Street had symbolised the prosperity of the 1920s. The stock market had seemed invulnerable. J.K. Galbraith has argued that even though the number of stock-market players was comparatively few, the idea of stock-market speculation had become central to the confidence of society. In other words, it had become almost a certainty, like a belief in the ideas behind the Declaration of Independence or even the pioneer spirit that had 'won the West'. Belief in the continued success of the stock market was an integral part of what it meant to be 'American'.

The warning voices had been ignored. People had chosen to listen instead to the soothing tones coming from the White House and big business. When those same voices continued in the wake of the Crash, they were no longer believed. Their credibility was fatally undermined – but more, they were despised as belonging to those who had let the nation down by destroying its fundamental beliefs. In this situation, national confidence sank to rock bottom. This in turn deepened the Depression to whose onset people had for too long been oblivious.

With the country increasingly in the grip of the Depression, with confidence shattered and new uncertainties pervading society, attention now began to focus on the president in the White House, Herbert Hoover.

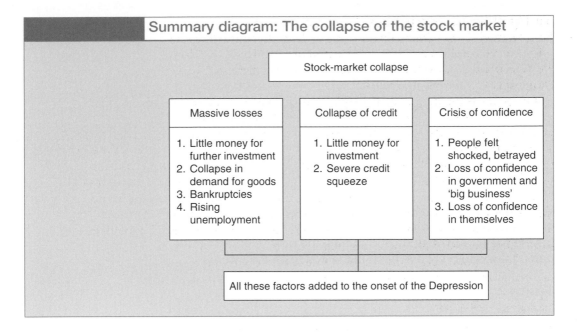

Summary diagram: The collapse of the stock market

Stock-market collapse

Massive losses	Collapse of credit	Crisis of confidence
1. Little money for further investment 2. Collapse in demand for goods 3. Bankruptcies 4. Rising unemployment	1. Little money for investment 2. Severe credit squeeze	1. People felt shocked, betrayed 2. Loss of confidence in government and 'big business' 3. Loss of confidence in themselves

All these factors added to the onset of the Depression

Study Guide: AS Questions

In the style of AQA

What was the most important factor in explaining the Wall Street Crash? Explain your answer.

> ### Study tips
>
> It is important that you understand what is required by this question. It asks you to analyse why the Wall Street Crash happened and make a judgement about which factor you consider the most important. It does not require an account of what happened. Remember that very few marks are given in an essay for description. The best answers will give more than just a list of possible causes and a description of each. In order to tackle the issue of relative importance of factors they will do some or all of the following.
>
> - Look at the different types of causes. For example, what were the triggers that set off the Crash and what were the underlying causes without which the Crash could not have happened? One way to tackle this is first to list the causes and then go on to categorise them into triggers and underlying causes. Generally the short-term causes are the triggers. If the long-term causes made things happen in themselves, they would not be long-term causes.
> - Place the causes in order of relative importance. To do this successfully you need to look at the circumstances in which they operated. If the market had been regulated more effectively, for example, would there have been so much overspeculation? How important was the comparatively weak central banking system?
> - Finally, make a judgement about which factor you consider to be the most important. There is no right answer to this question. The examiner is looking for the quality of your judgement, at how well it is supported by evidence and argument.

In the style of Edexcel

Study Sources 1–5 below and on page 81 and then answer the questions that follow.

Source 1

From Martin DeVries, as told to Studs Terkel in Hard Times, *a book of oral histories published in 1970.*

People were speculating. Now who are you gonna blame aside from themselves? It's their fault. See my point? If you gamble and make a mistake, why pick on somebody else? It's your fault, don't you see?...

Way back in the '20s, People were wearing 20 dollar silk shirts and throwing their money around like crazy. If they had been buying the $2 Arrow shirts and putting the other eighteen in the bank, they wouldn't have been in the condition they were in.

Source 2

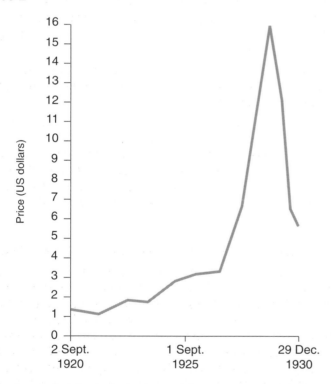

Profile of a stock: how a single share of General Electric bought in 1920 changed in value during the decade

Source 3

From: Frederick Lewis Allen a journalist whose history of the 1920s, Only Yesterday, *was published in 1931.*

As the price structure crumbled there was a sudden stampede to get out from under. By eleven o'clock traders on the floor of the Stock Exchange were in a wild scramble to 'sell at the market'. Long before the lagging ticker could tell what was happening, word had gone out by telephone and telegraph that the bottom was dropping out of things and the selling orders redoubled in volume. The leading stocks were going down between sales. Down, down, down …. Where were the bargain hunters who were supposed to come to the rescue at times like these? Where were the investment trusts, which were expected to provide a cushion for the market by making new purchases at low prices? Where were the big operators who had declared that they were still bullish? Where were the powerful bankers who were supposed to be able at any moment to support prices? There seemed to be no support whatsoever. Down, down, down. The roar of voices which rose from the floor of the Exchange had become a roar of panic.

Source 4

From: John Hersch, as told to Studs Terkel in Hard Times, *a book of oral histories published in 1970.*

The Crash – it didn't happen in one day. There were a great many warnings. The country was crazy. Everybody was in the stock market whether he could afford it or not. … It was a mad dream of get-rich-quick.

It wasn't only brokers involved in margin accounts. It was banks. They had a lot of stinking banks. The banks worked in as casual a way as the brokers did.

You had no governmental control of margins, so people could buy on a shoestring. And when they began pulling the plug you had a deluge of weakness. You also had short selling and a lack of rules. There were many cases of staid, reputable bankers making securities available on special deals – below the market price – for their friends. Anything went, and anything did go.

Source 5

From: Michael E. Parrish, Anxious Decades, *1992, page 234.*

The stock market was bound to collapse at some time as surely as Ponzi's scheme or the Florida Land Boom. In order to make a profit in a bull market, buyers must become sellers at ever-higher prices, but this process depends on a constant infusion of new players with new money who believe they can make a capital gain. A relatively small number of investors, perhaps 1,500,000 with active accounts and less than 600,000 margin traders, sustained the bull market of the late 1920s. Those with considerable means fuelled the boom … And given the poor distribution of national income by 1929, there were not enough to keep it rising forever.

(a) **Study Source 1**
    According to the speaker in Source 1 who was to blame for the Wall Street Crash? (6 marks)
(b) **Use your own knowledge**
    Use your own knowledge to explain why the Federal Reserve Board did not intervene as share prices rose in the stock market in the years 1927–9. (10 marks)

(c) **Study Sources 2 and 3**

Assess the value of Sources 2 and 3 for a historian enquiring into the causes of the Wall Street Crash. (10 marks)

(d) **Study Sources 4 and 5 and use your own knowledge**

To what extent does the evidence of Source 4 support Michael Parrish's view that the stock market was bound to collapse at some time as surely as Ponzi's scheme or the Florida land boom had? (24 marks)

Explain your answer, using these two sources and your own knowledge.

Exam tips

The cross-references are intended to take you straight to the material that will help you answer the questions.

1. For question **(b)** make sure you explain why the Federal Reserve did not want to get involved in regulation of the Stock Exchange. Notice that when the Federal Reserve did threaten to raise interest rates, Clarence Mitchell said his bank would pump $25 million into the market to keep prices high (pages 73–5).

2. For question **(c)**, remember you are being asked to evaluate the sources. What are the advantages and limitations of the value of one share? Think about whether we can assume the history of one share is typical. What are the advantages and limitations of a book written at the time of the events it describes? It lacks the advantages of hindsight and later interpretations, but it is also immediate in describing events the author may have seen at first hand.

3. Try questions **(a)** and **(d)** for yourself. Advice on how to tackle this *type* of question can be found on pages 29 and 62–3.

Study Guide: Advanced Level Question

In the style of OCR

'The Great Depression was well under way before the collapse of the stock market in October 1929.' How far would you agree with this assertion? (45 marks)

Exam tips

This question requires knowledge of the economy in the 1920s particularly in terms of pointers to a coming collapse, e.g. poor farm prices, the rate of business collapse, 'get-rich-quick' schemes and overproduction. This knowledge should be coupled with a section on the effects of the Crash so that a judgement can be made as to how far the Crash was a causal factor and how far an effect in itself of the Depression which hit the USA in 1929. Examiners are looking for a balanced and considered answer supported with relevant evidence and making use of the historical debate on this topic.

5

President Hoover and the Great Depression

POINTS TO CONSIDER
This chapter will consider the presidency of Herbert Hoover and how he attempted to deal with the Depression. It will focus on seven issues:

- The background and beliefs of President Hoover
- The USA during the Depression
- Why the Depression lasted so long
- Federal government policies: how President Hoover attempted to deal with the Depression
- The 1932 presidential election
- An assessment of Hoover as president
- Why, according to different historians, the Depression was so extensive and lasted so long

Key dates

1929	Presidency of Herbert Hoover
	Agricultural Marketing Act
1930	Hawley-Smoot tariff
1931	Moratorium on foreign debts
	National Credit Corporation set up
1932	Johnson Act
	Federal Home Loan Bank Act
	Reconstruction Finance Corporation set up
	Emergency Relief and Construction Act
	Bonus Army
	Hoover defeated in the presidential election

Key question
What impact did the Great Depression have on the reputation of Herbert Hoover?

1 | Introduction

In Hoover we trusted
And now we are busted
Popular slogan during the 1932 election campaign

In the 1928 presidential election campaign it is doubtful whether anyone could have beaten Herbert Hoover. In the 1932 campaign, he was generally criticised and had little chance of success. Hoover was a tragic figure, prematurely aged and the butt of cruel jokes throughout the country, such as the hitchhikers' placards that read, 'If you don't give me a ride, I'll vote for Hoover'.

In the 1928 campaign the main issues were Prohibition, the urban values and the Catholicism of the Democratic candidate, Al Smith. The economy was hardly an issue and, in any event, there was little difference between the candidates' policies.

By way of complete contrast, in 1932 the economy dominated. However, while in 1928 Hoover received 21,392,190 popular votes to Smith's 15,016,443, in 1932 Hoover's opponent, Franklin Delano Roosevelt, received 22,800,000 votes to his 15,750,000. This was actually a fairly respectable result for Hoover when one considers the attacks on him, his lacklustre campaign compared to Roosevelt's exciting one, and the fact that the election result seemed prejudged by most people. Hoover himself said, 'As we expected we were defeated in the election'.

Clearly the issue that destroyed Hoover was the Depression and his inability to deal with it with any degree of success. In this chapter we will consider why he failed so completely. To aid our understanding it is important to consider Hoover's background and attitudes before going on to look at the depth of the problems that faced him and how he responded to them. We need also to examine the 1932 election campaign to see what, if anything, his opponent offered the American people that Hoover had not.

Hoover has been called 'the last of the old presidents and the first of the new'. We need to investigate what is meant by this remark and consider how far it is justified by his response to the Depression. Finally, we shall consider the views of historians on the issues of why the Depression was so great and lasted so long.

2 | Herbert Hoover: His Background and Beliefs

Key question
How did Herbert Hoover's background affect the beliefs he brought with him to the presidency?

If anyone deserved to be president then that person surely was Herbert Hoover. Rarely has anyone been so well qualified for the task or had so much confidence placed in his ability. Hoover encapsulated the American Dream.

Herbert Hoover was shy and taciturn, uncomfortable with strangers and often shunned publicity. He was an administrator more than a politician, and avoided political tricks and infighting. He was respected rather than loved, but generally Americans had very high expectations of his administration. After all, it seemed the economy was booming and, as Secretary of Commerce, he was widely believed to have been one of the architects of the prosperity of the 1920s.

Hoover's beliefs
Hoover's tragedy was that he could not shift from his fundamental beliefs, which he acquired at an early age and never altered.

Profile: Herbert Hoover 1874–1964

1874	– born to a Quaker family in the small town of West Branch, Iowa
1895	– graduated from Stanford University as a mining engineer
1896	– began work as a mining engineer with the British firm, Berwick, Moreing and Company
1897	– surveyed gold mines in Australia
1989	– married sweetheart from University, Lou Henry
	– sent to China by his company
1902–7	– went around the world five times in mining work
1908	– began his own mining business, which became hugely successful
1914	– made chairman of the American Relief Commission for Relief in Belgium
1917	– appointed National Food Commissioner when the USA entered the First World War
1920	– appointed Secretary of Commerce in Warren Harding's government – served in the same role under Calvin Coolidge
1927	– organised large-scale flood relief when the River Mississippi burst its banks over a huge area; helped raise $15 million for Red Cross Relief
1928	– won the presidential election
1932	– lost the presidential election in the face of the Great Depression
1945	– became involved in American relief for Europe
1947	– Hoover Commission set up to look at increasing efficiency in Federal Government; made over 280 recommendations, most of which were implemented
1952	– memoirs published
1964	– died

Early career

Born in 1874 and orphaned by the age of nine, Hoover was raised by his uncle in a small rural settlement in Oregon. He studied mining engineering at Stanford University and gained a reputation for excellence in his field. Hoover travelled the world undertaking mining surveys and engineering projects. Often his family travelled with him, although their home base was London.

Hoover became famous in his work and was widely known as 'the great engineer'. He became a millionaire before he was 35 years old. He believed passionately in the values of hard work and enterprise. He once said that 'if a man has not made a million by the time he's forty he is not worth much'. Yet he was humanitarian too. When war was declared in August 1914, he headed the American Citizens' Relief Committee, arranging for thousands of compatriots caught up in war zones to be repatriated.

Through the reputation he acquired in this work, he later went on to head the Commission for Relief in Belgium where he made massive efforts to ensure victims of the First World War received necessary aid. When the USA entered the war in 1917, Hoover became Food Administrator. He was so successful in his work that American farmers produced surpluses with which it was possible to feed the hungry in war-torn Europe.

Secretary of Commerce

His reputation was such that both major parties were considering him as a possible presidential candidate. In 1920, he chose the Republicans. Defeated by Harding in the contest for candidate, he became Secretary of Commerce in his administration and quickly made his mark as a tireless worker. In fact, he became so influential that he was called by Coolidge 'Secretary of Commerce and undersecretary of everything else'. Coolidge kept him on but privately referred to him as 'the boy wonder' and later disparagingly said of him, 'That man has offered me unsolicited advice for six years and all of it bad'. This was simply not true. Among other things, Coolidge had accepted his advice on the need for farmers to work together rather than receive direct federal aid to solve their problems, the development of electric power by private industry and the use of the Labor Department to broker an end to industrial disputes. He also worked tirelessly to bring relief to those affected by disastrous Mississippi floods in 1928 and helped raise $15 million for Red Cross relief.

Hoover as president

Hoover's presidency was dominated by the Great Depression. Although he worked almost without rest to combat it and encourage recovery, he gradually lost credibility and many blamed him personally for the tragedy. Certainly he was blamed for not doing enough and not giving direct government aid even though he intervened in the economy more than any other president had before.

Later career

After his defeat in the 1932 presidential election, Hoover regained his status as an elder statesman. Although his wife died in 1944 he returned to public life. He headed a Commission to prevent world famine after the Second World War. In 1947 he was appointed head of a Commission to look into greater efficiency in federal government, and later examined what powers the federal government should and should not have. Most of his recommendations were implemented. Hoover spent his remaining years writing and also founded the Herbert Hoover Presidential Library. He died in his ninetieth year in 1964.

Self-reliance

He believed people should be responsible for their own welfare. This attitude was to make him inflexible in his handling of the Depression. He simply did not believe the government should try to solve people's problems. It was up to the government to give people the ability to solve their problems by themselves.

'American individualism'

Hoover's political philosophy was spelt out in his book, *American Individualism*, published in 1922. He never moved away from its ideas whatever the circumstances. He believed above all in equality of opportunity. He was a self-made man; he felt everyone else could be too. Everyone could, with hard work and initiative, become rich just as he had.

Having said this, he did not support strictly *laissez-faire* policies. He believed the government should co-ordinate the activities of capital and labour. He felt a balance should be struck between people's desire to do whatever they wanted themselves and the needs of the wider community.

The emphasis was always on the responsibility of the individual, the curbing of excesses in one's personal life and treating others fairly. Hoover's philosophy was an intensely moral one. He had a very high view of human nature – perhaps too high. He regarded 'American individualism' as the best system in the world. He saw the role of government as helping its development.

Together these ideas can be summarised as a belief in self-help and voluntary co-operation to solve problems. People should help themselves and each other

3 | The USA During the Great Depression

Statistics of the Depression are plentiful and tell their own story of the dramatic reduction in economic activity. However, they do not always illustrate the human cost. For this reason, the economic effects and the human dimension will be separated in the following account. It is also important to consider why this particular depression bit so deeply and lasted so long. The USA was, after all, quite used to depressions as part of the normal economic cycle – a cycle that Herbert Hoover was trying to break up so that prosperity would become the norm.

The economic effects

Key question
What was the economic impact of the Great Depression?

There are no totally reliable unemployment figures for this period because the federal government did not keep centralised records until the mid-1930s. However, there is no doubt that unemployment soared. One historian wrote that they resembled the casualty figures in the battles of the First World War. An official government source suggests unemployment rose from 3.2 per cent of the labour force in 1929 to 25.2 per cent by 1933; this meant that 12,830,000 were out of work. The Labor Research Association complained that these figures were underestimates and claimed that the real figure was nearer 17 million. Another

Unemployed waiting for admission to the New York Municipal Lodging House, 1930. Note the scale of numbers.

source suggested that by 1933 one-third of the workforce was unemployed. It was estimated that the national wage bill in 1932 was only 40 per cent of the 1929 figure. However, the figures do not show the numbers in part-time and unregistered work (pages 36–7). As we shall see, this was quite significant.

Uneven distribution of unemployment

Unemployment and underemployment were not evenly spread throughout the country. New York State alone had one million unemployed. In Ohio, the city of Cleveland had 50 per cent of its workforce unemployed and that of Toledo, a staggering 80 per cent. African-Americans and women were particular victims.

African-Americans

The magazine *The Nation* reported in April 1931 that the number of African-Americans out of work was four to six times higher than whites, and that poorly paid jobs traditionally reserved for African-Americans such as those of waiter and lift-attendant were now increasingly being offered to whites. African-American rural workers, of course, were used to depressed conditions. However, employment opportunities in the northern cities, which had opened up in the 1920s, was now generally closed to them. One commentator from Georgia said, 'Most blacks did not even know the Great Depression had come. They always had been poor and only thought the whites were catching up'.

Women

Women, particularly those of the working classes, also did badly. Those in unskilled jobs were likely to be laid off before men, and those in domestic service suffered because families could no longer afford to keep them on. Married women often needed to work to keep the family solvent. However, because they had a job they were often accused of being responsible for male unemployment. It was quite common for them to be dismissed and their work given to men. In 1930 over 75 per cent of American school authorities refused to employ married women.

Effects on individual industries

There were some areas that survived the onset of the Depression. A local military base, state university or seat of state government could delay it. Localised circumstances could also be significant, such as the temporary oil boom in Kigmore, Texas – which ironically led to a glut of oil and a collapse of prices in that industry. There were also 'depression-proof' industries, such as cigarette manufacture. This helped Louisville and Richmond from feeling the worst effects of the Depression until later. By 1933, however, nowhere in the USA could wholly escape its effects.

With fewer in productive work, the growth rate went into decline, from 6.7 per cent in 1929 to −14.7 per cent in 1932, representing a fall in gross national product (GNP) from $203.6 billion in 1929 to $144.2 billion in 1932. General price levels fell by 25 per cent during the period; farm prices fell by a half.

The separate statistics of decline indicate how individual industries fared. In the coal industry, production in 1932 was the lowest since 1904 and the workforce fell by 300,000; many of those in work were only part-time and wages could be as low as $2.50 per day. Seventy-five per cent of textile firms were losing money, while iron and steel production fell by 59 per cent and US Steel Corporation's workforce was wholly part-time by the end of 1932. Car sales fell from 4,455,178 in 1929 to 1,103,557 four years later.

The average number of people employed in the 'motor city' of Detroit fell by 21.5 per cent between 1928 and 1929. In Toledo, between May 1929 and spring 1932, Willis-Overland kept on only 3000 of their 25,000 strong workforce. In similar cases, the number employed by both General Electric and Westerhouse making electrical appliances was more than halved; the only electric goods not to suffer a significant decline in demand were lightbulbs, which need of course to be replaced.

The construction industry, already in decline before 1929, saw the number of residential units built fall 82 per cent between 1929 and 1932. Construction contracts were valued at $6.6 billion in 1929 but only $1.3 billion three years later.

Problems with credit and banking

Credit had all but vanished. The Stock Market went into serious decline despite occasional rallies as in December 1929 and in April 1930.

Table 5.1 shows the decline in industrial stocks. Bank closures multiplied. There had been 5000 in the entire period 1921–9, but there were over 10,000 between 1929 and 1933. Most of these

Table 5.1: Index of industrial stocks

November 1929	220.1
December 1930	196.1
December 1931	116.6
December 1932	84.81

were small banks that had overextended lending in the times of prosperity and now could not meet their depositors' demands for their money. When farmers, for example, could not meet their mortgage repayments, the banks had to evict them and take the farms over. In doing so, the banks lost liquid assets in the form of mortgage repayments and gained bankrupt, often unsaleable, farms in exchange.

Under these circumstances, depositors often lost confidence in their bank. This could lead to a 'run on the bank' to withdraw their money, which would force it to close down. Alternatively, many people simply needed to withdraw the money they had in their accounts; they may have lost their job, have been on short-time working or have needed to meet a debt. If enough people wanted their money at the same time, the result was the same; the collapse of the bank, with savings being lost for all those depositors who did not withdraw them quickly enough.

People often could not afford their loan repayments. This also led to banks not having enough money to pay to depositors, which in turn led to depositors losing confidence and rushing to withdraw all their money.

By 1933 the USA was a land of cash transactions, where those still in work fiercely protected their jobs, where credit was tight and no one was prepared to take a risk. It was also a land singularly unable to handle a major depression.

Social effects of the Great Depression
The human cost of the Depression was enormous.

Key question
What were the effects in human terms of the Great Depression?

Life for the unemployed
The USA was ill equipped to handle unemployment. Very little provision had been made for it. There was, for example, no federal unemployment benefit. The **work ethic** was very prevalent in America and unemployment among the able-bodied was generally held to be their own fault. For this reason alone, the psychological effects of mass unemployment were devastating. There are many cases of people pretending still to be in work, to go out early each morning with a briefcase or toolbag, packed lunch and the like – to keep up appearances

The strain on family life was intense. The number of marriages fell from 1.23 million in 1929 to 982,00 in 1932, with an accompanying fall in the birth rate from 21.2 per thousand in 1929 to 19.5 in 1932. Suicide rates increased greatly from 14 per 10,000 in 1929 to 17.4 in 1932.

Work ethic
The feeling that people should work hard and the unemployed should go out and find a job. It derived from the Puritan notion that how well one worked was a sign of one's worth, both personally and socially.

Key term

The extent of relief
The nature of relief varied greatly because it was provided variously by states, local authorities or charities. Most came from charities. In fact, before 1932 no state had any system of recognised unemployment insurance and only 11 operated any kind of pension scheme – with a total outlay of only $220,000, aiding a mere 1000 people.

At a time when the population was ageing, the majority of elderly people lived below the poverty line. There were very few private pension schemes – in 1925, only 36,000 pensioners were in receipt of benefits from 500 pension plans. This meant old people traditionally either had to keep working, live on their savings or rely on their children for support. The Depression meant that, in the main, these options were no longer viable.

To obtain any measure of relief, people often had to sell all their possessions, use up all their savings and become destitute. The stigma of receiving relief was deliberately intended to dissuade people from applying. Ten states, for example, removed the right to vote from relief applicants and some churches even banned those on relief from attending their services. *Fortune* magazine showed that only 25 per cent of those entitled to relief actually received any. Single people and childless couples were very unlikely to receive anything.

Hoboes

Many of the unemployed became **hoboes**. By 1932, it was estimated that there were between one million and two million of them, many of whom lived in shanty towns on the outskirts of settlements. Hoboes were usually given a hard time. The Southern Pacific Railroad claimed to have thrown 68,300 of them from its trains. The state of California posted guards to turn them away at its borders, and in Atlanta, Georgia, they were arrested and put into **chain gangs**.

Key terms

Hoboes
People who wandered around the USA in search of work.

Chain gangs
Groups of convicts chained together while working outside the prison, for example in digging roadside drainage ditches.

Hoboes aboard a freight train. Millions travelled around in search of work.

The strain on resources

For those who were entitled to relief, there was the added problem that the relief bodies were running out of funds. Charities naturally suffer a decline in revenue during a depression, at the very time when their funds were most needed. States too received less in taxes as unemployment rose. As a result, many had to cut rather than expand their services. In Arkansas, for example, schools were closed for 10 months in the year, while teachers in Chicago went unpaid during the winter of 1932–3. The simple truth was that charities could supply only six per cent of necessary funds in 1932, and states and local government agencies could not even begin to provide the shortfall of 94 per cent. In fact, in the years 1931 and 1932 when demand was greatest, most cut their relief appropriations. Michigan, for example, reduced funds from $2 million in 1931 to $832,000 in 1932.

The result was that many people went hungry or were starving. *Fortune* magazine estimated in September 1932 that as much as 28 per cent of the total population was receiving no income – and this estimate did not include the 11 million farm-workers, many of whom were in acute difficulties.

Rural poverty

According to US Department of Agriculture statistics, 58 farms in every thousand changed hands in 1929, of which 19.5 were forced sales due to banks repossessing farms as a result of non-payment of mortgages. By 1936 this figure had risen to 76.6, of which 41.7 were forced. Often the auction of foreclosed farm property attracted violence. But there were other ways in which those repossessing property could be thwarted. Local farmers would agree only to bid a few cents and then return the farm to its former owner. Sometimes there was intimidation. In the face of this, two state governors said that payments on farm mortgages could be postponed until circumstances improved.

Poverty in the midst of plenty

The tragedy was that people went hungry in one of the richest food-producing countries in the world. Farm prices were so low that food could not be profitably harvested. In Montana, for example, wheat was rotting in the fields. Meat prices were not sufficient to warrant transporting animals to market. In Oregon, sheep were slaughtered and left to the buzzards. In Chicago, meanwhile, women scoured rubbish tips for anything edible. Total relief funds in that city amounted to only $100,000 per day, which worked out at payments of only $2.40 per adult and $1.50 per child recipient per week. In 1931 there were 3.8 million one-parent families headed by a woman, with only 19,280 receiving any aid.

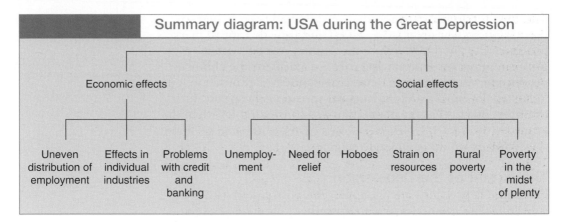

Summary diagram: USA during the Great Depression

Economic effects

Social effects

Uneven distribution of employment

Effects in individual industries

Problems with credit and banking

Unemploy-ment

Need for relief

Hoboes

Strain on resources

Rural poverty

Poverty in the midst of plenty

Key question
Why couldn't the Great Depression be brought to an end?

Key date

Hawley-Smoot tariff: 1930

4 | Why the Depression Lasted So Long

Various explanations have been given for the duration of the Depression, although they are usually closely interconnected.

Foreign economic crises

Herbert Hoover always blamed foreign economies for the Depression. It was their lack of purchasing power, he felt, that stifled trade and, as we shall see, many of his measures to combat the Depression were intended to strengthen foreign economies. Many historians would go along with his analysis up to a point. However, there is the countercriticism that, although the USA was the richest country in the world, it had not, in the 1920s, assumed the role of world economic leader. American tariffs had restricted international trade, and were to do so even more ferociously after the Hawley-Smoot tariff in 1930. In particular, the USA may be criticised for not devaluing its currency when others were losing value, thus making American goods even more expensive for foreigners.

The nature of American business

The vast growth of the American economy came during the years following the Civil War after 1865, when the country rapidly settled the continent and underwent a major process of industrialisation. However, government non-intervention meant that industries often came under the control of individuals or small groups who could control wages, prices and output to maximise their profits. While, on the surface, the system was highly competitive and dominated by market forces, in reality it was controlled by trusts and cartels (see page 6). This meant that in reality competition was limited.

Inevitably the two opposing forces of free and controlled markets would one day come into conflict. In the past, the growing population and territorial expansion that created enormous demand had hidden the tension between them in the past. However, by the late 1920s the amount of goods produced was greater than demand even though the population was still growing. Territorial expansion meanwhile had been halted so there were no new areas to be settled and provide captive markets for American goods. Therefore the country was left with a problem of overproduction and excess capacity or the ability to produce far more goods than were demanded by consumers. Relatively low wages and the unequal spread of prosperity, for example, meant that the population was consuming less than the economy produced. Unless new forms of demand could be found, the economy would continue to stagnate.

The extent of the Depression

Economic depressions are often unevenly distributed within a country. Some industries remain unscathed; others may even benefit. Some areas of the country escape. However, the extent of the Great Depression meant that no sector remained immune. This was to have two major effects that led to the Depression being prolonged.

- There was the absence of alternative employment opportunities. Every country that has been through an industrial revolution finds its old industries – coal, iron and steel, and textiles – lose their competitive edge in the face of competition from rivals whose more recent industrialisation means that their methods of production are more modern and efficient. However, as the old industries contract accordingly, the workforce can normally expect to find employment in the newer industries, such as car assembly and the manufacture of electrical appliances. But, as we have seen, because of overproduction and underconsumption, these industries were hit particularly badly during the Depression in the USA. As a result, employment opportunities were no longer available in there either. Clearly, this prolonged the Depression.
- The geographical extent of the Depression affected both rural and urban areas. Farmers, for example, had largely been depressed throughout the 1920s and so their purchasing power was poor. Because both rural and urban areas suffered neither could help the other.

Inadequate government intervention

A group of radical economists, including Rexford Tugwell and Adolph Berle later to be important supporters of Franklin D. Roosevelt (see page 104), argued that the Depression was caused by too many goods being produced and too few consumers being able to afford to buy them. A Brookings Institute Report of 1934, for example, showed that eight per cent of families had earned 42 per cent of the national wealth, while 60 per cent earned only 23 per cent. There was therefore a great inequality of wealth in the USA.

If the unregulated capitalist economy could not maintain a balance between the ability of people to buy goods and the level of earnings, then, it was argued, the government should intervene to do so. This clearly would involve such developments as increasing taxation of the rich to help make income more equal. With this increased revenue, the government could undertake public works to increase employment and 'kick start' the economy. In the USA, of course, the prevailing government policies had been the opposite of this, with economies in government spending and balancing the budget being seen as priorities.

Monetary policy

Associated in particular with the work of the economist Milton Friedman in the 1970s, monetarist theories argue that a decline in the amount of money in circulation often comes before a depression. Failure to increase this stock of money will prolong the depression as people have less money to spend. Altogether, the amount of money in circulation fell by about 33 per cent during the years 1929–33. Monetarists, meanwhile, have argued that a three per cent to five per cent annual increase in the amount of money in circulation is necessary to achieve a comparable rate of economic growth. Friedman argued, for example, that in October 1931 the rise in the discount rate from 1.5 to 3.5 per cent caused a 25 per cent fall in industrial production over the next year. According to monetarists, in other words, the tight monetary policy pursued by the Federal Reserve Board stifled recovery. This is because there was less money in circulation so people had less to spend, thus keeping the demand for goods low.

There is undoubtedly a large measure of truth in each of these explanations and they will be considered further in key debate section (see pages 106–10). Together they show that the Depression was a highly complex phenomenon with no easy solutions. However, increasingly, the federal government was expected to find the answers.

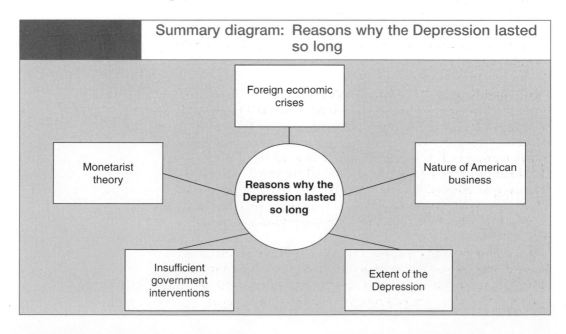

Summary diagram: Reasons why the Depression lasted so long

5 | Federal Government Policies

The role of President Hoover

President Hoover worked tirelessly to combat the Depression. As he left office in 1933 his face was lined and drawn. He worried constantly, had a humanitarian concern for suffering and misery, and gave generously to charity. He cut his own and state officials' salaries by 20 per cent to help provide revenues for his recovery measures. He worked very long hours. After rising before 6 am every morning he exercised with trusted advisers with a medicine ball. No doubt they discussed important issues as the ball was thrown to and fro. Hoover worked all day, every day and long into the night with scarcely a break for meals.

Hoover well understood the seriousness of the Depression, which overshadowed all but the first seven months of his presidency. In public, however, he had to be optimistic in spite of all the problems; this has led many to argue that he quite lost touch with reality. When, for example, he told the press that unemployment was falling, this created considerable resentment among many of the jobless. Many who believed Hoover's pronouncements argued that the unemployed were simply too lazy to get a job.

As a result of his constant public hopefulness, Hoover gradually lost all credibility. 'Hoovervilles' – the shanties were hoboes lived – were named after him as were 'hoover blankets' – the newspapers in which they wrapped themselves to keep warm.

Hoover's problem was that he would not abandon his two central beliefs of self-help and voluntary co-operation. Having said this, he involved the government more in the economy than

Key question
How did President Hoover's administration try to tackle the Great Depression?

Hooverville in New York City. Note the squalor in which people lived.

any other previous president. However, he could not bring himself to accept what many increasingly argued was necessary – direct government relief. He continued to believe that the economy had to right itself. 'Economic depression', he said, 'cannot be cured by legislative action or executive pronouncement. Economic wounds must be healed by the action of the cells of the economic body – the producers and consumers themselves'.

Hoover certainly understood the need for the government to take action to help this to happen. He had no patience, for example, with his Treasury Secretary, Andrew Mellon, who was advising businessmen who were still solvent to fire their workers and sell everything until the crisis was over. Hoover called these ideas 'childlike' and removed Mellon from his post by sending him to London as ambassador.

However, as we shall see, Hoover's policies were simply not far-reaching enough to address the scale and seriousness of the Depression. He was prepared to do something, but nowhere near enough.

Agriculture

Key question
How did President Hoover try to help the agricultural sector?

Key date
Agricultural Marketing Act: 1929

Hoover called a special session of Congress in April 1929, before the Wall Street Crash, to deal with the pressing problems of agriculture. He would no more accept the McNary-Haugen proposals (see page 52) than his predecessors, but he was prepared to help farmers to help themselves.

The Agricultural Marketing Act, 1929, established a nine-person Federal Farm Board with funds of $500 million to create farmers' marketing co-operatives called 'stabilisation corporations'. These were to be given the task of buying, storing and eventually disposing of farm surpluses in an orderly way. However, they had no power to order reductions in production. Huge surpluses in 1931 and 1932 both at home and abroad saw prices fall and the corporations paying above-market values for produce. The Grain Stabilization Corporation, for example, bought wheat in Chicago at 80 cents a bushel while the world price had fallen to 60 cents. By the time it ceased its purchases in summer 1931, it had paid an average of 82 cents per bushel for 300 million bushels while the world price had fallen to 40 cents a bushel.

The Corporation might have been helping farmers but it was also accused of throwing taxpayers' money away. It was buying farm produce at well over the market price and therefore was seen to encourage farmers to keep producing more, when, in fact, they should have been encouraged to produce less. By 1932 the world price of wheat was between 30 cents and 39 cents a bushel, less than harvesting costs in the USA. When Congress did propose a bill to subsidise farmers to reduce production, Hoover threatened to veto it because it undermined the principle of voluntary action. In the event, the bill failed without any need for a veto. It was too radical a measure for the time.

The agricultural policy failed mainly, then, for two reasons:

- It was paying American farmers artificially high prices and this could not continue in the long term.
- It treated agriculture as a domestic issue and, therefore, failed to take account of foreign considerations. Without high tariffs, there was little point in trying to keep the American price artificially high. The answer to the problem of cheap foreign imports, then, seemed to be even higher tariffs.

Tariffs

The Hawley-Smoot tariff, which came into force in June 1930, was the highest in American history with average duties of 40 per cent on both agricultural and industrial items. It led to most European nations abandoning free trade and to even fewer American goods being exported. This was of no advantage to farmers with their huge surpluses. Knowing this, farming interests in Congress fought hard against the measure, and it passed the Senate by only two votes. Hoover could have vetoed the bill but chose not to.

Repudiation of war debts

Hoover blamed the Depression on Europe but he was probably not entirely correct in doing so. Others have argued that it was the American Depression that spread to Europe and not vice versa. Certainly after the Wall Street Crash, American credit dried up. The Hawley-Smoot tariff made things worse. In the years 1929 and 1930 the value of international trade fell in total by $500 million and in the following year it fell by $1.2 billion. This led to European countries **repudiating their war debts**.

Germany was particularly affected by the withdrawal of American credit. When the German government became virtually bankrupt it announced the suspension of reparations payments and said that it might also have to refuse to pay back loans. Hoover feared a European war over this. He knew that the French, in particular, might resort to military action to get their reparations. Moreover, refusing to repay debts would badly affect American banks, which were already struggling to keep solvent.

On 21 June 1931 Hoover announced the USA would postpone the collection of its debts for 18 months if other countries would do the same. This, he hoped, would release monies for investment. It is generally known as the **Moratorium**. In the event, it was too little too late to stop the collapse of European economies.

Interestingly, when the proposed moratorium came up for renewal in December 1932, it was during the period of Hoover's **lame duck presidency**. Hoover advised Roosevelt to continue the moratorium. However, Roosevelt, sensing hostility in Congress, agreed to the passage of the Johnson Act. This made it illegal to sell in the USA the securities of any country that had refused to repay its debts. As the stock market was still stagnant, this had little effect except to make European countries even more

Key question

How did President Hoover try to improve matters through a moratorium on war debts?

Key dates

Moratorium on war debts: 1931

Johnson Act: 1932

Key terms

Repudiation of war debts
Where countries ceased repaying their war debts.

Moratorium
Term given to Hoover's offer to postpone debt repayment for 18 months.

Lame duck presidency
The period between one president coming to the end of his term and his successor taking over.

resentful of the USA. Finland was the only country that continued to pay its debts.

Promotion of voluntarism

Key question
How effective was voluntarism in halting the Depression?

At first, Hoover hoped to persuade businessmen and state governments to continue as if there was no Depression – to solve it through their own voluntary efforts. He called meetings of businessmen in which he implored them not to reduce their workforce or cut wages, but rather to maintain their output and urge people to buy. He encouraged state leaders to begin new programmes of public works as well as continuing with the old.

Key term

Voluntarism
The notion that business and state government should solve the Great Depression through their own voluntary efforts.

However, as the Depression worsened, business had little choice but to cut back. Workers were laid off, most investment was postponed and wages of those still in work were reduced. As we have seen, states also had to reduce their spending. The problems were simply too great for **voluntarism** to work, particularly when it went against customary business practice. Bankers, for example, set up the National Credit Corporation in October 1931 with the task of helping failing banks survive. It began with a capital fund of $500 million donated by the major financial institutions. However, with banks continuing to fail at unprecedented rates, the Corporation had spent only $10 million by the end of 1931. Bankers were simply too ingrained in their ways to begin investing in failing concerns. The Corporation died a death, showing again that individual financial concerns would almost always put their own interests before those of their country.

Key dates

National Credit Corporation set up: 1931

Federal Home Loan Bank Act: 1932

Reconstruction Finance Corporation set up: 1932

Unemployment relief

Key question
How effective were the measures taken to help the unemployed?

Hoover secured additional amounts from Congress to the tune of $500 million in 1932 to help the various agencies provide relief. However, this was wholly inadequate to meet the scale of the problem. He set up the President's Emergency Committee for Employment to help the agencies to organise their efforts. But, again, he would not countenance direct federal relief, arguing that this destroyed self-help and created a class of people dependent on the government for handouts. Even during the severe drought of 1930–1, which saw near-starvation conditions in much of the South, he baulked at direct relief. In the end, Congress allocated a pitifully small sum, $47 million, and even that was to be offered as loans that must be later repaid.

Federal Home Loan Bank Act

Key question
How effective was this measure in helping people pay their mortgages?

This measure, passed in July 1932, was intended to save mortgages by making credit easier. A series of Federal Home Loan banks was set up to help loan associations provide mortgages. However, as the maximum loan was only 50 per cent of the value of the property it was largely ineffective. It was simply another example of help that failed because it was insufficient to deal with the seriousness of the situation – in this case homes being repossessed.

Reconstruction Finance Corporation (RFC)

This was undoubtedly Hoover's most radical measure to combat the Depression and was a forerunner of the New Deal initiatives of Franklin D. Roosevelt. The Reconstruction Finance Corporation was established in January 1932 with authority to lend up to $2 billion to rescue banks, insurance companies, railroads and construction companies in distress. The new Treasury Secretary, Ogden Mills, said the RFC was 'an insurance measure more than anything else'. It was designed to restore confidence particularly in financial institutions.

Of its loans, 90 per cent went to small and medium banks, and 70 per cent to banks in towns with a population of less than 5000. However, critics of the RFC pointed to the size of individual loans not the actual number. They argued that 50 per cent of loans went to the seven per cent of borrowers who happened to be the biggest banks. Moreover, of the first $61 million committed by the RFC, $41 million was loaned to no more than three institutions. One alone, the Central Republican National Bank and Trust Company, received $90 million. This came soon after the return to the bank of its president – who had been seconded to run the RFC. The $90 million, incidentally, was almost as much as the bank held in total deposits at the time. Similarly, the biggest loans also went to the biggest railroads and public utilities.

The government argued its case by saying that the largest firms were the biggest employers so it made sense to help them in the war against unemployment. However, many critics saw the RFC as giving direct relief to large concerns while none was offered to individuals in distress. In fact, the clamour for direct relief became so great that in summer 1932 Hoover finally agreed. He gave his support to the Emergency Relief and Construction Act, which authorised the RFC to lend up to $1.5 billion to states to finance public works. However, to be eligible the states had to declare bankruptcy and the works undertaken had to produce revenues that would eventually pay off the loans. When Hoover agreed to this, many of his erstwhile supporters felt he had gone too far. In 1932 James M. Beck, a former Solicitor General, compared Hoover's government to that of Soviet Russia! Many members of the Republican Party believed strongly in policies of non-intervention. However, in the end, the RFC offered far too little far too late. By this time, in the words of Calvin Coolidge's former secretary, Edward Clark, 'Today, there seems to be no class nor section where Hoover is strong or where a decision is respected because [he] made it'.

Hoover's credibility, which was already severely damaged, was finally destroyed by his role in an event that made him seem cruel as well as unfeeling. This was the treatment of the 'Bonus Army'.

War veterans and the 'Bonus Army'

Ironically, it was Hoover who had set up the **Veterans' Administration** for those who had seen military service. Annual federal expenditure on veteran's disabilities was $675.8 million.

Key question
What was the RFC and how did it operate?

Key date
Emergency Relief and Construction Act: 1932

Key term
Veterans' Administration
Organisation to help ex-servicemen.

Key question
What was the 'Bonus Army' and how were they dealt with?

However, Hoover will always be remembered for what happened to the 'Bonus Army'.

Congress had agreed a veteran's 'bonus' in 1925. Based on the number of years of service, it was to be paid in full to each veteran in 1945. But, quite understandably, as the Depression hit many veterans said they needed it immediately. A march to Washington was organised to publicise their cause. By 15 June 1932, 20,000 people were camped in the capital, mainly around the Anacostia Flats region. On that day the House of Representatives voted by 226 votes to 175 to allow immediate payment of the bonus.

However, two days later, largely because of the cost, the Senate vetoed this. Feeling for the veterans' plight, but insistent that nothing could be done for them, Hoover offered $100,000 to pay for their transportation home.

But many refused to budge. Some were squatting in derelict buildings in Pennsylvania Avenue with the tacit support of the district Police Superintendent who sympathised with them. Hoover increasingly feared violence and even revolution. The White House was protected with barricades and its gates were chained.

The Secretary of War, determined to move the squatters, called in troops under General Douglas MacArthur. Tanks and infantry not only shifted the squatters, but chased them back to the main camp on Anacostia Flats where tear gas was used to disperse them. The camp was destroyed, many marchers were injured, and two babies died from the effects of the gas. A War Department official publicly called these men, who had previously been regarded as heroes, 'Tramps and hoodlums with a generous sprinkling of Communist agitators'.

Although MacArthur had gone beyond his authority in attacking the camp on Anacostia Flats, the deed was done and Hoover came out in his support. Later, in the election campaign he even blurted out, 'Thank God you have a government that knows how to deal with a mob'. However, Americans had been horrified at the scenes and whether they were his fault or not, Hoover was blamed. The violent dispersal of the Bonus Army by the military was a major political blunder.

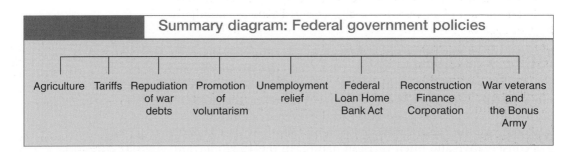

Summary diagram: Federal government policies

Agriculture — Tariffs — Repudiation of war debts — Promotion of voluntarism — Unemployment relief — Federal Loan Home Bank Act — Reconstruction Finance Corporation — War veterans and the Bonus Army

6 | The 1932 Presidential Election

The depths of the Depression undoubtedly led some to wonder whether the American system could survive. Extremism usually thrives on hopelessness and despair, and there was certainly enough of both during the Depression. However, there is very little evidence that the USA was anywhere near revolution and, unlike in European countries, extremist parties never received more than a small amount of support.

Key question
What were the extremist alternatives on the political Right and Left wings?

The extreme Right

There were the beginnings of an American Fascist movement, called the Silver Shirts. Despite the increasing interest shown in it by disaffected members of the Ku Klux Klan, its membership was estimated to be less than 700. Certainly its effects at this time were insignificant.

The extreme Left

Communists

American Communists expected the Depression to lead to revolution. They set up Unemployment Councils with the slogan, 'Fight – Don't Starve' and organised marches against unemployment. The Communists were a small, highly disciplined party in the revolutionary tradition of underground activity. They took their orders from Moscow. Officials there had insisted they refuse to work with Socialists or any non-communist organisation.

The Soviet government also had little understanding of the USA and some of the orders it gave demonstrated this. African-Americans, for example, were viewed as a persecuted nationality and the Party was persuaded to campaign for the creation of a separate African-American state in those parts of the South East where they were in the majority. Even when they did work with African-Americans to improve their living standards as in the Sharecroppers' Union, set up in 1931, their efforts achieved little. Local authorities often supported the violence and intimidation from the Ku Klux Klan, for example, that destroyed the Sharecroppers' Union members' will to fight. During the 1932 presidential election the Communists spent much of their time sniping at the Socialists. This helped to account for their poor showing in the election.

Socialists

The decade of the 1920s was a difficult one for the Socialists. Their opposition to American entry into the First World War and split with the Communists in 1919 had lost them the support of many intellectuals They had also been weakened by the 'Red Scare' of that year (see page 22), and they were committed to working with the American Federation of Labor (AFL), which was conservative and often racist in nature. In the 1932 election the Socialist candidate, Norman Thomas, polled fewer than one million votes. Many of his own supporters felt it was more important to defeat Hoover than to vote for Socialism.

Many gave their support to the Democratic candidate, Franklin D. Roosevelt simply for that reason. To others Roosevelt really did symbolise new hope, offering the real change they were clamouring for.

Profile: Franklin Delano Roosevelt 1882–1945

1882 – born at Hyde Park, New York
1905 – married Eleanor Roosevelt, a distant cousin
1910 – elected to New York State Senate
1913 – became Assistant Secretary of the Navy
1920 – Democratic nominee for vice-president
1921 – Polio left him crippled
1928 – became Governor of New York
1932 – elected president and began 'New Deal' programme
1936 – re-elected with massive majority
1940 – re-elected for third term of office
1941 – brought USA into the Second World War after the Japanese attack on Pearl Harbor
1944 – re-elected for a fourth term of office
1945 – died, still in office

Early life and career

Roosevelt was born into one of the most distinguished families in the USA. He could trace his roots back to the first Dutch settlers in the area of modern-day New York City. He had an idyllic upbringing on the family estate at Hyde Park in New York State. He was educated at the prestigious school of Groton, going on to Harvard University where he was popular without excelling himself academically. He trained to be a lawyer, but invested far more energy in the social activities than work. His real passion was sailing.

In 1905 he married his distant cousin, Eleanor, a niece of President Theodore Roosevelt. He entered politics as a Democrat in 1910 when he fought for a seat in the New York Senate. He was chosen mainly because his promoters had been looking for someone who could finance himself. Benefiting from infighting among his New York colleagues, he climbed the slippery pole of state politics with relative ease. In 1913 he was offered the post of Assistant Secretary of the Navy where he gained a reputation for enthusiasm and competence.

In the 1920 presidential election he was nominated as Democratic candidate for the vice-presidency. However, the Republicans won the election. The following year he was struck down by the disease that may in fact have been responsible for all his later energy, optimism and dynamism. He caught polio, then a killer disease. However, with the unfailing support of his wife, Roosevelt survived, although he was never to walk again except with the aid of painful leg braces. Through most of the 1920s he recuperated, grounded himself thoroughly in politics and showed a new determination to make something of himself.

Governor of New York

In 1928 Roosevelt became Governor of New York State. He was noted both as a reformer – he modernised the state's penal system, for example, building new prisons and revising harsh penalties – and for appointing able people to office rather than political cronies. However, it was with the onset of the Depression that he really made his mark.

No intellectual himself, Roosevelt was always ready to listen to those who were, and during his second term of office as governor he set up the 'Brains' Trust'. This was headed by academics such as Raymond Moley, Rexford Tugwell, Adolph Berle and Felix Frankfurter. Many of them would remain with Roosevelt throughout the rest of his career. It was they who convinced him that the government should intervene directly to combat the Depression.

Roosevelt already had an interventionist record in New York to try to improve the economy. In particular, he had set up the Temporary Emergency Relief Administration in 1931. This was given $20 million, financed from an increase in income tax, for work relief during the winter of 1931–2. The name of the organisation is significant. Roosevelt saw this agency very much as a temporary measure to meet a crisis. It was nevertheless the first state-run relief effort in the nation.

Roosevelt as president

No other president has ever served more than two terms of office. Roosevelt served four consecutive ones. His presidency can be divided into two periods; from 1933 to 1939 when attempts to deal with the Depression dominated and from 1940 to 1945 when USA became involved in the Second World War, first as a friend of Britain and then as a combatant against Japan and Germany.

Roosevelt began the New Deal programme to fight the Depression. This involved the federal government in American life to an unprecedented degree and changed forever the way people viewed the role of government forever. During the Second World War, the USA not only fought in many combat zones but also produced most of the weapons and supplies used by the Allies. It emerged from the war the world's richest and most powerful country. Roosevelt did not live to see this, however. He died in April 1945, one month before Germany surrendered and four months before atomic bombs were dropped on Japanese cities to end the war in the Far East.

The election campaigns

Roosevelt was by far the strongest Democratic nominee for candidate. Hoover was the only possible Republican nominee unless the party changed its policies. However, Hoover was too busy fighting the Depression to campaign effectively. The members of his re-election team were themselves short on ideas.

Key question
Why did Roosevelt win the 1932 presidential election?

One slogan they thought up but dared not suggest use was 'Boy! Wasn't that some Depression'.

Hoover generally had poor relations with the press: Roosevelt courted them. Hoover lacked charisma: Roosevelt exuded it. However, many historians have argued that there was little to choose between the candidates in terms of economic policies. Certainly, Roosevelt did not promise government action to solve economic problems. In fact, he even made a speech on 19 October attacking Hoover's 'extravagant government spending' and pledging a 25 per cent cut in the federal budget.

The most important factor was that Hoover expected to lose, while his opponent was determined to win. Many of Roosevelt's promises were vague and even contradictory. In San Francisco he made a speech advocating economic regulation only as a last resort, while, at Oglethorpe University, Georgia, he spoke of 'bold experimentation' to beat the Depression and of a redistribution of national income. However, Roosevelt did say things that captured the public imagination. In a national radio address in April 1932, before his nomination, he called for government to help 'the forgotten man'. In his acceptance speech, after receiving the nomination he repeated this idea:

> On the farms, in the large, metropolitan areas, in the smaller cities and in the villages, millions of our citizens cherish the hope that their old standards of living and of thought have not gone forever. These millions cannot and shall not hope in vain.
>
> I pledge you, I pledge myself, to a new deal for the American people. Let us all here assembled constitute ourselves prophets of a new order of competence and of courage. This is more than a political campaign; it is a call to arms. Give me your help, not to win votes alone but to aim in this crusade to restore America to its own people.

In this speech Roosevelt created a name for his programme, 'The New Deal' – we will discuss this in the next two chapters. Traditionally the victorious nominee waited at home for the party elders to visit him and to offer the nomination. However, Roosevelt took the unprecedented step of flying to Chicago, where the convention was being held, to accept it. This had the effect of showing to the rest of the USA that here was a man who meant business, who recognised there was a grave crisis and could not wait to get on with the job of solving it.

Roosevelt used the radio to great effect. It was as though he was speaking directly to individuals. Hoover was by comparison merely boring. One might say there was no contest. Roosevelt won by the biggest majority since Abraham Lincoln in 1864. However, it was not an overwhelming victory – 57 per cent of the popular vote is little more than half. Moreover, few really knew what Roosevelt stood for. Political columnist Walter Lippmann was possibly close to the truth when he wrote that Roosevelt was 'a pleasant man who, without any important qualifications for the office, would very much like to be president'.

However, Americans were voting above all for change. Whatever Roosevelt may have stood for, this, above all, is what he seemed to offer.

7 | President Hoover: An Epitaph

Key question
What were the main features of Hoover's presidency?

Historians have recently been more sympathetic to Hoover. He is now often viewed as a victim both of his own closed mind and of one of the most demanding crises in American history, which was also to prove beyond Roosevelt's powers to solve. But, whereas Roosevelt was prepared to listen to ideas and to show flexibility, Hoover never budged. This was his biggest failing.

He would consider many remedies, but he would not accept direct federal intervention. He believed the government should help make things happen but not do them itself. He believed it was the job of the government to create the circumstances within which self-help and community responsibility could thrive. In pursuing this policy, particularly during the Depression, Hoover did involve the government in more areas of life than ever before. Examples of this can be seen in the expansion of federal lending and encouragement of public works' schemes.

However, Hoover's legislation was limited because he would not countenance direct government action. There were very few theories at the time as to how a Depression of this severity could be solved. In later years economists such as John Maynard Keynes were to argue that direct government intervention was necessary. However, as we have seen, Hoover would not have supported this. As a result, what he offered fell far short of what was necessary. However, it must be remembered that neither Congress nor the business community were advocating wholesale federal government involvement either. Indeed, as government spending went into deficit partly as a result of measures he had taken, there was a widespread belief among both that Hoover should concentrate on balancing the budget.

Hoover was no exponent of *laissez-faire*. He believed that the government should be a positive force for good in society. It should facilitate, for example, equality of opportunity and clean living in its citizens. Unfortunately, Hoover's principal philosophies of voluntarism and self-help were wholly inadequate to meet the magnitude of the crisis facing the USA when he was president. Nevertheless, as we have seen, he believed that government should do far more than his immediate predecessors believed. In this respect, Hoover may well be described as the 'first of the new presidents' *and* 'the last of the old'.

	Summary diagram: President Hoover and the Great Depression	
Year	Economic factors and statistics	Government action
1929	Unemployment 3.2% GNP $203.6 billion Growth rate 6.7% October 1929, price of shares fell by $14 billion	Agricultural Marketing Act
1930	Unemployment 8.9% GNP $183.5 billion Growth rate –9.6% Serious drought SE of Rockies	Voluntarism, e.g. conferences to try to dissuade business from laying off workers Hawley-Smoot Tariff $49 million given in loans to victims of the drought
1931	Unemployment 16.3% GNP $169.5 million Growth rate –7.6%	Moratorium on collection of war debts for 18 months National Credit Corporation set up with capital funds of $500 million
1932	Unemployment 24.1% GNP $144.2 billion Growth rate –14.7%	Federal Home Loan Bank Act Reconstruction Finance Corporation set up with funds of $2 billion Emergency Relief and Construction Act Dispersal by force of 'Bonus Army'

1932 Presidential Election

Herbert Hoover	Franklin Delano Roosevelt
Self-help Voluntarism Community responsibility	'New Deal for the American People' Restoration of confidence in the USA
15.7 million votes	22.8 million votes

8 | The Key Debate

The economic cycle necessarily involves periods of depression in most industrial countries. However, the extent of the Great Depression, which coincided with the presidency of Herbert Hoover, was unprecedented. The reasons why it was so severe and why it lasted so long have been extensively debated both by historians and those involved at the time. In this section we will consider the various interpretations.

Why was the Depression so extensive and long-lasting?

Herbert Hoover

Hoover wrote extensively about the Depression in his memoirs.
He called it the nightmare of his years in the White House. He
insisted the Depression was European in its origin and was caused
by the effects of the First World War, which led countries to
continue to distrust each other.

The **Customs Union** founded by Germany and Austria in 1931
angered Britain and France. They had continued to distrust their
two former enemies who had been allies in the war. They now
feared the Customs Union could be the start of some wider
possibly military union between Germany and Austria.

Britain and France retaliated to the Customs Union by
demanding immediate repayment of bills owed to them by the
banks of those two countries. This led to bank collapses that
spread to other countries in Europe. The USA meanwhile could
not continue to lend money to European countries because of the
Wall Street Crash. The subsequent collapse of European banks in
turn spread to banks in the USA to whom the European banks
owed money that they could no longer repay.

Today there is some agreement at least in part with Hoover's
analysis.

Customs Union
Agreement to
abolish trade
barriers between
participating
countries and raise
those for other
countries.

Key term

Charles P. Kindleberger

Other historians place more blame on Hoover himself, however.
Writing in the 1980s, Charles P. Kindleberger argued the
Depression would have ended sooner if Hoover and the Federal
Reserve Board had been more willing to lend money to the
stricken banks. Hoover froze war debts and reparations payments,
but the Hawley-Smoot tariff reduced the levels of world trade and
triggered retaliations. The Depression therefore lasted so long
because trade was kept low.

Robert Sobel

Robert Sobel, an eminent historian of banking argued that the
Wall Street Crash did not in itself lead to any bank failures in the
USA. Large-scale business collapse did not really begin until
1930–1. Sobel argued that Hoover could have done more to
reform the financial system. It was effectively his inactivity that
was in part responsible for the collapse.

J.K. Galbraith

Writing in the mid-twentieth century, J.K. Galbraith felt that if the
economy had been sound, the effects of the Wall Street Crash
would have been relatively minor. However, the Crash made
deflation worse for two reasons:

• A major problem was represented by the problems of financial
  pyramids that existed only to buy and sell stock (see pages 44,
  54–5). As the value of stock slumped these collapsed. Their
  collapse in turn led to the failure of the companies they
  controlled, which actually produced goods (generally at the
  bottom of the pyramid). This led to greater unemployment.

- The public lost confidence in the economy and were no longer prepared to get into debt to buy goods even if they could afford to.

Galbraith also listed the evidence of too many small and weak banks, indebted foreigners and poor economic intelligence. The Fed, for example, believed the economy would right itself. If its members had loosened the money supply they could have stimulated the economy. In fact they made things worse by tightening the money supply by 33 per cent between 1929 and 1934.

Paul Johnson

Opposing the view that Hoover should have done more is the British historian Paul Johnson who felt that Hoover should have done less. Johnson disagreed that the economy was weak and believed it would have righted itself. However, he argued that Hoover asked employers not to cut wages while he reduced taxes and increased government spending. This led to a huge government deficit and began, in Johnson's opinion, the New Deal that Roosevelt continued. Indeed, he argued that Hoover started more public works schemes in his four years of office than had been done in the previous 40. Hoover had earlier reduced taxes. Now he increased them to pay for the public works schemes. According to Johnson this simply showed the inconsistency in Hoover's policies. The Hawley-Smoot tariff, which limited international trade, made things even worse. Meanwhile, by supporting insolvent companies and keeping people in work, Hoover simply extended the agonies of the Depression. He should have let the economy right itself.

David M. Kennedy

Kennedy, a modern historian, agreed in part with Hoover that economic problems in Europe made the depression worse in the USA. He sees as a catalyst the progressive abandonment of the gold standard. Keeping to the gold standard guaranteed the value of money across frontiers. Nations issued currencies in amounts fixed by the ratio of money to the amount in their gold reserves. In theory, incoming gold from other countries would expand the monetary base in the receiving country. This would mean the amount of money in circulation could be increased. This would in turn inflate prices and lower interest rates as more money for borrowing became available.

A fall in gold stocks had the opposite effect – it shrank the domestic money supply, deflated prices and raised interest rates. Any country whose supply of gold was falling was expected to deflate their economy, to lower prices to stimulate exports and raise interest rates. This would reverse the outflow of capital. By tying foreign economies together, the gold standard in theory ensured economic fluctuations in one country would be spread to others.

However, because of the Depression, by 1931 huge amounts of gold were lost. To protect themselves countries raised tariffs, imposed controls on the export of capital and abandoned the gold standard. Britain was the first country to do this in September 1931. Hoover felt that Britain was acting like a failed bank that cheated its creditors. This may be true – but Britain was also at the heart of the global financial structure. Therefore when Britain abandoned the gold standard other countries followed suit. This produced a crisis in the global economy and led to other countries protecting themselves through tariffs – like the Hawley-Smoot tariff in the USA. The value of global business fell from $36 billion in 1929 to $12 billion by 1932.

This affected the USA in three main ways:

- USA banks held worthless assets from foreigners as they had defaulted on repayment
- foreign investors began to withdraw capital from US banks
- insecurity led to domestic runs on US banks.

During the months of September to October 1931, following Britain's abandonment of the gold standard, 2294 US banks failed (double the number that did so in 1930). The Fed responded by further deflating the economy at a time it should have inflated it, for example, by increasing the stock of money. To stop the outflow of gold, the Fed raised the rediscount rates. If Hoover was at fault it was in his refusal to change his ideas. Many countries at least partially recovered after abandoning the gold standard. Hoover persisted with it.

Some key books and articles in the debate
H. Evans, *The American Century* (Jonathan Cape, 1998).
J.K. Galbraith, *The Great Crash* (Penguin, 1975).
J.K. Galbraith, *The Wall Street Crash*, *Purnell History of the Twentieth Century*, Volume 3 (Purnell, 1971).
H. Hoover, *Memoirs: The Great Depression* (Macmillan, 1952).
Paul Johnson, *Modern Times* (Phoenix, 2000).
Paul Johnson, *A History of the American People* (Phoenix, 2000).
David M. Kennedy, *Freedom From Fear* (Oxford University Press, 1999).
C.P. Kindleberger, *The World in Depression 1929–1939* (University of California Press, 1986).
R. Sobell, *The Great Bull Market* (Norton, 1968).

Study Guide: AS Questions

In the style of Edexcel

Study Sources 1–5 below and on page 112 and then answer the questions that follow.

Source 1

From: a speech by Herbert Hoover on 22 October 1928 during his campaign for the presidency.

Today there are almost nine automobiles for every ten families, where seven and a half years ago only enough automobiles were running to average less than four for every ten families.

The slogan of progress is changing from the full dinner plate to the full garage. Our people have more to eat, better things to wear and better homes. Wages have increased, the cost of living has decreased. The job of every man and woman has been made more secure. We have in this short period decreased the fear of poverty, the fear of unemployment, the fear of old age.

In seven and a half years we have added 70% to the electric power at the elbow of our workers and further promoted them from carriers of burdens to directors of machines. We have steadily reduced the sweat in human labor.

Source 2

From: an index calculated to show changes in farmers' incomes

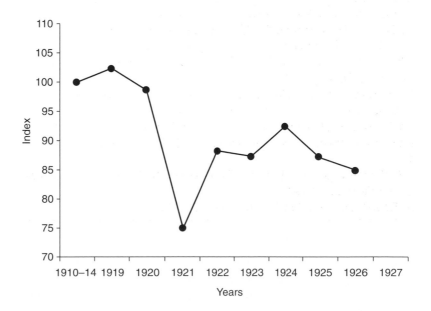

Source 3

From: Hugh Brogan, The Longman History of the USA, *1999.*

Already in 1928 the forces which were to destroy Coolidge prosperity were at work. Indeed the first signs of trouble came as early as 1926 when the sale of new housing began to slacken. The market was becoming saturated, like the market for farm products. Of course there were still tens of thousands of Americans who needed better housing than they were ever likely to get, but they had no money. By 1926, those who had money had usually obtained their houses; and though new buyers came on the market every year, they were not numerous enough to sustain the boom.

A faltering in the building industry was a bad signal. Others followed. By late summer of 1929, demand had slackened so much all the major indices of industrial production were turning down.

Such ebbs in commerce are wholly natural. In other circumstances, their impact and duration can be minimal. Unfortunately, two factors made the impact of this particular turndown catastrophic. The Coolidge-Hoover philosophy of government and economics forbade the federal government to take any preventative action, including stimulating demand. The federal government could have acted as governments have done so often since, and, by an extensive programme of public expenditure, maintained employment and stimulated demand. Unfortunately, such a policy was as yet unthinkable.

(a) **Study Sources 1, 2 and 3**
   How far do Sources 2 and 3 support Hoover's portrayal of a prosperous society in Source 1? (10 marks)
(b) **Study Sources 2 and 3 and use your own knowledge**
   Do you agree with the view that government policies were responsible for the severity of the economic crisis the USA faced from October 1929?

   Explain your answer, using these two sources and your own knowledge (24 marks)

Source: Edexcel, May 2002, questions (c) and (e)

Exam tips

The cross-reference is intended to take you straight to the material that will help you to answer the question.

(a) The key words here are 'How far'. You should notice that the sources support the statement in some ways and disagree in others. It is the examination of these factors that should lie at the heart of your answer. You could examine Source 2 to show that the problems faced by farmers had not been addressed and their condition in fact worsened over the decade. Source 3 discusses a variety of reasons why prosperity came to an end. However, to strike a balance it also mentions areas of continuing prosperity such as the fact that there were some new home buyers coming onto the market after 1926.

(b) Remember to use both the sources and your own knowledge in this question and note the length required from the fact that it carries 24 marks (about 40 per cent of the total for the exam). You need to examine the claims in Source 3, for example, that 'two factors made the impact of this particular turndown catastrophic' and examine evidence from Source 2. Use your own knowledge to agree or disagree with this.

You need to examine the factors that led to the extent of the depression (pages 93–6) and then come to a judgement in terms of how far government policies were responsible. You could consider, for example, world-wide causes and the failures in the banking system. At the end, however, a balanced and well-argued judgement is required in terms of how far government policies (or lack of them) were to blame.

Study Guide: Advanced Level Question

In the style of OCR

Assess the significance of reasons why the American economy collapsed between 1929 and 1933. (45 marks)

Exam tips

The cross-references are intended to take you straight to the material that will help you to answer the question.

This question invites you to evaluate reasons in terms of how significant they were rather than just describing them.

- You need to consider the interpretation that it was primarily the Wall Street Crash that caused the depression against other interpretations that state that structural weaknesses in the US economy (such as uneven distribution of wealth leading to overproduction and underconsumption) were a major factor (pages 48–58).
- In addition you need to consider the role of the Hoover administration in assessing the dramatic collapse of the US economy after 1929 against other factors such as the world-wide nature of the collapse, the unexpected depth of the depression and limitations placed on the Hoover administration by the US constitution and Congress (pages 93–6).
- You need to come to a balanced judgement in terms of which reasons were, in your view, the most significant.

6 Roosevelt and the First New Deal 1933–4

POINTS TO CONSIDER

This chapter is concerned with the following issues;

- The beginnings of Roosevelt's presidency and his presidential style
- The First 100 Days and the measures of the First New Deal in the context of the problems they were intended to solve
- The alternatives to the New Deal from the Right and Left
- An examination of the character of the First New Deal in terms of its coherence – was it a pre-planned programme of change or simply a series of measures attempting to deal with crises as and when they occurred?

Key dates

1887		Dawes Severality Act
1933		Presidency of Franklin D. Roosevelt
	March	Emergency Banking Relief Act
		Beer Act – abolition of prohibition
		Farm Credit Act
		Civilian Conservation Corps
	May	Glass-Steagall Act
		Truth-in-Securities Act
		Agricultural Adjustment Act
		Tennessee Valley Authority
		Federal Emergency Relief Act
	June	National Industrial Recovery Act
		National Recovery Administration
		Public Works Administration
		Home Owners Refinancing Corporation
	July	London Economic Conference
	November	Civil Works Administration
1934	January	Gold Reserve Act
	June	Silver Purchase Act
		Indian Reorganization Act
		Federal Housing Administration

1 | Beginnings of Roosevelt's Presidency

Key question
What was the
significance of the
New Deal?

Two weeks before his inauguration on 4 March 1933, Franklin
Delano Roosevelt addressed a gathering of American legionnaires
in Miami, Florida. Joseph Zangara, a bricklayer of Italian
extraction, fired five bullets at him from close range. All missed
their target, but Mayor Cermack of Chicago, who was with
Roosevelt, was killed. Zangara opposed capitalism and sought to
kill the man pledged to save it. Fittingly, Roosevelt did go on to
save the capitalist system in the USA through his New Deal
programme.

Historians speak of two and even three different New Deals in
the 1930s. In this chapter and the next we will consider these.
This chapter considers the period of the First New Deal beginning
with the 100 Days when a mass of legislation was passed.

The New Deal may by no means have been a cohesive
programme – indeed, it often seemed contradictory. It may even
be misleading to call it a programme at all. Possibly, it might best
be seen as a series of measures to deal with specific crises, with
little overall plan. Certainly, it is most easily categorised with the
hindsight of history. Historians can look back to see common
strands running through the legislation and its implementation.
They can see where it led and how its ideas were later developed.
There is little doubt that at the end of New Deal legislation, the
USA was changed forever and the role of government greatly
increased. However, whether this was intentional is a point for
debate.

Roosevelt's inauguration

Roosevelt's **inauguration** was in March 1933. This was four
months after the election in November 1932. The period of
waiting to take office is known as the lame duck presidency.
Hoover was still in office and clearly Roosevelt must have been
frustrated waiting to take over.

During this period, the Depression worsened considerably, with
the outgoing president, Hoover, unable to introduce effective
measures to combat it. Hoover did seek to involve Roosevelt in a
smooth transition and to agree on common policies. However,
Roosevelt was non-committal to these offers. He wanted neither
to be associated with Hoover, whose credibility was shattered, nor
to tie himself to shared policies with political opponents. Later
Hoover was to accuse Roosevelt of stealing his policies and taking
credit for them. Indeed, it was alleged by some critics that
Roosevelt wanted the Depression to get worse so he could take
credit for launching a rescue operation after his inauguration.
Hoover could then be accused of having done nothing to halt
the Depression.

It is unlikely that there was any truth to these accusations.
However, what is clear is that there was little difference at first
between the policies of Roosevelt and Hoover. It was the two men
who were different. Roosevelt came across as dynamic, charismatic

Key term

Inauguration
The ceremony that
begins the
president's term of
office.

and someone in whom people were ready to have faith. Hoover as we have seen, was tired, jaded and dull by comparison.

There was tremendous expectation and excitement about Roosevelt's presidency; people were willing it to be something special. Certainly no incoming president since the Civil War had faced so many problems. Roosevelt's inaugural speech seemed to offer everything that people wanted to hear. 'The only thing we have to fear,' Roosevelt said, 'is fear itself'. He called for 'action and action now'.

The first 100 days

Roosevelt asked Congress to grant him powers as great as those it would have given him had the USA been invaded by a foreign enemy. As far as the electorate were concerned, there was no problem with this demand. The influential political journalist, Walter Lippmann wrote, 'The danger we have to fear is not that Congress will give Franklin D. Roosevelt too much power but that it will deny him the power he needs'. Lippman need not have worried. Roosevelt called Congress into a special session, which was to last for 100 days. These first 100 days of Roosevelt's presidency were possibly the most frenzied and energetic of any presidency, with a considerable amount of emergency legislation and the setting up of many '**alphabet agencies**'. Many historians have categorised the measures into those intended to bring about 'relief, recovery or reform', but as we shall see it is dangerous to assume Roosevelt had a blueprint to transform American life greatly.

However, it is exaggeration to say that, intentionally or not, at the end of the 100 days the USA had been transformed.

Roosevelt's presidential style

One historian has claimed that the modern presidency begins with Roosevelt. There is little doubt that the New Deal expanded the roles of the president and state in the running of the USA. However, Roosevelt also brought a new style to the presidency. He appeared full of infectious optimism and confidence. As was written in one business journal a few weeks after Roosevelt's inauguration, 'The people aren't sure where they're going but anywhere seems better than where they've been'. Roosevelt's style differed from that of his predecessors in two ways: (1) his use of the media and (2) his appointment of personnel.

(1) Use of the media

Roosevelt was perhaps the first president to understand the power of the media. He developed the twice-weekly press conferences into cosy conversations. The writer John Dos Passos suggested that it was as if Roosevelt was sitting at a table talking to old friends. He got to know members of the press corps by name, he explained policies carefully and he invited questions. This contrasted with his predecessors, who had only accepted questions written out and presented in advance. Hoover's relationship with the press had been so frosty that he had been

Key term

Alphabet agencies
New government bodies set up to tackle problems. They were so-called because they became known by their initials, e.g. AAA, CCC.

Key question
What was different about Roosevelt's presidential style?

accused of using the secret service to investigate any leakage of information to the press.

The result of this new friendliness and 'openness' towards the press corps was that Roosevelt got them on his side. He could release information as and when he thought it necessary, forestall criticism and effectively control much of the newspaper reporting about him.

Fireside chats

Roosevelt was said to have 'the first great American radio voice'. He spoke directly to the electorate on issues in 'fireside chats'. These became so popular that those who did not have a radio would visit with those who did to ensure they did not miss the president. The mass media was still in its infancy. Until Calvin Coolidge went in for being photographed (see page 34), few Americans had ever seen a picture of their president let alone heard his voice. Now the reassuring voice of Roosevelt in living rooms throughout the nation restored confidence and helped people believe that everything was going to be all right. After he told people over the radio to tell him their troubles, it took a staff of 50 to handle his mail, which arrived by the truckload. By contrast, one person had been employed to deal with Herbert Hoover's correspondence.

(2) Appointment of personnel

Previously presidents had tended to appoint political allies or at best other members of their party to help them govern. Roosevelt tended to look for the best people for the job irrespective of political affiliations. Most of the 'Brains' Trusters' (see page 104) followed him to the White House. In addition, he appointed Henry A. Wallace, a farming expert, as Secretary for Agriculture; his father had held the same post in Warren Harding's cabinet. Harold Ickes, a former Republican, was to serve for 12 years as Secretary of the Interior, although he was always threatening to resign. His battles with Harry Hopkins over the running of rival 'alphabet agencies' were legendary.

Hopkins had done social work in New York before being appointed to run the state emergency relief administration while Roosevelt was governor. Although he was a hard-drinking gambler, he nevertheless had a vision of a country where the state cared for all those in need. This would put him in conflict with many of the more conservative members of the administration.

Roosevelt encouraged rivalry and disputes among his appointees. He would listen to their disputes and then make up his own mind between them. Sometimes he used personal appointees to investigate issues, by-passing proper channels. Often when appointing people to office he made their job specifications deliberately vague so their responsibilities would appear to overlap with others'. He knew this would make people more dependent on him as they asked him to intervene in disputes or sought his favour or support.

This strategy of personnel management worked. Roosevelt inspired intense loyalty. He could enthuse with a smile or small favour. As Harold Ickes said, no matter how jaded you were, you came out of a meeting with Roosevelt like 'a fighting cock'. His appointees would need their energy. The first 100 days of Roosevelt's administration set the scene for the transformation of the USA.

2 | The First 100 Days and the First New Deal

The measures undertaken in the first 100 days can be classified into different areas namely:

- banking and finance
- regulation of the Stock Exchange
- economies in government
- agriculture
- industrial recovery
- relief
- Native Americans
- housing issues.

We will consider each of these in turn.

Banking and finance

The most pressing concern was undoubtedly the collapse of the American banking system. By 1932 banks were closing at the rate of 40 per day. In October of that year, the Governor of Nevada, fearing the imminent collapse of an important banking chain, declared a bank holiday and closed every bank in the state. At midnight on 14 February 1933, the Governor of Michigan did the same. All 550 banks were closed for eight days. By the time of Roosevelt's inauguration, banks were in fact closed in many states.

One important effect of these bank closures was a flow of gold from the Federal Reserve and New York banks to local banks that were still functioning. This was both to support bank deposits elsewhere in the country and to meet the demands of panic-stricken foreign investors who wanted to remove their capital from the USA. Between January and the inauguration in March, the nation's gold reserves fell from $1.3 billion to $400 million. American banks had only $6 billion available to meet $41 billion worth of deposits. In the two days before the inauguration $500 million was withdrawn. The situation was so fraught that Washington hotels would not accept out-of-town cheques from inauguration guests.

Banking

On 6 March Roosevelt closed all the banks in the country for four days to give Treasury officials time to draft emergency legislation. The ensuing Emergency Banking Relief Act was passed by Congress after only 40 minutes of debate. All the measures it contained had already been considered by Hoover. However, they had been rejected because he feared the panic that may have

Key question
How were the problems in banking and finance overcome?

resulted from the closing of the banks. Roosevelt had no such fear. Although his action may have been unconstitutional, people were expecting him to act decisively and, while the banks were closed, they improvised using barter, foreign currencies and stamps as units of exchange.

The aim of the Emergency Banking Relief Act was simply to restore confidence in the American banking system. It gave the Treasury power to investigate all banks threatened with collapse. The Reconstruction Finance Corporation (see page 100) was authorised to buy their stock to support them and to take on many of their debts. In doing so the RFC became in effect the largest bank in the world.

In the meantime, Roosevelt appeared on radio to give the first of his 'fireside chats'. He explained to listeners, in language all could understand, the nature of the crisis and how they could help. The message on this occasion was simple; place your money in the bank rather than under your mattress. It worked. Solvent banks were allowed to reopen and others were reorganised by government officials to put them on a sounder footing. By the beginning of April, $1 billion in currency had been returned to bank deposits and the crisis was over. Raymond Moley, one of the 'Brains' Trusters' (see page 104), felt that 'American capitalism was saved in eight days'.

Roosevelt later drew up legislation to put the banking system on a sounder long-term footing. The Glass–Steagall Act of 1933 had the following effects:

- commercial banks that relied on small-scale depositors were banned from involvement in the type of investment banking that had fuelled some of the 1920s speculation
- bank officials were not to be allowed to take personal loans from their own banks
- authority over open-market operations such as buying and selling government securities was centralised by being transferred from the Federal Reserve Banks to the Federal Reserve Board in Washington
- individual bank deposits were to be insured against bank failure up to the figure of $2500 with the insurance fund to be administered by a new agency, the Federal Deposit Insurance Corporation (FDIC).

The banking legislation, despite its success, was not without its critics, notably supporters of Hoover. They felt that all these measures could have been applied before the inauguration with their chief's blessing and Roosevelt had therefore taken the credit that should have been due to his predecessor. On the other hand, some criticised Roosevelt for adopting Hoover's policies and for not being radical enough. Raymond Moley admitted that Hoover might have passed similar legislation if he had had the power. Moreover, the measures were carried out by officials appointed by Hoover such as Ogden Mills, whom Roosevelt had kept on.

While the Federal Reserve Board had been given more control, many critics nevertheless wanted to see more government supervision of banking possibly through nationalisation. Some felt that Roosevelt had even rewarded bankers for their past incompetence. Many banks had been given government subsidies to help them to stay in business. By requiring that state banks join the Federal Reserve system to qualify for insurance, large banks were given more control over smaller ones. Although this was to protect them from failure, it all seemed to favour the rich and powerful. However, what these critics failed to appreciate was that this was precisely Roosevelt's intention. He saw his task as the saving of, rather than the destruction of, American capitalism.

Finance

Roosevelt saw his role in finance as twofold:

- to stop the flow of gold out of the country
- to increase the amount of money in circulation in the USA, thus raising prices.

In a series of measures taken in March and April 1933, he effectively took the USA off the gold standard by forbidding the export of gold except under licence from the Treasury and prohibiting the trading-in of currency for gold. Those holding gold were required to turn it in to the Federal Banks for $20.67 an ounce.

The main objective of these measures was to bring down the value of the dollar abroad. Once the dollar was no longer tied to the value of gold, it could find its own level in international markets. This meant in theory that foreigners could afford to buy more American goods. The measure did seem to work, because the international value of the dollar fell to $0.85 in gold, meaning that foreigners could buy 15 per cent more American goods than before for their money.

Problems with Roosevelt's financial measures

This success did leave Roosevelt in a dilemma abroad. European counties in particular had great hopes that the London Economic Conference, which met on 6 July 1933, would help solve their financial problems. Delegates from these countries wanted a general stabilisation of currencies. Roosevelt believed the falling value of the dollar was revitalising the American economy and so refused to make any agreement. This led directly to the collapse of the Conference. It showed how Roosevelt was concentrating on American recovery and how the New Deal was essentially a domestic programme. The stabilisation of foreign economies was simply not on his agenda.

Roosevelt wanted the dollar to fall even further by being left to find its own level. On 22 October 1933 he announced that the Reconstruction Finance Corporation would buy gold above the market price, which was then $31.36 an ounce. As the price of gold rose, the value of the dollar fell because it needed more dollars to buy it. On 30 January 1934 the Gold Reserve Act pegged the price of gold at $35 an ounce, and the dollar had

Key question
What problems did these financial measures create?

London Economic Conference: 1933

Key date

effectively been devalued by nearly 60 per cent since March 1933 when gold had been worth $20.67 an ounce.

At home, the effect of all this was to increase the amount of money in circulation. This, it was hoped, would raise prices. The theory behind this was, as the volume of money rose, its relative value would fall simply because there is more of it around. On the other hand, if the value of money fell it bought less, thus causing prices to rise. It was hoped the rise in prices would in turn help revitalise American industry and agriculture. However, while prices did rise somewhat, juggling the price of gold and currency mechanisms did not effect any major economic recovery because the nature of the Depression was too complex for any single measures to work.

The Silver Purchase Act, June 1934

Roosevelt also sought to raise prices by introducing more silver into the coinage. He was persuaded in this by some of his supporters from silver-mining states such as Colorado. They had seen the value of silver fall to an all-time low and were looking for government help to improve this situation. Late in 1933 the federal government began to buy up all the silver produced domestically, at an artificially high price. The Silver Purchase Act of June 1934 stated that the Treasury would buy silver until its monetary value equalled 33 per cent that of gold; or alternatively the market price of silver reached what should be its monetary value. However, in effect this measure had little impact beyond subsidising the domestic silver industry. It offered a further lesson that prices could not be raised without real economic recovery.

Key question
How did Roosevelt try to ensure the Wall Street Crash would not be repeated?

Regulation of the Stock Exchange

To ensure that the excesses of the 1920s, which had caused the Wall Street Crash, were not repeated two measures were passed:

- The Truth-in-Securities Act, 1933, required brokers to offer clients realistic information about the securities they were selling.
- The Securities Act, 1934, set up a new agency, the Securities Exchange Commission. Its task was to oversee Stock Market activities and prevent fraudulent activities such as insider dealing, where brokers agreed to artificially raise prices before selling, as in the Bull Pool (see page 72). Roosevelt appointed Joseph Kennedy to head the Commission. Cynics held that Kennedy, who had been a major speculator in the 1920s, could exploit the situation. The Act was highly successful despite the opposition of Wall Street insiders – some of whom had threatened to move the Exchange to Canada if it was passed. When the system caught and imprisoned Richard Whitney for embezzlement in 1938, the Security Exchange Commission demonstrated it could now search out its own rotten apples. Wall Street had gained a new credibility.

Economies in government

Roosevelt was a conservative in financial matters and, like his predecessors, he believed strongly in a balanced budget. Care was taken to distinguish between the budget for normal government business and that for emergency relief to deal with the Depression. He expected the budget for normal business to balance. He also sought to make all his recovery programmes self-financing and often they began with loans rather than grants. It was hoped that as money began to be made from the programmes, these loans would be repaid.

The Economy Act, 1933, meanwhile, slashed government salaries and cut ex-soldiers' pensions. Roosevelt, like Hoover, refused to give the veterans their bonus. However, when a second 'Bonus Army' arrived in Washington, Roosevelt greeted them with refreshments and entertainment. His wife was sent to charm them without giving in to any of their demands. This time, they departed peacefully.

Key question
What were Roosevelt's views on government spending and how did he implement these?

Agriculture

Agricultural recovery was given a higher priority than industrial recovery. This was for a variety of reasons:

Key question
Why was agricultural recovery a high priority?

- 30 per cent of the labour force worked in agriculture. If agricultural workers could afford to buy more, industry would be stimulated.
- If agriculture became more profitable, there would be a reduction in farms being repossessed by the banks.
- As we have seen (page 50), the farming lobby in Washington had always been influential in the past but now felt under threat. Democratic politicians representing agricultural interests in the South and West had been among Roosevelt's earliest political supporters and he certainly felt he owed them something.
- Roosevelt took a personal interest in agriculture. He regarded the farmer as the backbone of the USA. This is an aspect of Roosevelt's thinking that is often forgotten. He remained passionately concerned with conservation and ecology, as illustrated by his personal interest in the work of the Civilian Conservation Corps (see pages 129–30).
- The increasingly militant **Farmers' Holiday Association** in the Midwest threatened farm strikes if effective legislation was not forthcoming. The same organisation had disrupted the repossession of farms. It both threatened and carried out acts of violence against officials trying to implement these.

Farmers' Holiday Association
Pressure group set up to increase pay and conditions for farmers.

Key term

In the long run, the aim of agricultural policies was to make farming more efficient by ending overproduction. This would be done by taking the most uneconomic land out of production and resettling displaced agricultural workers. However, in the short term, farming crises had to be addressed. This was done through a series of measures.

Key question
What were the short-term policies to aid recovery in agriculture?

Extension of farm credit

The Farm Credit Act of March 1933 brought all the various agencies dealing with agricultural credit into one body, the Farm Credit Administration. This helped the co-ordination of agricultural issues. In April, the Emergency Farm Mortgage Act loaned funds to farmers in danger of losing their properties. The Frazier–Lemke Farm Mortgage Act of June went a stage further. It lent money to farmers whose lands had already been repossessed so they could recover them; interest was set at only one per cent.

Agriculture Adjustment Act, May 1933

Overproduction had been the greatest problem of American agriculture. Neither the McNary-Haugen proposals of the 1920s (see page 52) nor Hoover's Federal Farm Board (see page 97) had addressed this problem. While industrial production had declined by 42 per cent in the years 1929–33, that of agriculture had fallen by only six per cent. It was extremely difficult to tell farmers to cut back their production. If the cutbacks were to be voluntary, individual farmers would be very unlikely to make the first move to do so in case none of his neighbours followed suit; if compulsory, there would need to be new and far-reaching enforcement agencies set up. Nevertheless, the main principle behind the Agricultural Adjustment Act was that the government would subsidise farmers to reduce their acreage and production voluntarily.

The overall aim was of the Agricultural Adjustment Act was to increase farmers' incomes. A new agency was set up, the Agricultural Adjustment Administration (AAA), which agreed to pay farmers to reduce their production of 'staple' items – initially corn, cotton, milk, pigs, rice, tobacco and wheat. The programme was to be self-financing through a tax placed on companies that processed food. It was assumed that these companies would in turn pass on the increased cost to the consumer.

Reduction of cotton production was perhaps the most pressing need. At the beginning of 1933, unsold cotton in the USA already exceeded the total average annual world consumption of American cotton. Moreover, farmers had planted 400,000 acres more than in 1932. They were, quite simply, paid to destroy much of this. A total of 10.5 million acres were ploughed under, and the price of cotton accordingly rose from 6.5 cents per pound in 1932 to 10 cents in 1933.

However, it was one thing to destroy cotton but it was far more contentious to destroy food when so many Americans were hungry. Six million piglets were bought and slaughtered. Although many of the carcasses were subsequently processed and fed to the unemployed, the public outcry was enormous.

In fact, the AAA destroyed only cotton and piglets. Drought helped to make the 1933 wheat crop the poorest since 1896, and agreements were reached to limit acreage in other crops in subsequent years as Table 6.1 shows.

Total farm income rose from $4.5 billion in 1932 to $6.9 billion in 1935. The percentage of farmers signing up for AAA

Table 6.1: Acreage removed from production

Year	Acreage removed (in millions)
1933	10.4
1934	35.7
1935	30.3

agreements was high at first – 95 per cent of tobacco growers, for example – and the Act was very popular with farmers.

Faced by drought, western ranchers sought to bring beef cattle under the protection of the AAA in 1934. By January 1935 the government had purchased 8.3 million head of cattle, in return for which ranchers agreed to reduce breeding cows by 20 per cent in 1937. Overall, it would appear that the AAA worked effectively to deal with the crisis of overproduction, although there were problems and these will be considered in the next chapter (see pages 158–9).

Tennessee Valley Authority, May 1933

The Tennessee Valley Authority (TVA) was one of the most grandiose schemes of the New Deal. It was created to harness the power of the River Tennessee, which ran through seven of the poorest states in the USA. It was hoped that by so doing the region of 80,000 square miles with a population of two million would become more prosperous. The TVA had several major tasks:

- to construct 20 huge dams to control the floods which periodically affected the region
- to develop ecological schemes such as tree planting to stop soil erosion
- to encourage farmers to use more efficient means of cultivation, such as **contour ploughing**
- to provide jobs by setting up fertiliser manufacture factories
- to develop welfare and educational programmes
- most significantly perhaps, to produce hydro-electric power for an area whose existing supplies of electricity were limited to two out of every 100 farms.

The designers of the TVA deliberately stated in the Act that the production of electricity was only a by-product. This was because they knew private companies would oppose the right of a government agency to manufacture and sell it. Moreover, the electricity generated was cheaper than elsewhere. The TVA

Contour ploughing Ploughing across hillsides so that the crested grooves retained the soil. Prior to this farmers had often ploughed up and down. In heavy rain the soil could get washed away.

Key term

The owner of the farm on the left agreed to become a test farmer using contour ploughing. Notice how more fertile his side appears. Photo courtesy of the Tennessee Valley Authority.

effectively became a central planning authority for the region. It was largely responsible for the modernisation and improved living standards that saw its residents increase their average income by 200 per cent in the period from 1929 to 1949.

Key question
How was industrial recovery dealt with?

Industrial recovery

Industrial recovery was a priority for the New Deal. However, it had only limited success due to the scale of the industrial collapse. Although the economy grew 10 per cent per year during Roosevelt's first term from 1933 to 1936, output had fallen so low since 1929 that this still left unemployment at 14 per cent.

Roosevelt's primary aims were to get people back to work and to increase consumer demand. To do this, he needed both to act quickly before the situation got even worse and to gain the co-operation of businessmen. He knew he could achieve little without the latter; there was simply no alternative structure to change things without the active support of businessmen. They would hardly consent to radical policies such as nationalisation or more anti-trust legislation.

The problem was that there was no consensus about how to go about ensuring industrial recovery.

Some businessmen still supported policies of *laissez-faire*; others wanted massive government intervention. Some felt competition should be ended; others believed it to be the keynote to recovery. Again, it is important to note that Roosevelt was in the business of saving the American system of capitalism, not replacing it. This came as a disappointment to many who had hoped for more radical objectives.

Roosevelt was forced to act quickly and under pressure, as Congress was about to pass a measure to restrict the working week to 30 hours with the hope of sharing out the existing jobs. He opposed this scheme because he feared that rather than raise overall purchasing power it would simply share out more thinly what already existed. Instead, he replaced it with the National Industry Recovery Act (NIRA) of June 1933. The Act came in two parts.

National Recovery Administration (NRA)

The NRA was set up to oversee industrial recovery. Headed by General Hugh Johnson, an argumentative, hard-drinking dynamo of energy, it seemed to offer something to all groups involved in industry. Powerful businessmen, for example, benefited from the suspension of anti-trust legislation for two years. The argument behind this was that if industrial expansion was to be promoted, it was crazy to maintain laws that, in fact, restricted it. Firms were encouraged to agree to codes of practice to regulate unfair competition such as price cutting, and to agree on such matters as working conditions and minimum wages in their industry.

Elsewhere in the NRA legislation, 'yellow dog' clauses (see page 57) were outlawed and Section 7(a) declared employees had a right to join labour unions and participate in **collective**

Key term
Collective bargaining
Discussions between employers and employees (usually represented by labour unions) about working conditions and pay.

bargaining. This meant that employers would have to recognise labour unions to negotiate on behalf of their members. Roosevelt had not welcomed this clause, which had been forced upon him by Congress. He was more interested in reducing unemployment than legalising unions. His fears that this could lead to industrial unrest seemed proved by the wave of violent strikes that alleviated only with further legislation.

A hectic promotional campaign took place to promote the NRA and the codes. At a mammoth NRA parade in New York, for example, the singer Al Jolson enthused before the newsreel cameras that this was the most exciting day of his life, more exciting, in fact, than the day of his own wedding.

The national response to the campaign was tremendous. Eventually, 557 codes were drawn up covering most industries, and firms which agreed to them were entitled to display what would become one of the most enduring symbols of the New Deal; a blue eagle, with the logo underneath, 'We do our part'. It was hoped that consumers would support those firms that bore the blue eagle and boycott those which did not. To hasten proceedings, Hugh Johnson had drawn up a blanket code known as the President's Re-employment Agreement. This was particularly intended for small firms to subscribe to in order to take advantage of the blue eagle and the increased custom it would presumably attract.

Problems with the codes

Problems with most of the operations of the NRA became quickly apparent. Many of the codes, for example, turned out to be unworkable. This was in part because they were adopted so quickly, often without proper thought or planning, but also because they were often contentious. Many large manufacturers, notably Henry Ford, never subscribed to them and yet, as we shall see, small firms complained that they favoured big business. Many small firms found it difficult to comply with all the regulations, particularly the minimum wages clauses. It was hoped, for example, that the firms signing the codes would introduce a minimum wage of $11 for a 40-hour week. Few small firms could afford this.

In March 1934 Congress set up the National Recovery Review Board to investigate whether small firms were disadvantaged by the codes. It was reported that they were indeed placed at a severe disadvantage. Moreover, the codes seemed to favour large companies that could take advantage of them to restrict competition and increase their profits. They could, for example, work together to draw up codes in which they agreed to raise prices while keeping wages low. Some agreed to limit output to raise prices and could therefore afford to cut back on their workforce or pay lower wages.

Unions said Section 7(a) was too weak for their needs and that many employers, including those who did subscribe to the codes, were still riding roughshod over them. Ford, who did not subscribe to any codes, kept a gang of union bashers on the payroll (see page 40). Johnson created labour advisory boards to mediate in disputes but because these were advisory, they had little influence.

The argument that the NRA favoured big business was a particularly persuasive argument. The codes were largely drawn up by representatives from big business, often with the assistance of inexperienced White House officials. One of the first tasks of a newly appointed young government official, for example, was to meet sharp company lawyers to draw up the petroleum codes, even though he knew nothing about the industry.

It was also felt that there was too much bureaucracy attached to the codes. Much of their credibility was lost when a dry cleaner was sent to prison for charging less than the agreed code price for pressing a pair of trousers. There was even a code for striptease artistes that stipulated the number of performers in each show.

Ultimately, despite the fanfare, the codes did not help economic recovery. This led Johnson to attempt a 'Buy Now' campaign in October 1933 to encourage people to spend and therefore stimulate production. He also advocated an overall 10 per cent wage increase and 10-hour cut in the working week. Neither was successful.

In reality, the NRA codes looked impressive but they could not bring about an economic recovery. Many critics argued that, in practice, they did little except give large firms the opportunity to indulge in unfair practices – the very opposite of what had been intended. Johnson, a successful businessman himself, believed very firmly in self-regulation by business. There were to be no new government powers over companies. Indeed, as mentioned earlier, the government had agreed to suspend anti-trust legislation for two years.

Johnson had made many powerful enemies with his high-handed ways. The press had a field day not only over his drinking but also over the high salary he gave to his secretary, Frances Robinson, whom he admitted was 'more than a stenographer'. He began to be an embarrassment to the administration and had to go. Roosevelt dismissed him in September 1934. After his departure some of the codes were relaxed but, as we shall see in Chapter 7, the Supreme Court dealt the death blow in May 1935 when it declared the NRA unconstitutional (page 157).

Public Works Administration (PWA)

The second part of NIRA set up an emergency Public Works Administration to be headed by the Secretary of the Interior, Harold Ickes. It was funded with $3.3 billion and its purpose was '**pump priming**'. It was hoped that expenditure on public works such as roads, dams, hospitals and schools would stimulate the economy. Road building would lead to increased demand for concrete, for example, which would lead the concrete companies to employ more workers, who would therefore have more money to spend, and so on.

Key term

Pump priming
Expression used to suggest government spending would lead to economic growth.

Ickes was a meticulous administrator who therefore made
progress very slowly. In fact, he was criticised for spending only
$110 million of his funding in the first six months. His strength
was that he demanded value for money and would only fund
worthwhile projects. He did not want to have the agency
jeopardised by criticisms that it was wasting taxpayers' money – or
'boondoggling' in popular speech. This viewpoint was fully
supported by the president. Moreover, public works projects
involve lengthy preparations with design, planning, submission of
contracts and so on. Eventually the PWA put hundreds of
thousands of people to work, building, among other things,
nearly 13,000 schools and 50,000 miles of roads.

It pumped billions of dollars into the economy and was
responsible for massive public works schemes, particularly in the
West, where it enabled dams to be built to help irrigate former
semi-desert land, electricity to be produced and four vast
National Parks to be created.

Relief

There were millions of needy people in the USA. One major
difference between Roosevelt and Hoover was the willingness of
the former to involve the government in direct relief measures.

Key question
What measures were
introduced to help the
poor?

Federal Emergency Relief Act, May 1933

This act established the Federal Emergency Relief Administration
(FERA). It was given $500 million to be divided equally among
the states to help provide for the unemployed. Half the money
was to be granted to states for outright relief and, with the
remainder, the government would pay each state $1 for every $3
it spent on relief.

Roosevelt chose Harry Hopkins to run this programme. He
had administered the relief programmes that the president had
introduced when Governor of New York. The Act said that each
state should set up a FERA office and organise relief
programmes. It should raise the money through borrowing, tax
rises or any other means. When some states such as Kentucky and
Ohio refused to comply, Hopkins simply threatened to deny them
any federal monies.

Many states were wedded to the idea of a balanced budget and
found expenditure on relief extremely distasteful. It was still felt
by many that to be poor was your own fault. Those requiring
relief were often treated abominably. One FERA worker reported
that in Phoenix, Arizona, over 100 claimants were jammed into a
small room in temperatures of over 100 degrees, while an
overflow queue was waiting in a nearby garage. In many places
there could be interminable waits and delays. Hostile policemen
often guarded the long queues of claimants, while uncaring
officials completed endless numbers of forms. Even after this
there were usually long delays before any kind of relief was
forthcoming.

The Governor of Oregon went as far as to advocate euthanasia
for the needy and sick while the Governor of Georgia offered the

unemployed a dose of caster oil. The bottom line was that they knew Hopkins could not refuse them funds as the only people who would suffer were those the funds were meant to help – the needy and unemployed themselves. One governor even boasted that he had cut relief spending but still received FERA funds.

In the face of such opposition, FERA's effectiveness was limited. Its workers were refused office space in some states and often their caseloads were numbered in thousands. Its funds were limited too. In 1935 it was paying about $25 per month to an average family on relief, while the average monthly minimum wage for **subsistence** was estimated at $100.

However, although its effects were disappointing, it did set the important precedent of federal government giving direct funds for relief.

Civilian Conservation Corps, March 1933

Unemployed young men between the ages of 17 and 24 (later 28) were recruited by the Department of Labor to work in the Civilian Conservation Corps (CCC) in national forests and parks and public lands. The Corps was organised along military lines, but its tasks were set out by the Departments of the Interior and Agriculture.

Key term

Subsistence
Minimum income necessary for survival.

CCC worker planting pine trees in soil that had been eroded. Pine trees were chosen because they grow quickly.

At an estimated cost of $5500 million in the first year, 250,000 recruits worked on reforestation, soil conservation and forestry management projects. Initially they served for nine months to give as many as possible the opportunity to join; they were paid $30 per month, of which $25 had to be sent home to their families. Among the first recruits were 2500 of the second 'Bonus Army' (see page 122); Roosevelt waived the age restrictions on their behalf.

The CCC was originally set up for two years but Congress extended this for a further seven years in 1935, when its strength was increased to 500,000. In the period of its life, the CCC installed 65,100 miles of telephone lines in inaccessible areas, spent 4.1 million man hours fighting forest fires and planted 1.3 billion trees. The CCC gave countless young men a new self-respect and, particularly those from the cities, valuable experience of both comradeship and life in the 'great outdoors'. In addition, 100,000 of its recruits were also taught to improve their literacy skills. However, this experience was primarily available to young *white* men and, of course, their time in the CCC was no guarantee that they would not return to the ranks of those on relief when it was over.

Civil Works Administration (CWA)

This agency was created in November 1933, with a $400 million grant from the PWA, primarily to provide emergency relief to the unemployed during the hard winter of 1933–4. While it put four million people to work on public works projects, it was closed down in March when the winter was over. However, FERA agreed to fund more public works projects itself.

Native Americans

The new Commissioner for the **Bureau of Indian Affairs**, John Collier, was determined to reverse government policy towards Native Americans. The current policy was based on the Dawes Severalty Act of 1887. This had as its lynchpin the twin notions of **assimilation** and **allotment**. Native American children, for example, were taught in Christian schools and forced to adopt 'Western' dress.

More significantly, the policy of allotment meant that the old tribal units were broken up and the reservations divided into family-sized farms of 160 acres. Surplus land was to be sold off.

The destruction of Native American culture had often left the people listless and apathetic. Allotment had been a failure particularly for those Native Americans who were not farmers by tradition. Moreover, much of the land allocated to them was unsuitable for productive farming. In fact, of 138 million acres owned by Native Americans at the time of the Dawes Severalty Act, 90 million acres had fallen out of their hands by 1932.

Many Native Americans lived in squalor and idleness. Often unscrupulous whites had swindled them out of their land or had acquired it below market prices. By 1926 a Department of the Interior inquiry found that the Act had been a disaster for Native

Key terms

Bureau of Indian Affairs
Government agency dealing with Native Americans.

Assimilation
Native Americans should adopt American lifestyles and values. Their traditional lifestyle should disappear.

Allotment
Each Native American family was given a plot of 160 acres to farm. This went against the traditional idea of common land ownership.

Key question
How were Native Americans helped?

Key date
Dawes Severalty Act: 1887

Americans and that the policy of allotment in particular should be reversed.

The Indian Reorganization Act, June 1934

It was not until 1934 that the Indian Reorganization Act did away with it, along with all other the terms of the Dawes Severalty Act. The new act recognised and encouraged Native American culture. Tribes were reorganised into self-governing bodies that could vote to adopt constitutions and have their own police and legal systems. They could control land sales on the reservations, while new tribal corporations were established to manage tribal resources.

These measures in no way relieved Native American poverty. Indeed, 75 out of 245 tribes voted against them. Moreover, there was concern that Collier did not really understand Native American needs. For example, he introduced the idea of voting by secret ballot both to see whether Native American tribal units were in favour of the Act in the first place and to establish democracy in the newly reorganised reservations. However, many Native Americans saw democracy as an alien 'white' concept. They wished to continue their own traditional tribal councils in which people spoke their minds openly rather than voted in secret.

Government policy of recognising Native American culture also came under attack from some quarters. Collier was accused of encouraging Native Americans to 'go back to the blanket'. Many felt that a return to tribal traditions was a backward move. It was argued that they needed assimilation to prosper in American society. Collier also seemed indifferent to Native American resistance to the efforts of big corporations to exploit natural resources on reservation land.

However, Collier did do his best to ensure Native Americans could take advantage of New Deal agencies such as the CCC and PWA. In addition, his work was important in affording a new respect for Native American culture even if the culture was often misunderstood. Having said this, one must remember that Native American poverty was so great that these measures for all their good intentions could at best have only a very limited effect. As New Deal programmes wound down in the 1940s, Native Americans began to set up pressure groups but often remained among the poorest people in the USA.

Key question
What measures were taken to improve housing?

Housing

Housing remained a problem because many homeowners were having problems repaying their mortgages, while there was a shortage of public sector accommodation

Home Owners Refinancing Corporation, June 1933

This agency helped homeowners in difficulties by offering new mortgages at low rates of interest over longer periods of time.

Federal Housing Administration (FHA)

This was established in June 1934 to offer federal insurance to protect the ability to repay low-interest, long-term mortgages taken out by those buying new homes. Clearly, this was an attempt to stimulate the building industry. However, the loans were solely for newly purchased single-family homes; they could not be used to renovate existing properties or for buildings set out as apartments where several people may live

The FHA therefore did nothing to help the increasingly poverty-stricken inner cities. In fact, one of the agency's unanticipated effects was to encourage the movement to the suburbs. And with 65 per cent of new houses costing over $4000 it was estimated that less than 25 per cent of urban families could afford to take out any kind of mortgage on them. The Act mainly benefited white, middle-class families. Increasingly, inner-city areas tended to be run down and left to poorer ethnic minorities who were forced to rent squalid properties.

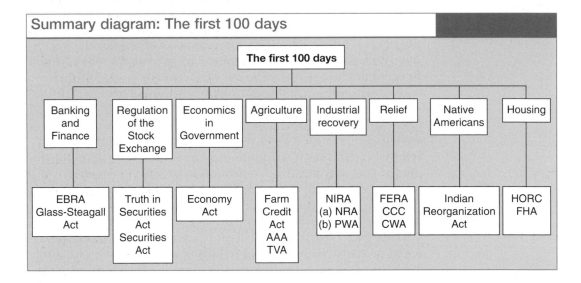

Summary diagram: The first 100 days

3 | Alternatives to the New Deal

The New Deal attracted much opposition – from the political right because it was too radical and from the political left because it was not radical enough. In this section the alternatives put forward by some of these opponents will be examined.

Liberty Leaguers

Many of the wealthy, who had supported Roosevelt in the darkest days of the Depression as the saviour of capitalism, now turned against him when it seemed that capitalism had, in fact, been saved. This was in part because of the increases in taxes, which they opposed, and also what they perceived as too much continued government involvement in the economy. The Liberty League was organised in April 1934 to promote private property and private enterprise unregulated by law. Increasingly, its members saw Roosevelt as a traitor to his class; some refused even to speak of him by name but used cruel jibes like, 'that cripple in the White House'. Some likened the New Deal to Communism in

Key question
Why did members of the wealthy classes oppose the New Deal?

the USSR. There is even a suggestion that the Far Right planned a *coup d'état* against Roosevelt in 1934 and that this was foiled by the very general who had been asked to lead it. The Liberty Leaguers attacked Roosevelt throughout the New Deal years and formed the basis of Right-wing opposition to him.

But, at the time, Roosevelt was more concerned about threats from the Left. This was particularly because Left-wing groups might join together to form a third party to challenge him in the next presidential election.

Key question
What were the Left-wing alternatives to the New Deal and how great a threat were they?

End Poverty in California (EPIC)

The novelist Upton Sinclair came up with a scheme whereby the unemployed would be put to work in state-run co-operatives. They would be paid in currency, which they could spend only in other co-operatives. For a time, Sinclair's ideas gained credibility and he won the Democratic nomination as state governor for California in the 1934 election. However, well-organised opposition, particularly from the movie industry in Hollywood, ensured that he was soundly defeated by the Republican candidate. Nevertheless, his many supporters remained and proved useful recruits for more serious alternative movements as discussed below

'Share Our Wealth'

Huey Long had done much for the state of Louisiana, ordering massive public works programmes – over 3000 miles of paved highways were built between 1928 and 1933, besides new public buildings and an airport at New Orleans – and ambitious adult literacy schemes. However, he did govern as a dictator and opponents were treated quite brutally by his bully boys.

In February 1934 Long moved on to the national scene with his 'Share Our Wealth' programme. He advocated that all private fortunes over $3 million should be confiscated and every family should be given enough money to buy a house, a car and a radio. There should also be old-age pensions, minimum wages so that every family would be guaranteed $2000–$3000 per year and free college education for all suitable candidates. Long's ideas proved very popular and 'Share Our Wealth' clubs grew to 27,431 in number, with 4.6 million members spread across the states. Long began to talk of joining forces with other radicals to form a third party to oppose Roosevelt in the 1936 presidential election.

In 1935, Postmaster General James A. Farley took a secret poll to assess Long's popularity and was shocked to discover that up to four million people might vote for him in 1936. This meant that Long might hold the balance of power in the election. The Louisiana Senator was, in fact, gunned down in September 1935. Rumours circulated by his supporters that Roosevelt's hand was somehow behind the assassination. While these accusations were unfounded, the president must nevertheless have breathed a sigh of relief at the news.

Profile: Huey Long 1893–1935

1893 – born in Winnfield, Louisiana
1913 – married Rose McConell
1914 – enrolled in law school in New Orleans
1915 – began to practise law
1918 – elected a member of the Louisiana Railroad Commission
1921 – became Chairman of the Louisiana Services Commission
1928 – became Governor of Louisiana
1930 – became US Senator
1935 – announced his intention to run for the presidency
       against Roosevelt
1935 – assassinated

Early life and career

Huey Long was born in the small town of Winnfield in Louisiana in the deep South of the USA, the eighth of nine children. He was rebellious at school and left early before he was due to graduate. Huey found a job selling vegetable oil door-to-door and met his future wife after she won a cake-baking competition he had organised to sell more oil. He was ambitious, however, and trained to become a lawyer as a springboard to a career in politics. Long completed the three-year course in less than one and gained a reputation as a lawyer who supported the poor against the rich and powerful.

Long was elected to the Louisiana Railroad Commission and later became Chairman of the Public Service Commission where he cut the prices of essential services such as gas and electricity. He began call himself 'Kingfish' after a character from the popular *Amos'n'Andy* radio show.

Governor of Louisiana

'The Kingfish' was elected state governor in 1928. His main policies were to build more roads and improve education although he also improved health provision. He was opposed by conservatives who did not like the cost of his programmes and the fact that they were taxed heavily to pay for them. His main supporters were the poor. He built up a large and ruthless political machine that ensured he stayed in power. He employed bribery, corruption and strong-arm tactics but also enjoyed genuine popularity amongst the poorer classes who saw him as a powerful ally against the wealthy.

US Senator

At first Long supported Roosevelt but began to oppose him over his failure to redistribute wealth in the USA. He developed his own scheme, 'Share Our Wealth' and decided to run against Roosevelt in the 1936 presidential election.

On 8 September 1935, Long was shot by Dr Carl Weiss. As Weiss was immediately killed himself by Long's bodyguards, his motives remain unclear although he was the son-in-law of one of Long's political enemies, Judge Benjamin Pavey. Long had spread rumours that Pavey had slept with black women and that his daughters (including Weiss's wife, whom Long did not know personally) were probably of mixed blood. This was scandalous in the racist South and Weiss may have thought himself defending his wife's honour. Long lived enough time to be told of the identity of his assassin. He did not know Weiss. On his deathbed he is alleged to have said, 'God, don't let me die! I have so much to do!'.

Old Age Revolving Pensions Inc

Francis Townsend was a retired doctor who advocated old-age pensions with a difference. Everyone over 60 years of age who was not in paid employment, should be given $200 per month on the understanding that every cent of it was spent and none saved. The idea was that this would boost consumption and thereby production and so pull the USA out of the Depression. Moreover, encouraging people to retire at 60 would provide more jobs for the young. Soon Townsend Clubs had 500,000 members and Congress was being lobbied to put the plan into operation. It was, of course, totally impractical; payments to recipients would have amounted to 50 per cent of national income and an army of bureaucrats would have been necessary to ensure pensioners were spending all their $200. Nevertheless, the level of support showed that the movement had to be taken seriously.

Father Charles Coughlin

Charles Coughlin was a priest whose radio programme, *The Golden Hour of the Little Flower* was enormously influential during the first half of the 1930s. It regularly commanded an audience of 30–40 million, and listeners contributed more than $5 million per year to his parish in Detroit. At first, Coughlin had supported Roosevelt, telling his audience, 'The New Deal is Christ's Deal'. However, he later felt that Roosevelt had not done enough to change the banking system – Coughlin believed that banks should be nationalised. He contradicted himself by arguing that the New Deal was both a communist conspiracy and a means by which Wall Street financiers could keep ordinary people enslaved. In 1934 Coughlin founded the National Union for Social Justice with the aim of monetary reform and redistribution of wealth. Roosevelt was afraid of Coughlin's influence, particularly when a possible alliance with Huey Long was mooted. However, Long was assassinated and Coughlin became increasingly anti-Semitic – he blamed Jews both for the New Deal and control of Wall Street. Inevitably, perhaps, he began to look with admiration to the European Fascist dictators and this, together with government-inspired attacks, led to Coughlin's influence declining as the decade wore on. This was due to many Americans' dislike of Hitler and Mussolini, and increasing fears of being involved in war against them.

Thunder on the Left

This is the name given to various political developments that are credited with moving Roosevelt and the New Deal further to the left in 1935 and 1936. Governor Floyd B. Olson of Minnesota, for example, led the Farmer–Labor Party which proposed far-reaching economic reforms. It advocated the state take control of idle factories to put the unemployed to work, nationalisation of public utilities and a postponement of farm mortgage foreclosures. However, the movement died with Olson, who developed terminal cancer in 1936. Robert Lafollette, Jr and his brother Philip founded a new Progressive Party, which had the support of eastern intellectuals and called for collective bargaining, unemployment insurance and old-age pensions.

Impact of the opposition

Although, with hindsight, we can see that these movements did not constitute a serious threat to Roosevelt, this was not how they were seen at the time. At best, from Roosevelt's point of view, their popularity showed the level of support there might be for more radical presidential measures to combat the Depression. At worst, there was the possibility that millions of Americans were so frustrated with the established order that they were prepared to vote for radical or even revolutionary change. Although few of Roosevelt's advisers seriously believed this, the prospect of a third party at the 1936 presidential election was worrying. In a three-

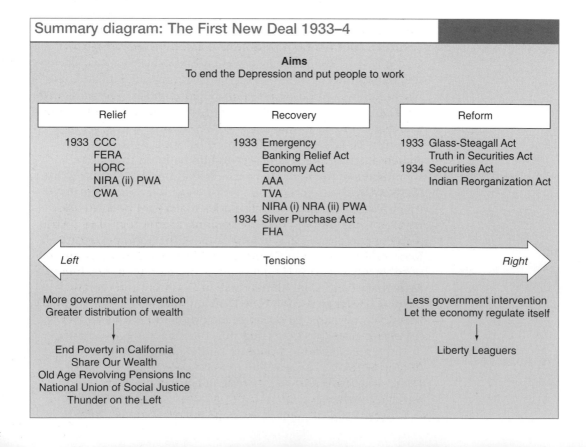

Summary diagram: The First New Deal 1933–4

Aims
To end the Depression and put people to work

Relief	Recovery	Reform
1933 CCC FERA HORC NIRA (ii) PWA CWA	1933 Emergency Banking Relief Act Economy Act AAA TVA NIRA (i) NRA (ii) PWA 1934 Silver Purchase Act FHA	1933 Glass-Steagall Act Truth in Securities Act 1934 Securities Act Indian Reorganization Act

Left ← Tensions → *Right*

More government intervention
Greater distribution of wealth
↓
End Poverty in California
Share Our Wealth
Old Age Revolving Pensions Inc
National Union of Social Justice
Thunder on the Left

Less government intervention
Let the economy regulate itself
↓
Liberty Leaguers

way presidential election it might hold the balance of power. Roosevelt may need to put forward many of the measures it favoured in order to get its support to hold onto office.

Roosevelt, meanwhile, had learned of the mood of the country. In the 1934 mid-term congressional elections, the Democrats had made gains in both houses, with 69 out of 96 seats in the Senate – the biggest Democratic majority to date. Roosevelt was preparing a second New Deal that was not only influenced by the demands of radical politicians but also by the increasing opposition of big business to his measures.

Key question
Was the First New Deal a planned programme or simply a series of unrelated measures to deal with specific problems?

4 | The Character of the First New Deal

The First New Deal transformed the USA. No government had previously been so energetic in peacetime; no government had taken so much upon itself. However, the main question to consider is whether the First New Deal was a coherent attempt to change the political, social and economic structure of the USA or whether it was simply an *ad hoc* series of measures taken to deal with crises as they arose.

It must be said from the outset that Roosevelt did employ some people who had a radical vision. They saw, for example, a permanent need for the government to take responsibility for the running of the economy, for people's welfare and so on. No doubt the New Deal was their blueprint for action. However, these people were not of one mind; they did not make up one radical group that was in agreement. They tended to offer different, often conflicting advice. Historians have distinguished four different schools of thought among prominent New Dealers.

Conservatives
Conservatives included Roosevelt's Director of the Budget, Lewis Douglas. He believed in only limited government interference in the economy, such as a public works programme to reflate the economy, but at heart wanted to leave existing structures unaltered.

Inflationists
Inflationists tended to see inflation as a means of boosting the economy. Advocating the use of silver as legal tender, they sought to reduce the gold content of the dollar. They were pleased when Roosevelt brought the USA off the gold standard, but this did not go far enough for them. They wanted an increase in the amount of silver in circulation and a reduction in that of gold because silver was the cheaper of the two. This would, it was hoped, allow the value of money to fall and hence prices to rise. The policy was largely unsuccessful.

Progressives
This group tended to share the ideas of the Progressive movement of the early part of the century (see page 6) and to seek in particular the break up of giant corporations. Their

leaders included Louis Brandeis of the Supreme Court and 'Brains' Truster' Felix Frankfurter.

Economic planners

These wanted the government to take a far more pro-active role in central planning. Some, for example General Johnson, wished to see a partnership between business and government, while others, such as Adolf Berle and Rexford Tugwell, wanted the government to take control. They opposed the idea of a balanced budget, believing the government should go into debt to bring about economic recovery. In particular, they supported ambitious public works projects and increases in taxation.

Roosevelt's way of making decisions

As we have seen (pages 117–18) Roosevelt's advisers had divergent ideas. He often treated them as rivals – which indeed they frequently were. He would ask them to prepare plans, listening to their arguments and then bouncing them off others, particularly those he thought would disagree with them. Finally, having weighed up all the arguments he would make up his own mind. Roosevelt played his cards close to his chest. Advisers who were with him for years often said they rarely knew what he was thinking.

It seems that Roosevelt himself had no radical blueprint for change during the early part of his administration. He was himself a conservative in economic terms, believing in the importance of the balanced budget. Certainly, in the short term, he kept on some of Hoover's appointees such as Ogden Mills. He maintained and extended the role of the RFC, which Hoover had created. He differentiated carefully between emergency measures and 'normal' government business, and readily spent federal funds on the former. However, as far as the latter was concerned, he cut federal salaries and refused the veterans their bonus. The very fact that he was prepared to differentiate between emergency measures and 'normal' government suggests that he responded to crises as they occurred and these crises required emergency measures to deal with them. Raymond Moley reported that 'he was improvising all the time. "Hit or miss".' This view is supported by Frank Marcus, an economist who worked for Harry Hopkins: 'it was not a clearly thought out program. There was much improvization'.

Roosevelt was no academic himself, but was interested in a variety of intellectual opinions. He welcomed and listened to advice. He encouraged people with radical ideas because even if he did not agree with them, they could be useful sounding boards. In this atmosphere of government improvisation and initiative, all sorts of people with ideas gravitated to Washington and it was undoubtedly an exciting time. Insiders spoke of the air of expectancy, the feeling that a wholly new era in government had begun. Economist Gardiner C. Means, who worked on various New Deal programmes, spoke for many when he said:

There was no question in our minds that we were saving the country. A student of mine remembered how exciting it was to him. He worked in the Department of Labor. He said 'Any idea I had, I put down on paper. I'd send it up and somebody would pay attention to it'.

There were radical agencies, for example the TVA who acted as a central planning agency for a vast region. The government did involve itself in direct relief. Many millions of dollars were spent on public works schemes.

One should not, however, be swept away by all these new ideas and approaches. Even if Roosevelt had supported wholesale change he had no authority to introduce it. He saw his role as saving capitalism, not replacing it with something new. In any event, neither the structures nor the personnel were available to effect major changes. Many of the measures we have discussed were based upon speed of implementation. They also needed the co-operation of businessmen, bankers, farmers and all those directly involved. Truly radical measures would probably have earned their hostility and would have been impossible to carry through. Indeed, they may well have been dragged through the courts as unconstitutional. As described by the Secretary of Labor, Frances Perkins, the motivation behind the New Deal was about helping 'the forgotten man', the wage earners, farmers and elderly who had been worst hit by the Depression.

This was accepted by most of the dominant elements in the Democratic Party in 1933.

The balance sheet

In the light of the evidence, therefore, many historians have argued that it seems best to regard the First New Deal as a series of measures in response to crises. There seems to have been no master plan or blueprint for radical change behind them, certainly on the part of the president. However, not all share this view. There is an argument that because the New Deal set so many precedents it did act as a blueprint for major change whatever the president may have wished. Never before, for example, had any government intervened to such an extent in the economy and society. Never before had people begun to look to the government for help to such an extent. Never before had there been such regulation. Never before had there been so many minds at work in Washington to effect change. Together these factors did, in fact, even if unintentionally, lead to significant changes in the role that many citizens expected of the government.

As it was, Roosevelt was building up both a considerable body of opposition to the measures he had taken and, conversely, powerful pressure for more radical change. Increasingly, as problems with his measures emerged, he found himself beleaguered and it is to these more difficult times that we must turn in the next chapter.

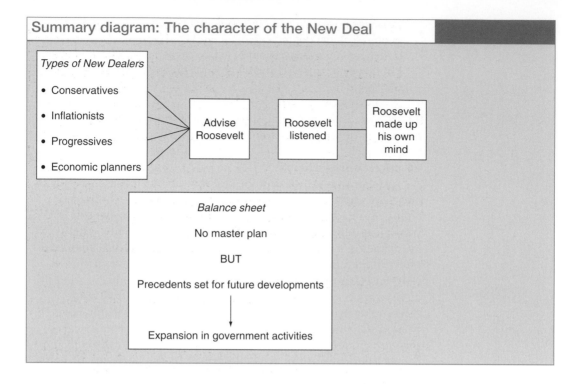

Summary diagram: The character of the New Deal

Types of New Dealers

- Conservatives
- Inflationists
- Progressives
- Economic planners

Advise Roosevelt → Roosevelt listened → Roosevelt made up his own mind

Balance sheet

No master plan

BUT

Precedents set for future developments

↓

Expansion in government activities

Study Guide: AS Questions

Note: this chapter has been concerned with the First New Deal (1933–5). Many of the problems with the legislation did not fully emerge until Roosevelt's second, more troubled administration and these will be considered more fully in Chapter 7. For this reason you should think of Chapters 6 and 7 as two parts of one whole; only when you are fully conversant with the contents of both will you be able to consider the New Deal in its entirety. Many exam questions will cover the complete period of the New Deal. However each examination board may set questions specifically on the First New Deal as the following examples show.

In the style of AQA

With what effect did the First New Deal combat the effects of the economic Depression?

Study tips

The cross-references are intended take you straight to the materials that will help you to answer the question.

In answering this question, it is important to avoid too much description of conditions during the Depression; these are only incidental to what is required.

- You could begin by considering the nature of the American economy before the New Deal and how the lack of government regulation meant there were few mechanisms to put it right.

Factors that may have helped recovery – government intervention through job creation and public works, for example – were not available. You would need to consider Hoover's measures to deal with the Depression and how effective they were (pages 96–102).

- You need to go on to the First New Deal to offer a contrast with what had gone on before. You could show how measures were developed to tackle the effects of the Depression such as banking legislation (pages 118–20) and the alphabet agencies (pages 122–32)
- You need to come to a judgement about their effectiveness and success. How far, for example, did the industrial and agricultural sectors recover as a result of New Deal legislation? You might consider how far Roosevelt was following Hoover's ideas, particularly in terms of banking legislation.

In the style of Edexcel

Study Sources 1 and 2 and answer the questions that follow.

Source 1

From: a conversation in 1934 with a Colorado rancher recorded by Laura Hickock, a roving investigator for the Agricultural Adjustment Agency.

The government paid $2.00 each for the ewes. They took six hundred of them. We had to kill and skin the other six hundred and hand over their fleeces. In my opinion, that was the silliest thing ever pulled by those in charge of dictating to the America Public, but that $2,400 did more good than any other I ever got hold of.

Source 2

From: a letter in 1942 from a Pueblo County official in Colorado to Paul Shriver, head of the State WPA (Works in Progress Administration).

I sometimes wonder just what Pueblo would have done if it had not been for the generosity of the Federal Government. Our parks are rated as some of the finest in the nation. We have miles of paved streets; miles of curbs and gutters and blocks of sidewalks have been constructed. We have new buildings for civic activities.

(a) **Study Sources 1 and 2**

What do these sources reveal of the ways in which the problems of the 1930s were addressed in the New Deal?

(10 marks)

(b) **Use your own knowledge**

Why was Roosevelt able to end the banking crisis in 1933?

(14 marks)

Source: Edexcel, May 2002

Exam tips

The cross-reference is intended to take you straight to the material that will help you to answer the questions.

(a) These questions require inferences from the sources. You need to show you understand what the sources say by explaining them in your own words. Don't look for extracts to copy out and don't include information not contained in the sources. The focus of your answer must be on what the sources say; you will gain no marks for going beyond them. Inference is the skill of working out the implications of what is said in the source. You might, for example, consider how problems were to be addressed by raising farm prices by cutting production and creating employment through public work schemes.

In this question the examiners are looking for the way the fall in farm prices was dealt with, in particular through the killing of sheep, and how the farmer responded to this. Key words such as 'dictating' should be noted. The best answers will realise that the second extract is retrospective, i.e. comes from later than the event it describes, to consider the long-term benefits of public works schemes.

(b) This question tests your knowledge and ability to explain the key features of an event you have studied. In this question examiners were looking for a mixture of legislation such as the Emergency Banking Relief Act, and Roosevelt's personal qualities that restored public confidence in the banking system through, for example, his fireside chats (page 117). It would also be useful to mention the extent of the power he had been given to deal with the crisis through the support of Congress.

Study Guide: Advanced Level Questions
In the style of OCR

Assess the view that the First New Deal (1933–4) brought 'relief, recovery and reform' to the US economy. (45 marks)

Source: OCR, January 2003

Exam tips

The cross-references are intended to take you straight to the material that will help you answer the question.

This question invites you to categorise the measures of the First New Deal into the headings of relief, recovery and reform (see the summary diagram on page 136).

- It is important that you don't go beyond the dates in question. However, you do need to evaluate the measures in terms of their success as to how far they brought relief or recovery or reform.
- You need to strike a balance in your answer. For example, while more was given in relief by the Federal Government than ever before, it was still limited in scope and depended on the support of the states; recovery again was partial at best and even in Roosevelt's first term of office NIRA was beset by problems. Meanwhile, reform was attempted in certain areas, notably banking and finance, but the issues of how radical or widespread reform should be was highly controversial.
- Some historians would argue that the First New Deal was largely a set of responses to different crises with no overall plan, and the issues of relief, recovery and reform are simply convenient labels used by historians. (This issue is discussed in more detail in Chapter 9, when the New Deal as a whole is evaluated on pages 190–3.)

7 Roosevelt and the Later New Deals 1935–9

POINTS TO CONSIDER

This chapter looks at the period of the Second and Third New Deals and how effective they were in addressing the continuing economic problems faced by the USA. It does this through five main themes:

- The Second New Deal: the reasons behind it and its effectiveness
- The 1936 presidential election: why Roosevelt won and what he promised the electorate
- The problems during Roosevelt's second term of office and the ways in which he attempted to overcome them
- The later New Deal
- The end of the New Deal

Key dates

1935	April	Emergency Relief Appropriation Act
	May	Resettlement Administration
		Rural Electrification Act
	May 25	Black Monday
	June	Revenue (Wealth) Act
	July	National Labor Relations Act
	August	Public Utility Holding Company Act
		Social Security Act
		Banking Act
1936		Roosevelt's battle with the Supreme Court (Judiciary Reform Bill)
1937		'Roosevelt Recession'
	July	Bankhead-Jones Farm Tenancy Act
1938	February	Second Agricultural Adjustment Act
	June	Fair Labor Standards Act
	Sept	Wagner-Steagall National Housing Act
1939		Executive Office of the President created

Key question
How did ordinary people at the time and how have historians since felt about the New Deal?

1 | Introduction

Dear Mr President,

This is just to tell you everything is all right now. The man you sent found our house all right and we went down the bank with him and the mortgage can go a while longer. You remember I wrote you about losing the furniture too. Well, your man got it back for us. I never heard of a President like you, Mr Roosevelt. Mrs — and I are old folks and don't amount to much, but we are joined with those millions of others in praying for you every night.

God bless you, Mr Roosevelt.

This is one of the thousands of letters Roosevelt received every day. He insisted that his staff answer every one of them. Many ordinary people regarded Roosevelt as their saviour. He once said that everyone was against him except the electorate. He never lost the support of the mass of the population and he was regarded by many of them with something akin to love. People believed he cared about and understood their problems. Although Roosevelt did not personally initiate labour relations legislation, an employee commented that Mr Roosevelt 'is the first man in the White House to understand that my boss is a son of a bitch'. Certainly he was the first president who spoke to the poor and hungry, the have-nots in society.

Many historians have argued that the New Deal became more radical in the years after 1935, that Roosevelt was genuinely trying to change the face of the USA and that he was favouring the poorer classes at the expense of the rich. They point in particular to the measures that made up the Second New Deal as evidence of this.

In the 1936 presidential election Roosevelt won a great victory. He was at the height of his success. And yet, after this the New Deal was beset with problems and according to some historians petered out in 1938 and 1939. They argue that it was ultimately a failure because it did not radically change the face of the USA. However, this can only be considered a failure of the New Deal if it was actually an objective of the New Deal.

2 | The Second New Deal

When the 75th Congress met early in 1935, Roosevelt presented it with a major legislative package. It was called by the contemporary journalist Walter Lippmann, 'the most comprehensive program of reform ever achieved in this country by any administration'. There was considerable excitement among the White House staff. Harry Hopkins said, 'Boys, this is our hour. We've got to get everything we want in the way of relief, social security and minimum wages'. Eighty-eight days later most of Roosevelt's objectives had been achieved. Some measures that he had not particularly supported had also been passed, for example, in the field of labour relations.

Some historians, notably Arthur Schlesinger, Jr, have seen the Second New Deal very much as a change in direction. They see the early New Deal as an attempt to reduce business competition in favour of greater co-operation through planning and government guidance. Clearly the NRA and AAA were examples of this in action (see pages 122–8). However, they believe the Second New Deal saw a reintroduction of competition but with regulations about fair play. Examples of this are:

- fair representation for all sides in industry through the National Labor Relations Act (see page 151)
- the Public Utility Holding Company Act that broke-up holding companies (see page 152)
- a national system of benefits for those groups who could not participate in the system, through measures such as the Social Security Act (see page 152).

Nevertheless, as we will see, in attacking big business the New Deal's bark was always worse than its bite.

Before considering the legislation of the Second New Deal, we need to examine in some detail the motivation behind it and the conditions that made it possible.

Reasons for the Second New Deal
Historians have suggested a variety of reasons behind the Second New Deal:

Key question
Why was a Second New Deal felt to be necessary?

- Roosevelt needed to respond to the radical forces described in the last chapter (pages 133–7). It has been argued that, quite simply, he was politically astute enough to understand the need to take the initiative from people such as Huey Long, Francis Townsend and Charles Coughlin. He did not wish to see possibly millions of voters supporting politicians with extreme views.
- The mid-term congressional elections in 1934 had returned a more radical House of Representatives, which was expecting wide-ranging legislative action and was prepared to support it. The Farmer–Labor Party (see page 136) could rely on possibly as many as 50 supporters in both houses. They were preparing their own programme that would have affected quite radical changes. For example, they spoke of maximum hours of work and minimum wages, greater investment in public works, higher taxes for the wealthy and social security. Meanwhile, radical senators such as Lafollette and Wagner were also preparing their own proposals.
- The climate in the new Congress was for action and Roosevelt wanted to prevent this. He did not, in other words, want to surrender the initiative in preparing New Deal legislation. He wanted to act in his own way with his own measures before others forced him to put forward ideas he may not have agreed with.
- Roosevelt was increasingly frustrated by the Supreme Court which was beginning to overturn New Deal legislation. He

believed it was opposing him. This in itself made him more radical in outlook. He also needed to introduce new measures to replace those such as the NRA, which the Supreme Court had declared unconstitutional (see page 157).

- Roosevelt was also increasingly frustrated with the wealthy and with the forces of big business, who were opposing him more and more. He was particularly angry when the **US Chamber of Commerce** attacked his policies in May 1935. He believed he had been elected to save American business and he felt let down by its lack of continued support. Moreover, small businesses had benefited little from measures so far adopted. We have seen, for example, how many of the NRA codes discriminated against them (see pages 126–7). New Deal officials in Washington were becoming aware that small firms had a crucial role to play in economic recovery. Many of the measures taken in the Second New Deal, for example the Public Utility Holding Company Act, operated to their benefit.
- Some historians have argued that politics in the USA was becoming more divided and extreme. Roosevelt was seeking the support of the political left.

Key term

US Chamber of Commerce
Non-governmental organisation responsible for speaking for business in the USA.

Each of these reasons contains elements of truth. Many of Roosevelt's supporters were forecasting widespread support, particularly for Huey Long if he chose to run for president (see pages 133–4). The new Congress was preparing a programme of far-reaching reforms. It should not be forgotten that it was Congress that actually initiated legislation in the USA.

However, increasingly Roosevelt was telling Congress clearly what legislation he required. Roosevelt sought to retain the initiative in new legislation, to lead rather than to follow the legislature. He sought, in other words, to introduce his own measures for Congress to pass rather than to rubber-stamp those introduced in and passed by Congress. He had no desire to see a rash of measures initiated by Congress that were too radical for his liking. He was also preparing to do battle with the Supreme Court, which he increasingly saw as conservative and out of touch.

We have already seen that members of big business – which Roosevelt still largely saw as the lynchpin of recovery – were organising opposition to him (see page 132). However, one should not overestimate Roosevelt's apparent shift of focus. On 22 May 1935 he again vetoed the veterans' bonus payments and also said the government had to be careful that it didn't spent public funds wastefully. Many of the ideas encompassed in the Second New Deal were not new to him. Indeed, as Governor of New York, he had considered several of them, such as old-age pensions and the regulation of public utilities. New advisers did not necessarily herald a change in direction. As discussed on pages 117–18, Roosevelt liked differences of opinion among his advisers and encouraged their rivalry. However, when it came to making decisions, he was his own man.

Finally, there was no more coherence to the Second New Deal than there had been to the first. Much of it emerged both in

response to new and continuing crises and because the first New
Deal had not brought about the economic recovery hoped for.

Legislation

As we move on to consider the actual legislation, the following
points should be borne in mind:

- we need to make judgements about how different it was from
  what had been passed during the first New Deal and how far it
  was more of the same
- we need to consider how radical it actually was
- finally, it is important to judge its effectiveness.

Emergency Relief Appropriation Act, April 1935

This measure saw the authorisation of the largest appropriation
for relief, at that time in the nation's history, to set up new
agencies to provide employment through federal works. The
$45.5 billion allocated was the equivalent of over $20 billion at
1930 values and well over $400 billion today. Harry Hopkins was
given control of the new Works Progress Administration (WPA).

Works Progress Administration (WPA)

The WPA recruited people for public works projects. It became a
major employer. At any one time it had about two million
employees and, by 1941, 20 per cent of the workforce had found
employment with it. Wages were approximately $52 per month,
which were greater than any relief but less that the going rate in
industry. The WPA was not allowed to compete for contracts with
private firms or to build private houses. However, it did build
1000 airport landing fields, 8000 schools and hospitals, and
12,000 playgrounds.

Although it was not supposed to engage in large-scale projects,
it did so. Among other things it was responsible for cutting the
Lincoln Tunnel, which connects Manhattan Island to New Jersey,
and building Fort Knox, home of the USA's gold reserves, in
Kentucky. Writers and photographers were employed to record
American life and culture, and it also encouraged the theatre. The
National Youth Administration (NYA) was set up to encourage
education and to provide part-time jobs for students so they
could complete their studies. The African-American educator,
Mary McLeod Bethune, was placed at the head of the NYA's
Division of Negro Affairs to make sure young African-Americans
got a fair chance. For example, she had her own fund specifically
for African-American students, and she encouraged state officials
to make sure African-Americans were signing up for programmes.
Eleanor Roosevelt also encouraged women and members of the
ethnic minorities to participate in government schemes.

Most people agreed with Hopkins when he said, 'Give a man a
dole and you save his body and destroy his spirit. Give him a job
and pay him an assured wage and you save both the body and the
spirit'. The WPA gave an employment opportunity to those who
would otherwise have been unemployed. It took people on for
one year only and did not compete with private enterprise. It

Key question
How did the WPA
help the problem of
unemployment?

employed no one who could have been employed elsewhere. Many of its projects such as surveying historic sites would not have been carried out by the private sector. In the south, some farmers complained that fieldhands and domestic servants were hard to find because of the WPA. If this, in fact, was the case, it suggests that they were exploiting their employees through low wages and poor working conditions rather than that the WPA was particularly generous.

The agencies came under attack from all quarters. Conservatives predictably argued that WPA projects were of dubious value and that little real work was involved. In 1939 Congressman Martin Dies, chairman of the newly formed House Un-American Activities Committee, actually accused the WPA-sponsored Federal Theatre of being a Communist organisation.

Rural Electrification Administration, May 1935

Key question
What measures were taken to help rural areas?

This act established the Rural Electrification Administration (REA) to build generating plants and power lines in rural areas. In 1936 only 12.6 per cent of farms had electricity, often because it was not profitable for private companies to provide it to out-of-the-way areas. Where rural co-operatives were formed to develop electricity, banks were reluctant to lend them money because the organisations could rarely afford the rates of interest. However, the REA offered loans at low rates of interest and farmers were encouraged to form co-operatives to lay on electricity. By 1941 35 per cent of farms had electricity; 773 systems, with 348,000 miles of transmission lines, had been built in six years.

Resettlement Administration, May 1935

It was decided to merge all rural rehabilitation projects into one new agency, the Resettlement Administration (RA). This was run by Rexford Tugwell who had ambitious plans to move 500,000 families from overworked land and resettle them in more promising surroundings elsewhere. This necessitated the agency buying good land, encouraging farmers to move to it and teaching them how to farm it effectively, using modern machinery and efficient techniques.

Key term

Greenbelt communities
New towns in rural areas based on careful planning with residential, commercial and industrial sectors separated.

Tugwell also envisaged the building of whole new **greenbelt communities**. In the event, partly due to underfunding, only three were ever completed – Greenbelt, Maryland; Greenville, Ohio; and Greendale, Wisconsin. Rural problems were too great to be solved merely by the construction of three new towns.

Overall, the agency only ever resettled 4441 families and as such could not be judged a success. The reasons for its apparent failure were partly to do with the costs involved and partly the reluctance of people to move. While the 1930s were a restless age and, as we shall see (page 160), there were significant migrations, the strength of the ties people felt for their own home region proved very powerful. Net migration from farms was lower in the 1930s than in the 1920s. One of the main reasons for people moving was not so much the promise of new communities as the lack of jobs in existing ones. With work in short supply

Oklahoma worker, formerly a farmowner, works in field at 30 cents an hour. He is one of the 'Grapes of Wrath' people, a name taken from the book of the same title by John Steinbeck.

everywhere, people tended to stay put despite the efforts of the RA. In addition, the government set up various schemes to help farmers remain on their land (see page 165). This left the RA policies at variance with those followed elsewhere in the administration.

Revenue (Wealth Tax) Act, June 1935

This act was implemented to pay for New Deal reforms and was perceived by those affected by it to be an attack on the fundamental right of Americans to become rich. The newspaper tycoon William Randolph Hearst called it the 'soak the successful' tax. However, Roosevelt's main aim was not to see any major redistribution of wealth but rather to reduce the need for **government deficit spending**. Quite simply, the government sought to raise more revenue through taxation and it seemed logical to do this by targeting those who could most afford it. Before this, it should be remembered, taxes on the rich had been minimal – those earning more than $16,000 per year paid on average less than $1000 tax.

Key question
What was the effect of the Revenue Act?

Government deficit spending
When the government spends more than it receives in income.

Key term

The Act, drafted by Treasury officials, caused long and heated debate. Many of their original proposals such as a federal inheritance tax were defeated. Legislation finally created a graduated tax on corporate income and an excessive profits tax on corporations. The maximum tax on incomes of over $50,000 was increased from 59 per cent to 75 per cent.

In fact, the new taxes raised comparatively little: about $250 million. For example, the laws regulating taxes paid by corporations contained loopholes, which clever lawyers could easily exploit. Only one per cent of the population earned more than $10,000 and so the increased income taxes did not raise large amounts of revenue. However, if Roosevelt had taxed the middle classes more, as he was urged to do by more radical colleagues, he would have cut their spending power and thus delayed economic recovery. While the Act did little in itself, it did act as a precedent for higher taxes during the Second World War.

Wagner-Connery National Labor Relations Act, July 1935

Key question
How were labour relations dealt with in the Second New Deal?

Roosevelt was reluctant to become involved in labour relations legislation. There are many reasons for this. In part he was simply uninterested in the subject. Certainly he had a very limited understanding of them. He was, it should be remembered, a country landowner at heart. His attitude to labour was more that of the benevolent squire than of the champion of the rights of collective bargaining.

Moreover, Roosevelt was reluctant to become involved because there was a mistrust of labour unions in the USA. This was particularly the case among conservative politicians such as the Southern Democrats whose support he needed. He had no more wish to become the champion of unions than to upset big business further – and big business generally loathed unions.

The Act, therefore, was not initiated by Roosevelt. Indeed, he approved it only when it had passed through the Senate and looked likely to become law. Nevertheless, the National Labor Relations Act is generally seen as an important part of the Second New Deal and was a milestone in American labour relations. It was born out of the disappointment with the Labor Board set up under the NRA. It was one thing to allow unionisation but quite another to get employers to accept it and the Board was generally felt to be powerless.

The Act guaranteed workers the rights to collective bargaining through unions of their own choice. They could choose their union through a secret ballot; and a new three-man National Labor Relations Board was set up to ensure fair play. Employers were forbidden to resort to unfair practices, such as discrimination against unionists.

It was the first Act that effectively gave unions rights in law and in the long term committed federal government to an important labour relations role. However, Roosevelt still did not see it that way and preferred to continue to take a back seat in labour relations.

Public Utility Holding Company Act, August 1935

There had been many problems resulting from the existence of giant holding-company structures (see page 44), as they were often powerful enough to bribe legislators either to stop legislation that threatened them or to promote beneficial areas. Rates paid to investors were often excessive.

Holding companies were built as pyramids. At the bottom were the actual companies providing the utility. Distribution and co-ordinating companies tended to be somewhere in the middle of the structure. Sitting at the very top there was often a company whose contribution to the structure was negligible. Despite this, it often received the lion's share of the profits. The actual utilities at the bottom of the pyramid, whose services fuelled the structure, were often kept short of funds. Nevertheless, they had to charge excessive rates to customers in order to survive themselves and to finance the rest of the pyramid.

The Public Utility Holding Company Act was quite severe in its operation. It ordered the breaking up of all companies more than twice removed from the operating company (some of Samuel Insull's companies, it will be remembered, were more than 24 times removed from the operating company). This destroyed the pyramid structure referred to above. It did this by making all holding companies register with the Securities Exchange Commission (SEC), which could decide their fate. Any company more than twice removed from the utility that could not justify its existence on the grounds of co-ordination of utilities or economic efficiency was to be eliminated by 1 January 1940.

The SEC was also given control of all the companies' financial transactions and stock issues. Despite furious lobbying from the companies concerned, the Act became law. Although some holding companies did refuse to register until the Supreme Court upheld the Act, within three years the great holding companies had been broken up. The Act helped rid the capitalist system of the exploitation associated with these companies. Most commentators agree that by doing so the Act's major effect was to strengthen the capitalist system rather than to weaken it as the lobbyists had claimed. This is because it rid the system of structures that were obviously unfair.

Social Security Act, August 1935

It has already been suggested (see pages 90–1) that the provision made by states for social security was wholly inadequate. For example, only Wisconsin provided any form of unemployment benefit and this was to be paid by former employers as a disincentive to laying-off their workers. Roosevelt had long been interested in a federal system of social security. However, what he came up with was both conservative and limited in its provision. Certainly it was not as generous as Townsend's, whose popularity was of concern to Roosevelt and to many members of Congress.

Whatever its limitations, the Social Security Act was the first federal measure of direct help as a worker's right and would be built upon in the future. The Act provided for old-age pensions

Key question
How were holding companies broken up?

Key question
What was the impact of direct government schemes to help the needy?

to be funded by employer and employee contributions, and unemployment insurance to be paid for by payroll taxes levied on both employers and employees. While the pension scheme was a federal programme, it was anticipated that states would control unemployment insurance.

The scheme was very complicated. Employers were encouraged to participate through an incentive of 90 per cent exemption from **payroll tax** if they contributed to the state unemployment scheme. They would pass on their contributions in the form of increased prices for their products. Employees would pay direct contributions through the payroll tax. It was then assumed that recipients would largely pay for the benefits themselves through their own contributions and higher prices.

Reduced real wages and increased prices were two of the reasons cited for the coming recession that will be discussed later (see pages 162–4). There was also much resentment that the wealthy were not made to contribute more to the scheme. In considering this criticism we need to remember that, despite what many might have wished, Roosevelt was not really interested at this time in a major redistribution of wealth.

Limitations of the Act

The Social Security Act was generally inadequate to meet the needs of the poor. Pensions were paid at a minimum of $10 and a maximum $85 per month according to the contribution that recipients had paid into the scheme. They were not to be paid until 1940 so everyone first receiving them had paid something in. Unemployment benefit was a maximum of $18 per week for 16 weeks only.

Assistance programmes for the blind, disabled and families with dependent children were also set up by the Act. However, although states received the same amount per child from federal government, the amounts paid varied widely – in 1939 Massachusetts paid poor children $61 per month while Mississippi paid $8 per month. Those needing most help, such as agricultural workers, domestic servants and those working for small-scale employers, were actually excluded from the Act. This was because it was felt employers could not afford to pay the contributions and it would in any event cost the Treasury too much to collect them. It was hoped that these workers would be included in the schemes later, once the Act had had time to embed itself. Health insurance was not included largely due to the opposition of the **American Medical Association**, which would not agree to any measure that limited its right to decide what fees to charge patients.

Although the Social Security Act had serious flaws, it should not be forgotten that it was a major break with American governmental tradition. Never before had there been a direct system of national benefits. But it is important to stress that this was not relief. Roosevelt refused to allow general taxes to subsidise the system. It had to be self-financing. Recipients had to pay into the system. The pensions were not paid at a flat rate

Key term

Payroll tax
Tax paid by employers for each of their employees.

Key term

American Medical Association
US doctors' professional association, governing medical practices.

but according to how much the worker had previously contributed. Unemployment benefits were low and paid for a very limited period.

Many conservatives argued that even this was too much. It would destroy individual initiative. It would make people dependent on the state. It took powers away from individual states and concentrated them in Washington. Many states compensated for unemployment benefits by cutting back on other schemes of relief. They increased residence qualifications and they made **means-tested benefits** more rigorous. However, despite the limitations and drawbacks, the Act signified a massive break with the traditional role of federal government. It was also sending out a loud message that it cared about people. It was said that Roosevelt took more satisfaction in this measure than anything else he had achieved on the domestic front.

Banking Act, August 1935

This Act was intended to give the federal government control of banking in the USA. The Governor of the Federal Reserve Board, Marriner Eccles, felt that Wall Street exercised too much power in national finance and sought to repeal the 1913 Federal Reserve Act, which governed the American banking system (see page 55).

Eccles faced powerful opposition from bankers, and, in the event, the final Act was a compromise. Each Federal Reserve Bank could elect its own head but that person had to be approved by the Federal Reserve Board. The decisions on reserve requirements and rediscount rates were also to be given to the Federal Reserve Board. All large banks seeking new federal deposit insurance were required to register with the Board and accept its authority.

In these ways the control of banking was removed from private banking to central government and the centre of financial management shifted from New York to Washington.

Assessing the Second New Deal

The Second New Deal saw an important expansion of the role of federal, state and local government. There was much that was new.

- The banking system was centralised.
- Some of the worst excesses of capitalism, such as the colossal power of the holding companies, were addressed. The attack on unfair competition helped small businesses.
- Labour unions were given a legal voice.
- The Social Security Act created the first national system of benefits, although individual states operated the parts they had control over very differently.
- There was also the further development of existing policies, as with the creation of the WPA to aid both relief and recovery.
- The REA helped the process of modernising the rural areas of the USA.

However, not all of the legislation was particularly effective. The REA enjoyed only limited success. The Revenue Act of 1935

Key term

Means-tested benefits
Where the levels of welfare benefits are based on the recipient's income.

Key question
How was banking dealt with in the Second New Deal?

Key question
What was the impact of the Second New Deal?

angered people out of all proportion to its actual effect. Some historians have argued that the Second New Deal differed from the first in that the first was primarily about relief and recovery from the Depression, while the second was about the creation of permanent reforms.

Whatever the merits of individual pieces of legislation, whatever the significance of the Second New Deal in terms of its philosophy, the key element was that the administration was seen to be acting, to be doing something and to be addressing issues and concerns. The Second New Deal continued, of course, to involve itself particularly in everyday issues that were important to those individuals whose concerns probably would previously have been ignored. It was for this reason that the administration could enter the 1936 presidential election with confidence.

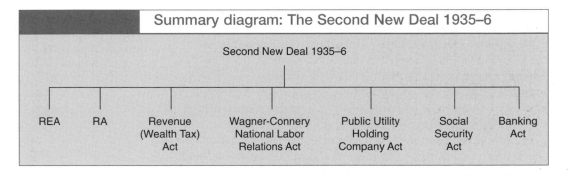

Summary diagram: The Second New Deal 1935–6

Second New Deal 1935–6

REA · RA · Revenue (Wealth Tax) Act · Wagner-Connery National Labor Relations Act · Public Utility Holding Company Act · Social Security Act · Banking Act

Key question
Why did Roosevelt win the 1936 presidential election?

3 | The 1936 Presidential Election

All parties agreed that the 1936 presidential election would be significant. If the electorate voted for Roosevelt for a second term, they would be supporting the changes in the role of government he had made.

There was little doubt that Roosevelt would be reselected as the Democratic candidate. The economy was improving. In 1936 the volume of industrial production was twice that of 1932 and the value of farm products had increased from $4 billion in 1932 to $7 billion in 1936. Unemployment, while still comparatively high, had fallen by 4 million if those on the various relief schemes are excluded from the unemployment figures. The Republicans were in some disarray. It was easy to attack them, to tar them with the brush of the Liberty Leaguers (see pages 132–3) – after all they were objecting to having to pay for measures that benefited millions of ordinary people.

In the event, the Republicans chose Alfred Landon, Governor of Kansas, to run against Roosevelt. While he was not associated with the vote-losing policies of Herbert Hoover, he was nevertheless rather dour and colourless. Henry Ford called him 'A Kansas Coolidge'. He had little chance of winning.

In July Roosevelt compared his critics to a 'nice old gentleman rescued from drowning in 1933 by a friend but who subsequently complains that although saved, his fine silk hat had been lost'.

They were against him now only because they felt secure again after he had saved them from disaster.

One essential issue of the election was the changed role of government. Roosevelt said, 'Government in a modern civilisation has certain inescapable obligations to its citizens among which are the protection of the family and the home, the establishment of a democracy of opportunity and to aid those overtaken by disaster'.

Following the assassination of Huey Long (see page 134), the Left formed the Union Party in which Coughlin and Townsend supported the candidacy of Congressman William 'Liberty Bill' Lemke of North Dakota. Lemke unfortunately had a glass eye, wore outrageous clothes and had a shrill, high-pitched voice. One commentator wrote that, 'he had the charisma of a deserted telephone booth'. His policies, according to Roosevelt, appealed to 10–15 per cent of the electorate at most. Leaders such as Coughlin found it difficult to co-operate effectively with others and arguments abounded.

More significantly perhaps, while there was undoubtedly considerable support for particular issues such as Townsend's scheme for pensions, this simply did not translate into a mass willingness to vote for overwhelming change. Few Americans wanted to change the 'system', particularly when Roosevelt, steering a middle line, was so popular.

In the election Roosevelt was triumphant. With the smaller alternative parties barely raising a million votes between them, Roosevelt won 60.8 per cent of the popular vote to Landon's 36.5 per cent and carried all but two states, Vermont and Maine, which were memorably shown in a subsequent cartoon to be in the doghouse. As ever, Roosevelt had offered little in the way of concrete promises in his election speeches but people expected much of him. His celebrated inaugural address in 1937, seemed to promise much.

> In this nation, I see tens of millions of its citizens – a substantial part of the whole population – who at this very moment are denied the greater part of what the very lowest standards of today call the necessities of life … I see one third of the nation ill housed, ill clad, ill nourished … We are determined to make every American citizen the subject of his country's interest and concern. … The test of our progress is not whether we add more to the abundance of those who have much; it is whether we provide enough for those who have too little.

The implication was clearly that these people would be Roosevelt's priority; but he actually said little about precisely what he was going to do for them.

4 | Problems in the Second Term

Roosevelt had fought the election largely on his personality and the trust ordinary people had in him. He was certainly aided by the disorganisation of his opponents and the fact that the Republicans could not possibly gain support by attacking measures that had benefited so many. Perhaps his victory made him overconfident and even arrogant. However, during his second term problems multiplied until his presidency seemed at times on its last legs.

The Supreme Court

Key question
How and why did the Supreme Court threaten New Deal Legislation?

Key dates
Black Monday:
25 May 1935
Judiciary Reform Bill:
February 1936

Given Roosevelt's flexible ideas on the workings of the constitution, it was perhaps inevitable that he would come into conflict with its guardian, the Supreme Court. Although he had not directly attacked the Court during the election campaign, he was very concerned about its operations and felt it was in need of reform. Although the Court had supported New Deal laws in the days of crisis, it had increasingly declared legislation unconstitutional as Roosevelt's first term of office came to an end. In the 140 years before 1935, the Supreme Court had found only about 60 federal laws unconstitutional; in 18 months during 1935 and 1936, it found 11 to be so.

Indeed, on one day, 'Black Monday', 27 May 1935 the Supreme Court attacked the New Deal in several ways. For example, it found the Farm Mortgage Act (see page 123) unconstitutional. It argued that the removal of a Trade Commissioner, which Roosevelt sought, was the responsibility not of the president but of Congress. Most importantly it found the NIRA to be unconstitutional through the 'sick chicken' case.

The 'sick chicken' case

This was possibly the Court's most serious decision and it motivated Roosevelt into action. The case involved the Schechter Brothers, a firm of butchers in New York who were selling chickens unfit for human consumption. Prosecuted by the NIRA for breaking its codes of practice, the Schechter Brothers appealed against the verdict to the Supreme Court. It decided that their prosecution should be a matter for the New York courts not the federal government, and the poultry code was declared illegal.

Key term
Inter-state commerce
Trade between different states.

In effect, the decision meant that federal government had no right to interfere in internal state issues. While recognising that the federal government had powers to intervene in **inter-state commerce**, the court found that it had none to do so in the internal commerce of states.

Moreover, if the federal government could not prosecute individual firms for breaking the NIRA codes, it followed that all the codes themselves must be unconstitutional. This was because they were developed by federal government but affected individual firms in individual states. The argument went that the Executive had acted unconstitutionally in giving itself the powers to implement the codes in the first place. This was because it had not authority to intervene in matters that were the preserves of individual states. Given that the codes were at the heart of NIRA, it could not survive without them. More significantly, the ruling seemed to imply that the government had no powers to oversee nation-wide economic affairs except in so far as they affected inter-state commerce.

Judiciary Reform Bill

Roosevelt believed the justices on the Supreme Court were out of
touch. Of the nine judges, none were his appointments. He
increasingly saw the issue of the Supreme Court as one of
unelected officials stifling the work of a democratically elected
government, while members of the Supreme Court saw it as them
using their legal authority to halt the spread of dictatorship. The
scene was set for battle.

On 3 February 1936 Roosevelt presented the Judiciary Reform
Bill to Congress. This proposed that the president could appoint
a new justice whenever an existing judge, reaching the age of 70,
failed to retire within six months. He could also appoint up to six
new justices, increasing the possible total to 15. The measure had
been drawn up in secret, although, ironically, the idea of forcibly
retiring judges had first been proposed by one of the existing
members of the Supreme Court in 1913.

Roosevelt gave as the reasoning behind his proposal that the
Supreme Court could not keep up with the volume of work and
more justices would help. However, everyone knew that it was
really a proposal to pack the court with his own nominees who
would favour New Deal legislation.

In the event, the whole thing backfired. It was not a matter of
the most elderly justices being the most conservative; in fact the
oldest, Justice Brandeis was, at 79, the most liberal. Nor was the
Court inefficient. Chief Justice Hughes could show that the Court
was necessarily selective in the cases it considered and that, given
the need for considerable discussion on each, a greater number of
justices would make its work far more difficult.

Roosevelt had stirred up a hornet's nest. Many congressmen
feared he might start to retire them at 70 next. He had also
greatly underestimated popular support and respect for the
Court. In proposing this measure, Roosevelt was seen as a
dictator. In July the Senate rejected the Judiciary Reform Bill by
70 votes to 20. However, it was not a total defeat for Roosevelt.
Justice Van Devanter, who was ill, announced his retirement. The
Supreme Court recognised that Roosevelt had just won an
election with a huge majority. Most of the electorate clearly
supported his measures. Therefore the Court had already begun
to uphold legislation such as the National Labour Relations and
the Social Security Acts – possibly, as one wag commented,
because 'a switch in time saves nine'. As more justices retired,
Roosevelt could appoint his supporters, such as Felix Frankfurter,
to replace them, but he did not again attempt to reform
the Court.

Problems with agriculture

Although the AAA (see pages 123–4) was generally regarded as
successful, various problems had emerged as time went on. At the
local level, the AAA was usually run by county committees, and so
tended to be dominated by the most powerful landowners. If, for
example, they were paid to take land out of production, they
thought little about turning out their sharecroppers or tenants

Key question
How did Roosevelt try to reform the Supreme Court?

Key question
What problems did Roosevelt face in regard to agriculture and rural poverty?

A dust storm in Oklahoma. What would conditions be like inside these houses?

despite the attempts of AAA officials to mediate. Where the treatment of African-Americans in the South was concerned, officials from Washington and others who came to help were regarded as interfering busybodies trying to destroy Southern ways. Where the displaced tried to organise themselves – as in Alabama where they formed the Alabama Sharecroppers' Union – they were met with violence that was condoned by state officials. Roosevelt was reluctant to intervene because he relied so much on the support of Southern Democrats.

In addition, there was an increasing feeling that the AAA only really benefited the wealthy. While farm income doubled overall during the 1930s, it had only reached 80 per cent of the amount farmers were receiving before 1914. By and large, the agricultural sector remained depressed.

The dustbowl

To add to the problem, there was a natural catastrophe taking place over much of rural America. Years of overploughing in the agricultural regions, particularly in the Midwest, had made much of the soil fine and dusty. This had been of little importance in years of heavy rain, but in dry years that were coupled with high winds, the topsoil literally blew away. There was a series of droughts in the early 1930s, which one weather scientist described as 'the worst in the climatalogical history of the country'.

Beginning in the eastern states, the drought headed west. By the winter of 1933–4 the snowfall in the Northern Rockies was only 33 per cent that of normal times and in the southern peaks there was hardly any. High winds led to massive erosion; the topsoil blew away in great clouds. The Natural Resources Board estimated in 1934 that 35 million acres of previously arable land had been destroyed and the soil of a further 125 million acres was exhausted. One storm between 9 and 11 May 1934 saw an estimated 350 million tons of soil transplanted from the west of the country and deposited in the east. Chicago received four pounds of soil for every one of its citizens.

The effects were horrendous. Day became night as whole landscapes were covered with swirling dust. Homes were buried and formerly arable land was exposed as bare rock. Thousands lost their farms and were forced to migrate. It has been estimated that the state of Oklahoma alone lost 440,000 people during the 1930s, while Kansas lost 227,000. Many left to try their luck in neighbouring states. Usually their quest was unsuccessful. The plains states had little large-scale industry. Unemployment stood at 39 per cent in Arkansas in 1933, and about 30 per cent in Missouri, Oklahoma and Texas.

Around 220,000 people migrated to California in search of work. The 'Golden State' did not welcome them. The authorities patrolled their borders, sending migrants back. They also expelled many Mexican immigrants. Despite these efforts, the state still had a drifting population of 200,000 migrant agricultural labourers, 70,000 in the fertile San Joaquin Valley alone. Farmers there were still reeling from a series of strikes in 1933 and 1934 in which the Cannery and Agricultural Workers Industrial Union had successfully seen wages rise by as much as 100 per cent. Farmers retaliated by forming their own organisation, the Associated Farmers of California, which worked with the authorities to break strikes and destroy the unions, often by violence. They often used 'Okies' – as the migrants from the plains were called, whatever their state of origin – as 'blackleg' labour.

Certainly the migrants were desperate for work. They followed the harvests throughout the state, travelling as far as 500 miles per year. Normally, they lived in filthy, squalid roadside camps with no facilities and high infant mortality rates. In one county as many as 50 'Okie' babies died of diarrhoea and enteritis during the harvest season. They were often condemned as dirty and almost subhuman by the richer Californians. The state was extremely reluctant to help, seeing them as an unwanted burden. They looked to the federal government for help, who had also seemed reluctant at first to take their part.

Government measures

To combat erosion, the government had set up the Soil Erosion Service in August 1933. This was later renamed the Soil Conservation Service and became part of the Department of Agriculture. It divided farms into soil conservation districts, and encouraged farmers to consider new ideas such as contour ploughing to hold the soil (see page 124). Test farmers were used and evidence of their efforts were publicised to promote the effectiveness of their methods. The CCC planted trees and shelterbeds. However, all in all it was too little too late – and indeed if the land was reclaimed, farmers often began to overplough again and the dustbowl returned in the postwar period.

When the rains finally did come, they would not stop. On 23 January 1937 *The New York Times* reported that floods across 12 states had made 150,000 people homeless. Nearly 4000 were killed in the windstorms and floods.

Although these events were disastrous for farmers in the short term, in the long term they were beneficial for American agriculture. Many of the surplus workforce left and many of the remaining farms became bigger and more efficient. The Agricultural Bureau estimated that in 1933 about one in every 10 farms changed hands and that about half of those sales were forced. This figure did not notably fall at any time during the 1930s. The human cost was incalculable, despite the fact that measures were taken to alleviate some of the misery during the latter years of the New Deal.

Labour relations

Key question
What problems arose in industrial relations?

The mid-1930s was a time of difficult labour relations. Labour unions wanted to exercise the rights afforded them by Section 7(a) of NIRA and the Wagner Act. However, many employers did not recognise these. At a time when many large-scale employers such as Henry Ford employed strong-arm men, strikes could often result in violence. There was also considerable anger at the use of 'blackleg' labour during disputes, particularly if the 'blacklegs' were of different ethnic group to the strikers.

There was, moreover, an important new development in American labour unionism. The **AFL** traditionally favoured craft unions and did not encourage the semi-skilled and unskilled to unionise. John Lewis, President of the United Mine Workers, in particular, wanted to see large industry-wide unions set up rather than small individual craft-based ones. If this happened it would be possible for any dispute to paralyse an entire industry. When the AFL continued to show little interest in this idea at its 1935 conference, Lewis and others who thought similarly broke away to form the Congress of Industrial Organisations.

Key term
American Federation of Labor (AFL) Organisation representing American labour unions.

This was later renamed the Committee of Industrial Organisations (CIO). It did encourage whole industry-based unions. Its first battle took place in Dayton, Ohio where rubber workers struck at the giant Goodyear plant. After the firm capitulated to the strikers' demands, the United Rubber Workers' Union became the first to join the CIO. In December 1936, a battle on a larger scale was to take place to gain union recognition in the automobile industry. At General Motors, there were 'sit-in' strikes for six weeks to gain employer recognition of the United Automobile Workers' Union (UAW). General Motors had produced 15,000 cars per week. During the strikes it was down to 150 and on 11 February 1936 the company recognised the UAW. Chrysler followed suit but Ford, using muscle men to beat up unionists, held out against the UAW until 1941.

Policemen tussle with pickets as disorder breaks out at the gates of the Pontiac Fisher body plant.

Using the threat of massive strikes, the CIO had achieved union recognition in the automobile, steel, rubber, electricity, textile and farm implement industries by the end of 1937. Firms could not afford long drawn-out strikes at a time of economic recovery. Union membership rose from 4 million in 1936 to 7 million in 1937. The number of strikes rose from 637 in 1930 to 2172 in 1936 and 4740 in 1937. Managers were worried by this and the accompanying threat to their profits.

The unions meanwhile were concerned about the level of violence used against them, which was often condoned and even perpetrated by the authorities. Both sides looked to Roosevelt for help, but he upset both by doing nothing. He felt that the two sides had to solve the problems for themselves. He had never been especially sympathetic to labour unions; hardly any of the New Deal legislation supporting them had been initiated by him. Indeed, as we have seen, he had only given his support to the Wagner Act when it had already passed through the Senate (page 151). However, as the unions gained in strength, Roosevelt could not continue to ignore them, and by 1940 they made the largest contribution to the Democratic Party's campaign funds and in return their leaders expected consultations at the highest levels.

The 'Roosevelt Recession' 1937–8

Federal expenditure was cut in June 1937 to meet Roosevelt's long-held belief in a balanced budget. He hoped business had by this time recovered sufficiently to fill the gaps caused by government cutbacks. It had not. The cutbacks led to what

Key question
What were the effects of the downturn in the economy?

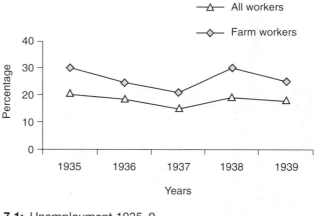

Figure 7.1: Unemployment 1935–9

Roosevelt Recession
Downswing in the economy associated with Roosevelt's cutbacks in government spending in 1937.

became known as the '**Roosevelt Recession**'. Figure 7.1 shows how unemployment rose, particularly among farm workers in 1937–8. With the numbers of unemployed rising to 7.5 million in 11 months, social security payments swallowed $2 billion of the nation's wealth.

The same problems of human misery that had been witnessed in the early years of the decade returned in full force.

- In the manufacturing industries, employment fell by 23 per cent and the production of such items as motor cars fell by as much as 50 per cent.
- Overall, national income fell by 13 per cent. Recovery suddenly seemed as far away as ever.
- According to the Federal Reserve Board's index of industrial production, 66 per cent of the gains made during the New Deal years were lost.
- The fall in the index from 117 in August 1937 to 76 by May 1938 was in fact faster than at any time during the earlier depression of 1929–33.
- Farm prices fell by 20 per cent.

Big business was made a scapegoat for the collapse. A Temporary National Economic Committee (TNEC) was speedily set up to investigate price fixing among large corporations. Many government officials thought these practices were responsible for the recession.

In the event, the mass of evidence that the Committee had collected led to little in the way of government action because by the time it reported, the recession was over. In any case, there was little political will to take on the giant corporations. While there was much popular sympathy for small companies and their difficulties, people increasingly realised the benefits of large ones with their relatively cheap, mass-produced goods that small companies could not provide.

In this sense, the New Deal always supported big business, even though it often verbally attacked it. This perceived hostility led to a lack of morale among businessmen and accounts for their frequent opposition to the New Deal. However, we must remember that, despite his attacks, Roosevelt expected big business to lead the USA out of the recession. However it was ill disposed to do so because of the attacks. Representatives of big business in their turn blamed too much government and high taxes for their problems. Many sought a return to the policies of the 1920s.

Roosevelt's attempts to end the recession

Roosevelt seemed undecided in the face of the mounting economic problems. His Treasury Secretary, Henry Morgenthal, was advising him to balance the budget, while the chief of the Federal Reserve Board, Marriner Eccles, insisted that he return to deficit spending. In April 1938 Roosevelt finally chose the latter and asked Congress to vote him a $3.8 billion relief budget with the lion's share going to the PWA and WPA. However, recovery was slow and in 1939 unemployment still stood at 9 million. Roosevelt did appear to be moving towards policies of massive government intervention in the economy and deficit spending. However, his conversion was slow and reluctant. Yet, by the later 1930s he did seem to give more credence and support to those advisers such as Harry Hopkins and Frances Perkins who had advocated this, and conservative Democrats were increasingly frozen out. As the decade drew to a close, the European war began to dominate Roosevelt's policies. War contracts and the opening of markets unable to be met by those at war brought about recovery and concealed the failings of the New Deal.

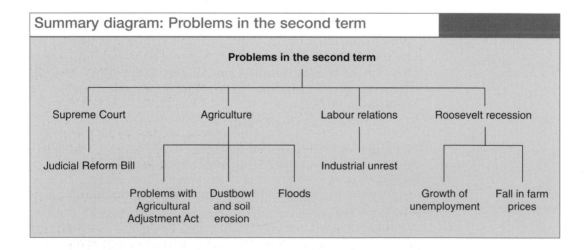

Summary diagram: Problems in the second term

Problems in the second term

- Supreme Court
  - Judicial Reform Bill
- Agriculture
  - Problems with Agricultural Adjustment Act
  - Dustbowl and soil erosion
  - Floods
- Labour relations
  - Industrial unrest
- Roosevelt recession
  - Growth of unemployment
  - Fall in farm prices

5 | The Later New Deal

Some commentators have spoken of a 'Third New Deal' between 1937 and 1939. This, they argue, was characterised by Roosevelt adopting the idea of permanent government spending to solve economic problems. They cite as a particular example his response to the 1937 recession. However, this argument may not be sustainable. It could imply a consistency where there was none.

Key question
Were the measures of the Third New Deal more radical than those that had gone before?

It could be counter-argued that the measures of the later New Deal were more piecemeal than ever. As it turned out, much of Roosevelt's programme failed to pass through an increasingly hostile Congress. The national mood was for a reduction in government spending, not expansion. This naturally limited the scope of what was passed.

We have seen above how the 'Roosevelt Recession' took his administration by surprise and he seemed uncharacteristically uncertain as to how to address it. However, problems in getting legislation through Congress were already appearing before this. There is broad agreement that Roosevelt's second administration was something of a disappointment. The increasing hostility of Congress, compounded by the president's increasing concentration on foreign affairs, have led some to argue that it ran out of steam.

Certainly, Roosevelt was frustrated in many of his legislative requests. He wanted, for example, the encouragement of more privately built housing and the creation of seven more planning authorities on the lines of the TVA (see pages 124–5). Nothing came of either. As we will see, he went through with his plan to reorganise the Executive in the face of congressional disapproval. This is not to suggest that pressing concerns were not addressed or that advances were not made. However, on the whole the legislation of Roosevelt's second administration seems nowhere near as comprehensive as that of his first.

Key question
How was agricultural dealt with in the Third New Deal?

Agriculture Acts
Bankhead-Jones Farm Tenant Act, July 1937
This was passed partly in response to a report showing that as banks foreclosed on farms, farm ownership was declining. The Act created a Farm Security Administration (FSA), which replaced the RA. Its primary aim was to help tenants acquire low-interest loans to buy and restock their farms. The Act was, of course, contrary to the RA, which was intended to resettle farmers elsewhere. The FSA was intended to redress some of the ill effects of the first AAA mentioned on pages 158–9 and helped tens of thousands to stay on their land. It also established about 30 camps to provide temporary accommodation for displaced families.

The FSA also provided medical and dental centres, and funded loans to enable owners of small farms to purchase heavy machinery. By 1947, 40,000 farmers had bought their own farms through its efforts and 900,000 families had borrowed $800 million to rehabilitate their farms. Because of the return to prosperity as a result of the Second World War, the vast majority of the loans were repaid.

Second Agricultural Adjustment Act, February 1938
This was based on storing surplus produce in good years for distribution in poor ones. It established that quotas in five staple crops – rice, tobacco, wheat, corn and cotton – could be imposed by a 66 per cent majority of farmers in a vote. Those who then

kept to the quotas received subsidies. By concentrating on quotas the Act was meant to be fairer to small farmers than the first AAA, which had given most subsidies to those with the most land. In case of overproduction, a Commodity Credit Corporation could make loans to enable the farmer to store his surplus produce. If, in other words, the market price fell, the farmer could store his crop. When the price rose the farmer could repay the loan and sell the surplus. Moreover, the Food Stamp Plan allowed for farm surpluses to be distributed to people on relief – they would receive 50 cents worth of such commodities for every $1 spent on other groceries.

The AAA's complexity left the county committees with too much to do and so they had little time to explain its provisions to individual farmers. It was widely distrusted therefore and believed to be unfair. This was particularly true for the small farmers it was designed to help. They had no time to study its details and had to rely on the county committees largely made up of the large-scale farmers they distrusted. It also came into operation too late for some farmers. They had already overproduced before they knew of the quotas for 1938. The resentment of the farmers was expressed in the 1938 Congressional elections, when Republicans and opponents of the New Deal made sizeable gains. The two politicians who introduced the measure into Congress were both defeated. Nevertheless, the principles behind the Act – that of subsidies for farmers adhering to quotas – essentially remained in force until recent years.

Wagner-Steagall National Housing Act, September 1937

Key question
What was the purpose of housing legislation?

This act was designed to meet the needs for slum clearance and the building of public housing. It was largely the brainchild of Senator Wagner. Roosevelt had little enthusiasm for the scheme because he did not understand the scale of the problem of housing in the cities and preferred to support home ownership schemes. The measure established the US Housing Authority (USHA) to act through the public housing bureaux in large cities to provide loans of up to 100 per cent at low rates of interest to build new homes.

Congress allocated $500 million, only half of what had been requested. The biggest problems lay in the great north-eastern cities. However, in a slight to them, it was stipulated that no more than 10 per cent of USHA could be spent in any one state. By 1941, 160,000 homes had been built for slum dwellers at an average rent of $12–15 per month.

However, this was wholly inadequate to meet the problem. It was a clear example of Congressmen from the west and south failing to agree on the needs of the northern cities. They increasingly saw these as getting the lion's share of the benefits of New Deal legislation. They were determined to reverse this trend. In addition, conservatives feared public housing was a threat to capitalism, driving away the private landlord.

The result of the limitations of the Act was that millions of people remained in poor housing. It was only when urbanisation developed throughout the USA in the postwar period that Congress began to provide adequate means for public housing developments.

Key question
How did the government help pay and working conditions?

Fair Labor Standards Act, June 1938

This Act fixed minimum wages and maximum hours of work in all industries engaged in inter-state commerce. The minimum wage was set at 25 cents per hour, intended to rise eventually to 40 cents, and maximum hours should be 44 per week, with the hope that they would fall to 40 within three years. The wages of 300,000 people were immediately increased and the hours of 1.3 million were reduced. The inter-state shipment of goods made by children working under the age of 16 was forbidden. Children under 18 years were forbidden to work in hazardous employment.

To supervise the legislation, a Wages and Hours division was set up in the Department of Labor. This had the power to impose hefty fines. However, to get the Act accepted, particularly by Southern politicians, Roosevelt had to make exemptions, notably domestic servants and farm labourers. As with the Social Security legislation, it was hoped that these would be included in the future. However, as the omissions were mainly jobs associated with African-Americans, it could be argued that this group were losing out yet again. It was another example of New Deal legislation bypassing them, an issue that will be more fully addressed in the final chapter.

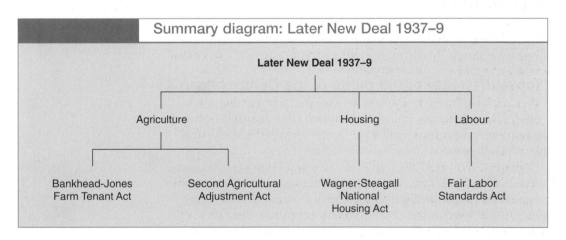

Summary diagram: Later New Deal 1937–9

Later New Deal 1937–9

Agriculture	Housing	Labour
Bankhead-Jones Farm Tenant Act / Second Agricultural Adjustment Act	Wagner-Steagall National Housing Act	Fair Labor Standards Act

Key question
How and when did the New Deal come to a close?

6 | The End of the New Deal

In the mid-term elections of 1938 the Republicans doubled their seats in the House of Representatives and also made gains in the Senate. The tide appeared to be turning against Roosevelt politically. Although he was to break with tradition and stand for a historic third (and later a fourth) term of office, this was not known at the time.

Increasingly as his second term drew to a close, he was seen as a 'lame duck' president whose New Deal policies had failed to deliver economic recovery to the extent hoped for. There were no new New Deal measures passed after January 1939. Increasingly thereafter foreign affairs began to dominate. However, one can discern a shift in Roosevelt's thinking. He began to realise that a balanced budget might not be possible in the modern world and that involvement in the economy and in the provision of relief might become permanent features of American government.

This was quite different from his earlier ideas. In fact, some commentators have argued that when the USA was ready for radical change in 1933, Roosevelt adopted a conservative stance but when he tried to impose radical change during the later 1930s, the country was too conservative to accept it. In 1939, for example, opinion polls found that only 20 per cent of Americans were prepared to accept the idea of an unbalanced budget. Roosevelt faced three significant defeats during this period.

Revenue Act 1938

The Revenue Act states how the government aims to raise money that year. Roosevelt's Revenue Act of 1938 was considerably weakened when Congress removed the proposed tax on company profits. Allowing firms to keep more of their revenue, would, it was hoped, help stimulate industrial recovery. Nevertheless, the message seemed to be that Roosevelt could not rely on the support of the legislature, that it was 'business as usual', and the mood was for lessening government involvement.

In other words, Roosevelt had, in his increasing radicalism, gone beyond the mood of the politicians in Congress. The message from the legislature suggested that many of the powers he had accumulated in the past were now going to be taken away from him.

Roosevelt's attempted purge of the Democrats

When Roosevelt tried to purge his own party by getting rid of conservatives this also failed. In summer 1938 the mid-term primary elections for Democratic candidates to Congress took place. The president travelled the country supporting liberal candidates and opposing conservative ones. However, the conservative candidates he opposed still made a show of publicly supporting him. Moreover, these elections tended to be very much about local issues. Roosevelt's interventions had little effect but they did make the president seem ham-fisted. The attempt also made for difficult working relationships with the new Congress when it met.

Executive Office of the President

Roosevelt recognised that the increased role of government would be permanent. He planned to accommodate this through the creation of the **Executive Office of the President**. This would lead to an expanded White House staff, a system of promotion by merit in the civil service and development of more government

Executive Office of the President
The president's staff.

Key term

Creation of Executive
Office of the
President: 1939

Executive Order
Right of the
president to force
through his
decision.

departments. He was surprised by the general hostility to the
idea. There was a fear that he was seeking to acquire too much
power, that he wished to become a dictator and that his
appointees would use their new unelected positions to stay
in power.

Others felt that the president was encroaching on the powers of
Congress, which was supposed to initiate legislation. Some, of
course, opposed it simply because it was promoted by Roosevelt.
In any event, the House of Representatives rejected the measure
in April 1938 by a vote of 204 to 196. Roosevelt, in fact, created
the Executive Office by **Executive Order** in September 1939 as
was his right. But it is important to note that this was in defiance
of Congress.

Summary diagram: Roosevelt and the New Deal 1935–6

Pressures on Roosevelt		Second New Deal 1935–6
Radical outsiders e.g. Coughlin, Townsend		Emerging Relief Association Act Resettlement Administration National Labor Relations Act Rural Electrification Act Social Security Act Banking Act Revenue (Wealth) Act
Reforming members of Congress e.g. Senator Wagner		
Conservative opposition e.g. Liberty Leaguers, wealthy businessman		

Problems of second term	How addressed	Level of success
Supreme Court opposed New Deal legislation	Judicial Reform Bill	Bill rejected in Congress – but Supreme Court do begin to pass New Deal legislation

Agriculture
1 Working of AAA unfair to tenant farmers and sharecroppers
 	
2 Dustbowl
	1 (a) AAA officials try to persuade local committees to act more fairly
	   (b) Second AAA
	2 (a) Farm Tenant Act
	   (b) Farm Security Administration
		1 (a) Largely failed
		   (b) Mainly helped large farmers
		
		2 (a) Partial success
		   (b) Partial success

Labour relations	(a) Did little to intervene in industrial disputes (b) Fair Labor Standards Act	(a) Upset both sides (b) Affected industries involved in inter-state commerce but many sectors excluded
'Roosevelt Recession'	$3.8 billion in relief	Inadequate to meet needs or to inflate the economy

Effects of these defeats

Although each of these attempts to impose his will ended in defeat, collectively they made more people suspicious of Roosevelt's intentions. In August 1938 a Gallup Poll showed that 50 per cent of Americans feared the development of dictatorship in the USA, compared with 37 per cent in a similar poll the previous October. With anxious eyes looking towards Europe and the growth of dictatorships, the tide seemed to have turned against Roosevelt and the expansion of American government. Moreover, Roosevelt was blamed for the recession, which is why it was named after him.

Roosevelt's personal popularity with the electorate was not in doubt. However, there was a feeling that the New Deal had run out of steam. It was in part Roosevelt's realisation that he had no successor in the Democratic Party who would continue his work, along with the events in Europe, that made him decide to stand for an unprecedented third term of office. As has already been stated, the European war and its effects in the USA overtook the New Deal and subsumed it. However, this should not blind us to the significance of the New Deal.

Study Guide: AS Questions

In the style of AQA

Explain the degree to which opposition to the New Deal was effective in the period 1935–41.

Study tips

The cross-references are intended to take you straight to the section that will help you to answer the question.

You need to consider the range of opposition both from the left and the right of the political spectrum (pages 132–7).

- You need to consider why the Left opposed the New Deal, for example because it did not go far enough, and the Right, because it went too far.
- You need to consider the dispute with the Supreme Court, for example over state–federal government powers (pages 157–8) and how far the later New Deal was a response to criticisms of earlier legislation (pages 164–7).
- Most important, you need to come to balanced judgements supported by analysis in terms of the key terms 'the degree to which' and 'effective'.

In the style of Edexcel

How far did the opposition of the Supreme Court weaken Roosevelt's ability to carry out New Deal policies in the years 1935–41? (36 marks)

> ### Exam tips
> *The cross-references are intended to take you straight to the section that will help you to answer the question.*
>
> The key issue here is a balanced judgement relating to the issue of 'how far' the opposition of the Supreme Court harmed Roosevelt's ability to get his policies passed. The need is then to reflect this in the response:
>
> - the Supreme Court had declared some of his legislation, such as the NIRA, unconstitutional (page 157)
> - Roosevelt was diverted from other issues during his battle with the Supreme Court (page 158)
> - his Judicial Reform Bill was defeated (page 158)
> - however, after 1936, the Supreme Court opposed his measures less (page 158).
>
> The focus needs be on an evaluation in terms of the key issue. The question of 'how far' needs to be central to your answer.

Study Guide: Advanced Level Question

In the style of OCR

Discuss the extent of opposition to the New Deal in the years 1933 to 1937. (45 marks)

Source: OCR, June 2003

> ### Exam tips
> *The cross-references are intended to take you straight to the section that will help you to answer the question.*
>
> What matters here is the quality and breadth of discussion. You need to consider the range and extent of opposition across the political spectrum and the reasons for it (pages 132–7). The emphasis is on evaluation. Don't forget to include historical debate within your answer.
>
> - Why was opposition so widespread and from so many different groups? Why, for example, was the Supreme Court opposed to the New Deal (pages 157–8)?
> - How much a threat was this opposition? Huey Long appeared to threaten Roosevelt's position in the Democratic Party, for example, but after his death Democratic opponents performed badly (pages 155–6).
> - You might also consider whether Left-wing opposition drove Roosevelt to a more radical position in the later 1930s (pages 156–70).

8 American Foreign Policy 1920–41

POINTS TO CONSIDER

This chapter examines the political aspects of foreign policy between 1920 and 1941. It charts how the USA moved from a position of strict neutrality and non-involvement with the other affairs of other nations to full participation in the Second World War. It examines the following issues:

- Foreign policy in the 1920s and whether it was possible for the USA to be isolationist
- Roosevelt's foreign policy
- US response to the war in Europe
- US relations with Japan
- How US foreign policy changed between 1920 and 1941

Key dates

1917	14 Points drawn up
1921	Washington Naval Conference
1928	Kellogg–Briand Pact
1933	World Economic Conference
	Montevideo Conference
1936–7	Neutrality Acts
1937	Chinese–Japanese War
	US gunboat Panay sunk
	Ludlow Amendment
1939	Outbreak of the Second World War in Europe
1940	Roosevelt elected for a third term of office
	Greater East Asia Co-Prosperity Sphere set up
	US destroyers traded for British bases
1941	Lend-lease Act
	Atlantic Charter
	American involvement in Second World War

1 | Introduction

Key question
Did the USA pursue a policy of isolationism?

Britain and France declared war on Germany on 3 September 1939. The news caught the USA sleeping – literally, because of the different time zones. However, when Roosevelt was roused he told his Cabinet that the USA was not going to get involved. He repeated this message in both a press conference and radio fireside chat the following day. A Gallop Poll showed that 94 per cent of Americans agreed. There was a strong feeling that the USA had cleared up the mess European countries had created for themselves during the First World War and they would not do the same thing now. In Europe, too, American neutrality was expected. Neither side had considered that the USA might get involved. Hitler indeed had dismissed the USA as 'hopelessly weak' a few weeks before he ordered the invasion of Poland.

Many historians have noted that the USA pursued a policy of **isolationism** between the wars, ignoring crises and trying to stay clear of foreign entanglements. However, the truth is more complex. The USA was far too powerful and influential a nation to remain isolated. This chapter will examine its foreign policy and track the movement from strict neutrality to full-scale involvement in the Second World War. We have already discussed its economic involvement with other countries (see pages 46–7) and the issue of war debts and their repayment (see pages 55–6 and 98–9). The chapter is primarily concerned therefore with political issues.

Key term

Isolationism
The policy by which USA detached itself from the affairs of other states.

Key question
How far was it possible for the USA to pursue a policy of isolationism in the 1920s?

Key terms

Interventionism
To interfere in the affairs of other states to protect US interests.

Open door policy
Policy of granting equal trade opportunities to all countries.

2 | US Foreign Policy in the 1920s

American foreign policy traditionally veered between isolationism and **interventionism**. On the surface foreign policy in the 1920s appeared isolationist. However, American interests meant that this policy could not always be maintained. At the end of the First World War, for example, the USA was the world's largest exporter and creditor, and owned the world's largest merchant fleet. She was owed almost $12 billion in war debts.

While the USA pursued an **open door policy** to stimulate trade, export its own technology and thereby improve its own economic performance, many countries were too impoverished after the First World War to take full advantage of this. Many found recovery difficult because of the burden of their debts to the USA. This issue, probably the most contentious one in USA's relations with other countries during the 1920s, has already been discussed (see pages 55–6). However, the USA was the most important trading nation in the world and its global dominance certainly helped create the overall prosperity in the USA.

The motive for intervening in the affairs of other countries may have been the USA looking after its own interests abroad rather than any real desire for foreign involvement for its own sake. Nevertheless intervention resulted during the 1920s in terms of disarmament treaties and prolonged controversies about the repayment of war loans. Decisions made in political and financial circles in the USA had significant effects throughout the world.

There were two major themes in US foreign policy in the 1920s. Both were concerned with the maintenance of peace and avoidance of American involvement in any future wars. These were:

• the American rejection of the peace treaties and membership of the League of Nations
• disarmament.

The American rejection of the peace treaties

By January 1917 President Wilson had realised that Allied victory would be wasted if they sought only revenge. He devised his **14 Points** and attended the Paris Peace Conference personally to try to get them adopted as the basis for peace. Among these points were proposals that:

- Small nations should govern themselves.
- Trade barriers and armaments should be reduced. It was felt, for example, that countries that co-operated by trading together would not go to war.
- A **League of Nations** should be set up to encourage co-operation between nations and to arbitrate in disputes to avoid future wars.

However, in attending this conference, Wilson appeared to turn his back on problems in the USA. Soldiers were returning home to unemployment as war industries closed. As wartime controls were abandoned, millions went on strike. There was racial conflict in many cities such as Chicago and St Louis. Western wheat farmers claimed they had been treated unfairly because the prices of their produce had been controlled during the war, whereas prices for Southern cotton producers had been allowed to find their own levels so they had made greater profits. Western farmers mainly voted republican while Southerners favoured the Democrats. In 1918 Republicans won victories in both Houses of Congress. This meant that the Democratic President Wilson could no longer count on support from the legislature.

Treaties with foreign countries have to be passed by the Senate by a two-thirds majority but Wilson had not even taken any Republicans with him to the Paris Peace Conference. The peacemakers among the victorious nations began to argue and the treaties they came up with seemed to be compromises that pleased no one. Germany in particular was treated very harshly, losing land and being forced to pay reparations (see page 56). This led to criticisms in the USA about their country's involvement in the peace process.

Many critics were already suggesting, even before they were signed, that the peace treaties would simply lead to further wars. However, Wilson returned home to drum up support for them and American membership of the League of Nations.

In the meantime 37 Republican Senators had signed a document condemning the League of Nations and suggesting its creation should be delayed until peace with Germany had been finally concluded by the signing of a peace treaty that was satisfactory to all parties. With Wilson determined to have his way, the scene was set for a trial of strength. This focused on the question of US membership of the League of Nations.

Wilson's Republican opponents to US membership of the League of Nations tended to be divided into three camps:

- The 'Irreconcilables' led by Willian Borah of Idaho, who opposed membership completely.

Key question
What were the USA's concerns about the peace treaties and why did it refuse to join the League of Nations?

Key dates

14 points drawn up: 1917

USA refused to join the League of Nations: 1921

Key terms

14 Points
President Wilson's blueprint for a peaceful postwar world.

League of Nations
International organisation to encourage co-operation between nations and keep the peace between them.

- The milder reservationists, who were prepared to support membership if the USA had more of a say in the drafting of 'its Charter'.
- The stronger reservationists, who worried about the loss of **sovereignty** as a result of membership. Senator Henry Cabot Lodge was associated with this latter group. He drew up his own '14 reservations'. One of these stated that the government of the USA should not give up any of its authority to the League.

Key term

Sovereignty
A nation's control over its own affairs.

During his nation-wide campaigning Wilson's health broke down. In the meantime, opposition to the peace treaties grew among Americans, for example from those of German origin who thought Germany was being treated unfairly.

In the Senate vote on membership of the League, Lodge won his vote by 55 to 38 simply by keeping his party united. To get over the problems of refusing to sign the peace treaties, the USA simply issued the Parker-Knox resolution declaring the war was over. In October 1921 the Senate passed the peace treaties but refused to accept membership of the League of Nations.

The rejection of the League of Nations did not, however, mean that the USA was strictly isolationist during this period. It was to involve itself in various disarmament conferences and treaties in the belief that this would prevent future wars. There was an increasing feeling within the USA that war in itself was wrong and it should not have got involved in the First World War.

Key question
Why did the USA support disarmament?

Washington Disarmament Conference 1921

President Harding largely left foreign affairs to his very able Secretary of State, Charles Evans Hughes. The USA was a prime mover in attempts at **disarmament**. In November 1921, for example, delegates from the USA, UK, France, Japan and Italy met in Washington to discuss issues concerning the balance of power in East Asia. Agreements were signed on naval disarmament and easing of tensions in the region. In terms of naval disarmament, each country agreed to reduce tonnage of battleships for 10 years in an approximate ratio of five for USA and UK, three for Japan, and 1.75 for Italy and France, respectively.

Key dates

Washington Disarmament Conference: 1921

Kellogg-Briand Pact: 1928

Key term

Disarmament
Getting rid of, or reducing weapons.

One key intention of the Conference was to maintain the balance of power in the Pacific. There was a concern that Japan was becoming too powerful and China, beset by civil war, too weak. The USA had colonies in the Philippines but worried that it would not be able to defend them in the event of attack. At the conference, the UK, USA, France and Japan signed the Four Power Treaty by which they agreed to respect each others' interests in the Pacific and confer in the event of any other country behaving aggressively in the region.

While this may sound very impressive, the treaties were in fact 'toothless'. There were no penalties for defaulters and, as Harding assured the Senate, there was 'no commitment to armed force, no alliance, no written or moral obligation to join in

defence'. While Japan, for example, abided by the treaty for
several years, she began to expand her influence in the 1930s. As
events were later to show (see pages 184–5), naval limitations did
make it impossible for the USA to defend the Philippines and
also left vulnerable the US naval base at Pearl Harbor.

China
Japan learned that the USA would not intervene in China, which
was increasingly plagued by civil war. A senior official in the State
Department said, in 1924, 'We have no favorites in the present
dog fight in China. They all look alike to us'. Even when there
were anti-foreigner riots in Shanghai and a senior American
official was killed in Nanking, the USA did not intervene.
President Calvin Coolidge realised Americans would not tolerate
the deaths of American troops in China and even praised Chinese
attempts to rid themselves of foreign influence. The Japanese,
however, saw this as a sign of American weakness. Japan was
to remember this in the 1930s when she had her own designs
on China.

Kellogg-Briand Pact 1928
The USA wanted to maintain peace. There were conferences and
competitions for peace plans throughout the decade. In 1923 the
future President Franklin D. Roosevelt submitted one for
$100,000 prize while he was recovering from polio. In 1928 the
US signed the Kellogg-Briand Pact, renouncing war as a means of
settling international grievances. While again it had little
substance and no sanctions attached for signatories who did in
fact go to war, the Senate passed it 85:1.

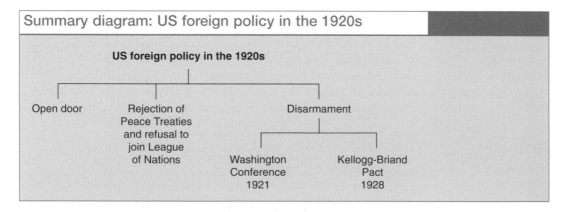

Summary diagram: US foreign policy in the 1920s

3 | Roosevelt's Foreign Policies 1933–9

Roosevelt's priority was in solving the Depression. We have
already seen how he told the 1933 World Economic Conference
that the USA would go its own way (see pages 120–1). He had no
illusions about the European dictators. Indeed, as early as 1933
he told the French Ambassador that 'Hitler is a madman and his
counsellors, some of whom I know personally are even madder
than he is'. However, he had no intention in getting involved in

Key term

'Good Neighbour'
Policy of cultivating
good relations with
Canada and Latin
America.

European affairs. In the early 1930s he agreed with the
traditional policy that the USA could act as a moral force for
good if it avoided foreign entanglements and any accusation of
taking sides. He encouraged economic co-operation through
'**Good Neighbour**' policies and increased trade. His Secretary of
State, Cordell Hull, in particular believed about the beneficial
effects of trade between nations as 'the greatest peacemaker and
civilizer within human experience' In this sense foreign policy was
all about economics. This can be seen in US policies towards its
Latin American neighbours.

Good Neighbour foreign policies

Key question
What were the effects
of the 'Good
Neighbour' policy?

Key date

Montevideo
Conference: 1933

Although Roosevelt first mentioned the idea of 'Good Neighbour'
policies in his inaugural address in 1933, it had predated his
presidency. For example, American troops were withdrawn from
the Dominican Republic in 1924 and in Nicaragua they remained
only for as long as it took to train a native police force to
maintain order while democratic elections were held. The
American military withdrawal from Latin America encouraged
trade and good will. By 1929 the volume of American trade with
Latin America totalled $3.2 billion. This was twice that of US
trade with any other region in the world. This was reduced by
30 per cent during the Depression years.

Roosevelt ordered American troops to leave Haiti where they
had served since 1901. The USA agreed at the 1933 Montevideo
Conference that no country had the right to intervene in either
the internal or external affairs of another. The USA even resisted
the temptation to intervene in Mexico when, in March 1938,
President Cardenas nationalised mainly British- and American-
owned oil companies. The leaders of the American oil companies
at first demanded military action and then demanded $260
million compensation from the Mexican government. With their
own government refusing to take action the companies eventually
settled for $24 million.

As a result of 'Good Neighbour' policies, Hull was able to
negotiate trade agreements with 10 Latin American republics by
1938, which led to a 166 per cent increase in the volume of
American exports to these countries.

Roosevelt had been advised that stern action over oil
nationalisation would have created problems for other US
business interests in Mexico. However, there is no doubt that his
attention in foreign policy was more focused on what was
happening in Europe and the Far East.

Neutrality

Key question
How did the USA
attempt to stay out of
foreign crises in the
1930s?

There was in the USA a strong feeling that involvement in the
First World War had been a mistake that must not be repeated in
any future conflict. We have seen how President Hoover blamed
the war for the Great Depression. In the early 1930s, as we shall
see later, there was considerable research into how the USA had
got involved in the war. Many were looking for someone to
blame. One scapegoat was the arms manufacturers.

'Come on in, I'll treat you right.' Isolationist cartoon. How is the cartoonist making his point?

In 1931 Henry Stimson, Hoover's Secretary of State, tried to introduce an **arms embargo** law for the president to use whenever there was an international conflict. It would have been applied against all **belligerents**.

A study of arms manufacture in the USA by the Senate under the leadership of Gerald P. Nye concluded that arms manufacturers had tricked the USA into entering the First World War, so they could make fortunes from the sales of their products. This conclusion was supported by an influential article in *Fortune* magazine in 1935 entitled 'Arms and Man', which suggested that

Arms embargo
Government order prohibiting the movement of weapons.

Belligerents
Those who were fighting a war.

Key terms

the motto of arms manufacturers was, 'when there are wars, prolong them: where there is peace, disturb it'.

Walter Mills in his book, *The Road to War* published in 1935 argued that the USA had been drawn into the war as a result of:

- British propaganda
- heavy purchases of US arms by the Allies
- Wilson's favouring the Allies and therefore upsetting Germany unnecessarily.

Neutrality Acts

Key date

Neutrality Acts: 1936–7

The message was clear; involvement in the war could and should have been avoided. The lesson was that USA should avoid involvement in future wars. This led in part to a series of Neutrality Acts passed by Congress:

- 1935 Neutrality Act forbade the sale of munitions to all belligerent nations whenever the president proclaimed a state of war existed between them. It even went so far as to say that Americans travelling on ships of belligerent nations did so at their own risk. This was to avoid a similar outcry to the 1915 sinking of a British ship the *Lusitania* with hundreds of American nationals on aboard.
- In 1936 a second Neutrality Act banned all loans to belligerents.
- A third extended the provisions to civil war specifically to avoid American involvement in the Spanish Civil War, which had begun in 1936.
- A fourth forbade US citizens to travel on ships of belligerent nations and said the sale of all goods to belligerents should be on a cash-and-carry basis. This meant that countries paid for the goods before receiving them and were then responsible for carrying them home without US help.

Non-involvement reached its peak in 1937 when a survey found that 94 per cent of Americans felt that US foreign policy should be geared towards keeping out of wars rather than helping prevent them from breaking out in the first place.

After this, however, as the world became a much more dangerous place, Roosevelt began to shift his policy. Nevertheless, most of his countrymen still sought to avoid any involvement. Roosevelt's dilemma was that privately he was increasingly at variance with public opinion and he had to educate the American people to change their minds. This was particularly difficult for him as many of the most loyal supporters of the New Deal, for example the less well-off, were the most isolationist in outlook.

Events that occurred over this period included the following.

Key dates

Outbreak of Chinese-Japanese war: 1937

Ludlow Amendment: 1937

- In 1937 full-scale war erupted between Japan and China, although neither side made a formal declaration of war therefore the Neutrality Acts were not invoked. Roosevelt realised China was dependent on US arms and it supplied the forces of Chiang Kai Shek with them. Chiang Kai Shek was the Chinese leader who opposed both the Japanese and the

Communists, and the Americans had pinned their hopes on him as the most promising future leader of a peaceful and united China.

However, the USA showed considerable restraint when an American gunboat the *Panay* was sunk by Japanese aircraft in the Yangste River. It accepted Japan's apology. Critics were more concerned with why the gunboat had been placed in danger than what the Japanese had done.

- Fear of war led to the Ludlow Amendment, which suggested that war should be declared only after a popular referendum rather than by the president. The proposal was only narrowly defeated in Congress.
- By 1937 Roosevelt was concerned about the rise of the dictators and their aggressive foreign policies. In October he decided to test public opinion in a speech in which he condemned aggression and spoke rather vaguely of 'quarantining' aggressor nations. He was beginning to believe that US intervention might one day be necessary, although he knew that most Congressmen supported isolationism. He was right. The speech brought a storm of protest from the isolationist press.

It is easy with hindsight to say that the USA should have done more to stop the dictators, but the European democracies, notably Britain and France, were not doing much either. There were also limits as to what action Roosevelt could have taken, given the support for isolationism within the USA and the Neutrality Acts. The USA was also militarily very weak.

Rearmament

The military weakness of the USA was mainly due to financial cutbacks. The mainland US Army stood at less than 100,000 men and their standard weapon was the 1903 Springfield rifle. The Air Corps and Navy between them had less than 1600 combat aircraft, many of them biplanes; this figure compared with 3600 in Nazi Germany. The USA was clearly in no position to start a war.

US arms manufacturers, however, did well when the war in Europe began. They were, for example, selling aero-engines to France, a fact that emerged when a bomber earmarked for sale to the French crashed on a test-flight killing an official from the French air ministry. However, US businessmen were also openly trading with Nazi Germany. The Ethyl Gasoline Corporation, for example, helped the Germans develop materials essential for their air war plans. Overall, US investment in Germany increased by 40 per cent from 1936 to 1940.

In December 1938, Roosevelt began to rearm the USA. In January 1939, for example, Congress allocated $500 million for military spending. While the president said this was for purposes of defence, it included the development of 'Flying Fortress' bombers, which showed he must have had an offensive war in mind at some time in the future. By 1941, military budgets were four times that of 1940 and the USA was on its way to becoming

Key question
How powerful was the USA militarily?

an armed giant. This spending also restored employment to pre-Depression levels and saw an end to New Deal programmes as prosperity returned.

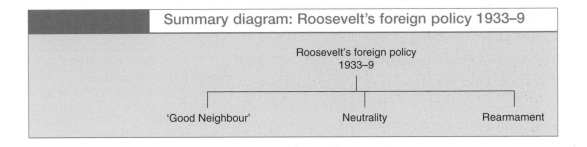

Summary diagram: Roosevelt's foreign policy 1933–9

Roosevelt's foreign policy
1933–9

'Good Neighbour'   Neutrality   Rearmament

Key question
How did the USA react to the war in Europe?

4 | US Response to the European War

When Britain and France went to war with Germany in September 1939, Roosevelt summoned Congress into special session to repeal the arms embargo terms of the Neutrality Acts. Most Americans sympathised with the Allied cause and wanted to see Germany defeated. This was because they disliked the aggression of Nazi Germany. Many feared that if it conquered the European continent it would threaten the USA next. Already there was evidence that it was infiltrating agents into Latin America where many leaders appeared sympathetic to Hitler. As can be imagined, many American Jews also disliked the Nazis.

In November, in a vote on party lines, Congress agreed to sell arms on a strictly cash-and-carry basis. No American ships would carry weapons. However, it was felt the sales would benefit the Allies rather than Germany as British warships could protect their own vessels and destroy German carriers. Clearly Congress had not anticipated the threat to British shipping from German **U-boats**.

Most Americans wanted Britain and France to win but as German successes mounted, this seemed decreasingly likely. The problem was compounded in the summer of 1940 when France was defeated and Britain stood alone against Germany. Britain had placed orders for 14,000 aircraft and 25,000 aero-engines, but was increasingly unable to pay. Roosevelt had overestimated Britain's wealth and began to realise that USA would have to help more if Britain was to stay in the war. This would involve a re-education of the American people.

- The media gave five times as much time to interventionist programmes as isolationist ones. This meant, for example in cinema newsreels and radio programmes, Americans were made to feel sympathy with the allies. Many Americans were moved by Edward Morrow's radio reports from London during the Blitz.
- A pro-intervention series of documentaries *The March of Time* was commissioned.

Key date

Britain and France declared war on Germany: 1939

Key terms

U-boats
German submarines.

The March of Time
Series of documentaries produced to show the Allied cause sympathetically.

- Movies in which Nazis were portrayed as villains were plentiful and their infiltration of American life was depicted in such films as *Confessions of a Nazi Spy*.
- Newspaper and magazine articles fuelled fears of Nazi Germany. Fears were voiced that the Germans had developed long-range aircraft that could bomb the US and drop gas bombs that could kill everyone in Manhattan.

The **America First Campaign** was set up by isolationists meanwhile to keep USA out of the conflict. Among its leaders was the aviator Charles Lindbergh. Much of the campaign's finance came from the German Embassy. An American Nazi Party, the Volksbund, upset many Americans by its paramilitary style and attacks on Jews. Increasingly out-and-out isolationists were seen, fairly or otherwise, as supporters of Germany. This diminished their support.

In 1940, Roosevelt 'traded' Britain 50 destroyers for six Caribbean bases. British bases on Bermuda and Newfoundland were also leased to the USA. This was good business for Roosevelt. He had swapped some elderly destroyers for valuable bases. Nevertheless, it marked a shift to active support for Britain in the war that allowed her to continue to defend her merchant ships.

The 1940 election

Although the Republicans and their candidate, Wendell Willkie, were seen as the party of non-involvement, support for neutrality did cross party lines. Roosevelt decided to stand for a third term partly because there seemed no suitable successor within the Democratic party. He repeated to audiences how much he hated war. Indeed, in Boston in September, Roosevelt made a famous speech in which he assured listeners that American 'boys were not going to be sent into any foreign wars'. However, Roosevelt was beginning to appeal more to businessmen who would do well out of war and less to his more traditional supporters whose boys would be fighting in one. Despite what he said, the USA was moving ever closer to war.

Although his victory was smaller than in 1936, by 27 to 22 million votes, Roosevelt decided to act more boldly after winning. In a fireside chat of 29 December 1940 he called the USA ' the arsenal of democracy', meaning the provider of arms to Britain. This was effectively a turning point in his policy and he began to prepare Americans for **Lend-lease**.

Lend-lease and the Atlantic Charter

Lend-lease was introduced with Congressional approval in May 1941. Britain would be 'loaned' the means to keep fighting. Roosevelt likened it to lending a neighbour a garden hose to fight a fire that might otherwise have spread to his own property, but everyone knew you did not lend weapons. The USA was effectively giving Britain the means to remain in the war. This too showed a switch in policy. Roosevelt had been reluctant

Key terms

America First Campaign
Campaign to keep the USA neutral.

Lend-lease
Scheme whereby the USA loaned goods and weapons to Britain until the war was over.

Key dates

US destroyers traded for British bases: 1940

Roosevelt elected for a third term of office: 1940

Lend-lease introduced: May 1941

to give Britain weapons in 1940 in case she was defeated and Germany subsequently used America's own weapons against her.

In the meantime, in August, Roosevelt had met with the British Prime Minister, Winston Churchill, on the British battleship, *Prince of Wales*, anchored off the Newfoundland coast of Canada. After three days of talks, they issued the **Atlantic Charter**. This was a powerful expression of a vision of what the world should be like after 'the final destruction of Nazi tyranny' with international peace, national self-determination and freedom of the seas.

Churchill had also sought a declaration of war from Roosevelt but this was not forthcoming. The president was even vague about agreeing to the setting up of an international organisation to promote peace in a postwar world. He remembered American responses to the League of Nations. Roosevelt did, however, agree to send aid to the USSR, which had been invaded by Germany in June 1941. In November 1941, Lend-lease was extended to the USSR. While the USA was clearly now giving all aid short of war to the Allies, it did find itself increasingly in direct conflict with Germany in the Atlantic Ocean.

Key term

Atlantic Charter
Joint declaration by Roosevelt and Churchill for a peaceful postwar world.

Key question
How far was the USA involved in the conflict with Germany in the Atlantic Ocean?

The undeclared naval war

The American Navy was fighting an undeclared war against Germany in the Atlantic. In January 1941, US ships had begun to patrol the North Atlantic warning the British convoys against U-boats and on occasion engaging them in battle. In April 1941 USA occupied Greenland and in July Iceland, in order to prevent their bases becoming U-boat harbours. In September 1941 an American destroyer sank the U652, which it had been tracking. The Navy began escorting British convoys as far as Iceland. In October 1941 the American ship *Reuben James* was sunk by a German submarine. Thereafter, Congress allowed merchant ships to be armed.

As discussed, Roosevelt was clearly giving Britain 'all aid short of war' but he still was not prepared to formally go to war with Germany. He had no wish to be a president who took his country into war. He had made great play throughout his career of how much he hated war. Indeed, his horror of the sights when he had visited the trenches of the First World War had stayed with him all his life. He realised that, while the majority of Americans supported Britain, they still wished to keep out of the conflict – although a Gallup Poll in May 1941 showed only 19 per cent of respondents thought he'd gone too far in helping Britain. He felt indeed that the USA would have to be attacked before it went to war but, the conflict in the Atlantic notwithstanding, the Germans were anxious not to give the USA this excuse. It was in fact the Japanese who caused full-scale American involvement with their attack on the American naval base at Pearl Harbor.

5 | Road to Pearl Harbor

The USA and Japan were increasingly at loggerheads in the Pacific. Neither side wanted war. However, their relations were worsening and Japan in particular felt it had little room for manoeuvre.

Japan and US relations had deteriorated since the Japanese invasion of China, which had begun in 1937. Japan declared the open door policy obsolete. Roosevelt retaliated by lending funds to China to buy weapons and by asking US manufacturers not to sell planes to Japan. Japan was dependent on supplies of industrial goods from the USA and if these dried up it realised it needed to find new suppliers by force if necessary.

In July 1940, Congress limited supplies of oil and scrap iron to Japan. After the signing of the **Rome-Berlin-Tokyo axis**, Roosevelt banned the sale of machine tools to Japan.

In spring 1941 Secretary of State Cordell Hull met with the Japanese Ambassador Kichisaburo to resolve differences between the two countries. Hull demanded Japan withdraw from China and promise not to attack Dutch and French colonies in South-east Asia. Japan did not respond because the USA offered them nothing in return.

The European powers were involved in the war in their own continent and could not defend their Asian possessions, for example, in the Dutch East Indies. When France was defeated by Germany, the Japanese marched into the French colonies in Indochina. Japan subsequently announced the setting up of the **Greater East-Asia Co-Prosperity Sphere**. This was effectively a means by which Japan could economically exploit countries under its control.

In July 1941, the USA responded by freezing Japanese assets in the USA and an embargo on oil. Japan was almost wholly dependent on US oil.

As the military increasingly took over in Japan, the new Japanese Ambassador in Washington, Nomura, told Hull that Japan would halt any further expansion if US and Britain cut-off aid to China and lifted the economic blockade on Japan. Japan, indeed, promised to pull out of Indochina if a 'just peace' was made with China. Some historians believe today that Japan, bogged down in its Chinese war, was genuinely seeking a face-saving way out. However, few feel that Japan would actually have honoured any agreement it made with China.

Attack on Pearl Harbor

Few in the USA at the time trusted Japan. The USA did not respond to the Japanese offers and so the Japanese made preparations to attack the US naval base at Pearl Harbor. This objective of this attack was to immobilise the US Navy so it could not stop Japan's expansion into East Asia, to areas such as the Dutch East Indies with their supplies of oil. Japan had not told its European allies of its intentions.

Key question
Why did Japan go to war with the USA?

Key dates

Chinese-Japanese War: 1937

Greater East Asia Co-Prosperity Sphere: 1940

Japanese attack on Pearl Harbor: 1941

Key terms

Rome-Berlin-Tokyo axis
Friendship agreement between Italy, Germany and Japan.

Greater East-Asia Co-Prosperity Sphere
Economic alliance of countries set up by Japan.

In the early morning of Sunday 7 December 1941, when most of the garrison were asleep, the Japanese launched a ferocious attack on Pearl Harbor. Catching the defenders by surprise, their fighter planes and bombers destroyed 180 American aircraft, sank seven battleships and 10 other vessels. Over 2400 American servicemen were killed. However, the American aircraft carriers were out at sea and avoided being attacked. Further, the Japanese had missed the American fuel stores, which if hit would have meant the entire naval base would have had to return to the USA, thus leaving the region entirely undefended against further Japanese aggression.

On 8 December, USA declared war on Japan. On 11 December, honouring his treaty obligations, Hitler declared war on USA as did his ally, Italy.

The USA had shifted from a policy of strict neutrality to full-scale involvement in one of the most terrible wars in history. American involvement saw an end to the New Deal and by 1945 the USA would emerge as by far the most powerful nation on earth.

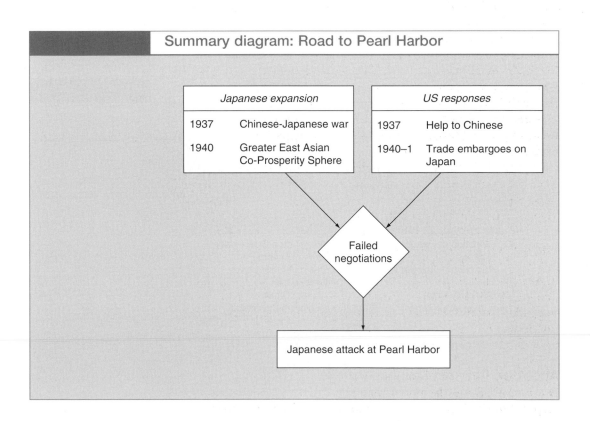

Summary diagram: Road to Pearl Harbor

Japanese expansion	
1937	Chinese-Japanese war
1940	Greater East Asian Co-Prosperity Sphere

US responses	
1937	Help to Chinese
1940–1	Trade embargoes on Japan

Failed negotiations

Japanese attack at Pearl Harbor

6 | US Foreign Policy: An Overview

While the USA sought to avoid getting involved in foreign treaties, it certainly did not wish to see another war and was happy to participate in disarmament conferences, as at the 1921 Washington Naval Conference. Its leaders felt trade was beneficial to international co-operation and generally promoted this idea except when their own economy was under threat as during the Depression. Roosevelt's initial priority was to fight the Depression at home and he disappointed many by his attitude at the 1933 World Economic Conference when he said the USA would not co-operate with other nations. However, his Secretary of State, Cordell Hull, encouraged trade with Latin America as a result of the 'Good Neighbour' policy.

Roosevelt wished to stay out of European entanglements in the 1930s but they were forced upon him as Britain and France declared war on Germany. There was no question that Germany was regarded as a potential enemy and the USA had to give increasing support to Britain to keep her fighting. This not only involved supplying Britain with goods and weapons but actively helping her in her naval war in the Atlantic. However, it was the Japanese attack on Pearl Harbor that finally brought the USA into the conflict.

Key question
How far did US foreign policy change between 1920 and 1941?

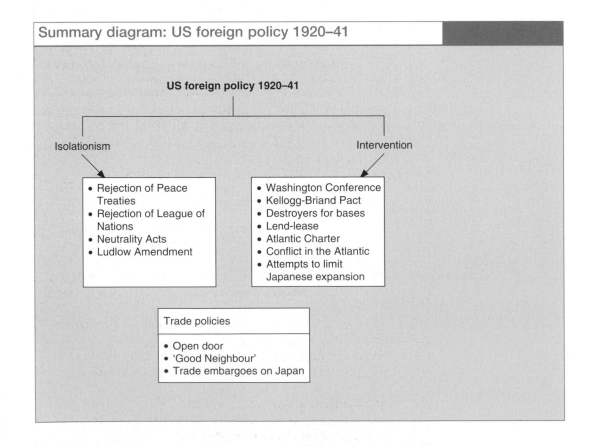

Summary diagram: US foreign policy 1920–41

Study Guide: AS Question

In the style of AQA

Read the following source and then answer the questions that follow.

Adapted from: D. Merrill, Major Problems in American Foreign Relations, *2000.*

German and Japanese aggression in the 1930s presented Americans once again with questions of war and peace, neutrality or alliance.

(a) What is meant by 'neutrality' in relation to American foreign policy in the 1920s and 1930s?   (3 marks)

(b) Explain why President Roosevelt developed the Lend-lease programme   (7 marks)

(c) 'American foreign policy completely changed during the period from 1919 to 1941'. Explain why you agree or disagree with this opinion.   (15 marks)

Source: AQA, June 2003

Exam tips

The cross-references are intended to take you straight to the material that will help you to answer the questions.

(a) This is clearly a short question just requiring a few sentences. However to get to the higher levels you need to link the concept of non-involvement to events such as America's failure to join the League of Nations and/or Neutrality Acts (pages 173–5 and 179–80).

(b) You need to show that you understand a range of factors that led to the adoption of Lend-lease such as the fear that Britain might lose the war without American supplies and Roosevelt's victory in the 1940 election.

(c) Examiners are looking for a balanced judgement supported by well-selected evidence in support. You might consider for example that:

- Before 1941, the USA was officially neutral in political issues but did involve itself in economic and disarmament issues (pages 175–7).
- As the European war developed, Britain appeared to be losing. This prompted Roosevelt to give more and more help (pages 181–3).
- USA became fully committed to the war after the bombing of Pearl Harbor (pages 184–5).
- The USA maintained its interests in Latin and South America throughout the period, for example, through its 'Good Neighbour' policies (page 177).
- Your conclusion might consider the factors that appear to support and those which appear disagree with the quotation before coming to a balanced judgement.

Study Guide: Advanced Level Question

In the style of OCR

Discuss the extent to which US foreign policy altered during the period 1921–41.   (45 marks)

Source: OCR, June 2003

Exam tips

The cross-references are intended to take you straight to the material that will help you to answer the question.

Examiners are looking for the breadth and quality of your discussion. You need to cover a wide range of issues and focus on debate in terms of the question.

- How far was US policy consistent and how far did it change during the period under discussion. You could consider for example how far isolationist policies were followed in the 1920s (pages 173–6).
- Remember that isolationist policies did not mean total non-involvement in the affairs of other countries – US involvement in disarmament and trade was significant. If you give the impression that the USA moved from complete non-involvement in foreign affairs to full-scale involvement in war, your answer will be over-simplistic.
- How far was Roosevelt interventionalist? (pages 176–84). It could be that Roosevelt simply tried to continue the policy of avoiding foreign entanglements until it was no longer possible to do so, after the summer of 1940 when Britain increasingly needed US help to continue fighting. Lend-lease, for example, is hardly the act of a neutral power.

9 The New Deal in Retrospect

KEY POINTS

This chapter examines the New Deal from the perspective of distance. It considers:

- How effective the New Deal was in terms of its own aims of providing relief, recovery and reform
- What the New Deal achieved in terms of race and gender
- The impact of the Second World War
- The political legacy of the New Deal
- How historians have assessed what the New Deal achieved
- The impact the New Deal had on changing the USA

Key dates

1939   Beginnings of research in the USA into nuclear weapons
1942   Japanese bombing raids on USA
        Internment of Japanese-Americans living in the West Coast area
        Executive Order 8802
1943   Smith-Connally War Labor Disputes Act
        Race riots in Detroit
1944   Supreme Court decision forbidding the internment of loyal Japanese-Americans
        Roosevelt began his fourth term of office
1945   Death of Roosevelt
        End of the Second World War

1 | Introduction

Key question
How have economic statistics of the New Deal been interpreted?

According to Ed Johnson, the Democratic Governor of Colorado during the 1930s, the New Deal was 'the worst fraud ever perpetrated on the American people'. While this view may be extreme, it can be argued that on the surface at least, the actual achievements of the New Deal do seem rather slender. In 1933, 18 million Americans were unemployed and in 1939, nine million were still out of work. The national total of personal income stood at $86 billion in 1929 and only $73 billion in 1939. This was despite a population increase of nine million during the course of the decade. The government seemed reconciled to a permanent unemployment figure of at least five million.

One in five Americans required some sort of relief in 1939. Table 9.1 shows the prices indices. Wages averaged $25.03 per week in 1929 and $23.86 10 years later.

On the surface, these figures are not impressive. However, the significance of statistics can often be assessed in different ways. One could argue, for example, that the New Deal decreased unemployment by 50 per cent; the New Deal saw farm incomes rise by the same amount; and that four out of five Americans did not require relief by 1939. Furthermore, because prices fell more than wages, people in work could afford to buy more as a result of the New Deal.

Clearly any evaluation of the New Deal needs to go beyond statistics. Nor should one forget the enormity of the problems facing Roosevelt in 1933. No incoming president faced greater economic difficulties; and these were compounded by a desperate loss of confidence among both producers and consumers.

Table 9.1: Price indices

Year	Index
1926	100.0
1929	95.3
1933	65.9
1937	86.3
1939	77.1

2 | Relief, Recovery and Reform

Key question
How successful was the New Deal?

The differing aims of relief, recovery and reform offer a convenient way of assessing of the New Deal. However, they should not be seen as strictly separate. Many measures overlapped. The WPA, for example, offered both relief to the unemployed and a boost to economic recovery through public works schemes. No measure was started solely to fit into any one category. New Deal legislation, it should be remembered, came about largely in response to crises. Little thought went into the niceties of where in any blueprint it might fit. However, as these goals of relief, recovery and reform were mentioned by Roosevelt himself as being the aims of the New Deal, it seems appropriate to use them for purposes of evaluation.

Relief

Key question
How effective was the New Deal in bringing about measures of relief?

One of the greatest achievements of the New Deal was in changing the role of federal government. This was particularly true of help for the less fortunate members of society. Relief agencies such as FERA and the WPA were set up to offer hope to millions. There were new departures in governmental responsibilities. The Social Security Act was not strictly a relief measure as it was financed through contributions paid by recipients. However, it did set up a national system of old-age pensions and unemployment benefit for the first time.

It is true that the amounts spent were inadequate for the needs of a population suffering from a prolonged depression. Nevertheless, important precedents were set by this legislation. It could be built on in the future. Never before had the federal government become involved in granting direct relief or benefits. Roosevelt initially saw relief agencies as only temporary expedients until economic recovery was achieved. However, in offering direct relief he significantly increased the role of federal government.

This led in turn to a greater role for state and local governments as partners – however unwillingly at first – in many of the programmes.

The effects of the expansion of Welfare provision

The growth in expenditure on welfare tells its own story. Before 1930 states spent virtually nothing on relief measures. In 1930 together they spent $9 million; by 1940 this figure had risen to $479 million. A further $480 million was spent on unemployment benefit. Before this they had spent nothing. Millions of people began to see the federal government as their saviour. It was through social reform that it first directly spoke to them. It was through the provision of relief and benefits that many people first became aware of a president not as a distant figure who meant little to the likes of them but as someone who was interested in them and who cared about them.

More people took part in presidential elections in the 1930s than had done so previously. In 1920 and 1924 only 49 per cent of the electorate bothered to vote in the presidential elections; in 1928 and 1932 the figure rose to 57 per cent, and by 1936 and 1940 it was 62 per cent The increase was partly due to the Depression that had destroyed much of what people had previously believed in, and partly through the programmes of the New Deal which helped them. Because of the provision of relief and benefits, more and more people felt they had a stake in their country. It made them feel they belonged.

Key question
How successful was the New Deal in helping the USA recover from the Depression?

Table 9.2: Budget deficit

Year	Deficit
1936	$4.4 billion
1937	$2.7 billion
1938	$1.2 billion

Recovery

The New Deal was less successful in achieving economic recovery. This was partly because many of its measures were contradictory. Roosevelt believed in a balanced budget. He was therefore reluctant to spend excessively on federal projects. He failed to see that massive government expenditure might be necessary to offset the reduction in spending in the private sector.

The two last figures shown in Table 9.2 were lower than the $2.8 billion deficit Hoover had run up in 1932 and over which Roosevelt had criticised him in the 1932 presidential election.

Roosevelt was dubious about the effectiveness of public works programmes. The British economist J.M. Keynes came out of a meeting with him in 1934 very disappointed, saying he doubted the president had really understood what he was saying. When Roosevelt reversed earlier policy in the wake of the 1937 recession and offered $3.8 billion for public spending, it was not enough to make much of a difference.

The New Deal was designed to save the capitalist system in the USA. Roosevelt hoped his measures would restore capitalist confidence and expansion. We have already seen how many of his measures favoured big business. For example, the NRA codes were largely drawn up by the representatives of big business.

In the later years of the New Deal, Roosevelt was annoyed with big business because of its ingratitude for all the New Deal had done for it. However, he never doubted that the answer to economic problems lay largely in the hands of large corporations. Again, it was his faith in capitalism and the **market structure** that led him to maintain fiscal conservatism and not adopt a plan of permanent massive state spending. It is interesting to note that the countries that did so, notably Sweden and Germany – albeit in the case of the latter on military expansion – overcame the Depression first. In contrast, by 1939, the USA was the slowest of the major countries to recover from depression.

Market structure
How the capitalist system worked through supply and demand.

Key term

Reform

The New Deal was, when viewed as a whole, a programme of reform. The reforms were economic, political and social.

Key question
How successful was the New Deal in changing the USA?

Economic reforms

Economic reforms were mainly intended to rescue the capitalist system from its worst excesses and to provide a more rational framework in which it could operate. For example, the banking system was reformed and made more efficient, particularly through the centralisation of banking in 1935. The evils of Wall Street and the holding companies were exposed and reformed. Roosevelt allowed trade unions to take their place in labour relations and reluctantly recognised that federal government had a role in settling industrial disputes. In this sense the triangular partnership in labour relations between employers, employees and government was created.

Political reforms

Reluctantly, Roosevelt came to realise that the expansion of government he had created was to be permanent. He set up the Executive Office of the President to help manage this expansion and ensure that the federal bureaucracy could cope with the demands being made upon it both at that time and in the future. His attempted reform of the Supreme Court failed but the Court nevertheless became more sympathetic to New Deal legislation, recognising the political realities of the later 1930s. The New Deal also saw an expansion in the functions of state and local government. The system again became more modern and able to address the needs of citizens in the twentieth century.

Social reforms

People increasingly expected that the government would take responsibility for their problems. The Social Security Act and the relief and job creation agencies expanded the role of government considerably.

However, having said this, it is important to repeat that the New Deal should not be judged by targets it did not set itself. It did not intend to change the capitalist structure. Some commentators criticised it as a lost opportunity to bring in a **socialist economic system** with greater equality of wealth and fully centralised planning. They wanted the New Deal to be about these things. Unfortunately for them, it was not.

Socialist economic system
An economy run by the state where all large-scale enterprises are managed by the government.

Key term

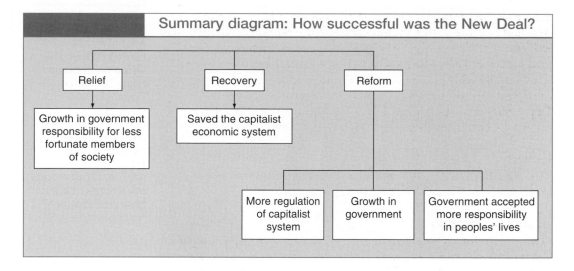

Summary diagram: How successful was the New Deal?

Relief → Growth in government responsibility for less fortunate members of society

Recovery → Saved the capitalist economic system

Reform

More regulation of capitalist system

Growth in government

Government accepted more responsibility in peoples' lives

3 | Race and Gender

We have already seen that the New Deal did more for Native Americans than past administrations, but critics have argued that it did little for African-Americans and women.

African-Americans

Key question
What did the New Deal achieve for African-Americans?

Roosevelt needed the vote of Southern Democrats who were often racist. A realist, he said, 'I did not choose the tools with which I must work'. Certainly, early in the New Deal, Southern politicians were often his most loyal supporters. Not surprisingly, therefore, the New Deal saw no civil rights legislation. Many measures – the AAA for instance – worked against African-Americans.

African-Americans suffered particularly badly in the Depression, often being the last to be taken on and the first to be fired. Many poorly paid, menial jobs previously reserved for them were now taken by whites. NRA codes allowed for African-Americans to be paid less than whites for doing the same jobs. Some African-Americans called the NRA the 'Negro-run-around' because it was so unfair to them. The CCC was run by a Southern racist who did little to encourage African-Americans to join: those who did faced strict segregation. Anti-lynching bills were introduced into Congress in 1934 and 1937, but Roosevelt did nothing to support either and both were eventually defeated.

Changing voting behaviour of African-Americans

Despite these negative points, one of the most important political features of the New Deal years was the shift in the voting behaviour of African-Americans in the North who were able to vote (less than 5 per cent of African-Americans in the South could vote). Traditionally African-Americans voted Republican because this was the party that had fought the Civil War in part to end slavery. In 1932, of 15 African-American **wards** in nine major cities, Roosevelt won only four; in 1936, he won nine, and by 1940, all 15. In some African-American areas of cities, notably

Key term

Wards
Electoral districts in the USA.

African-American sharecroppers being evicted from their home in 1939. This was a photograph taken by Arthur Rothstein who created a photographic survey of the nation paid for by the Farm Security Administration. How might this photograph reflect upon what the New Deal did for African-Americans?

Harlem in New York, Roosevelt won 85 per cent of the vote. A Gallop Poll in 1936 showed that nationally 76 per cent of African-Americans intended to vote for Roosevelt. Many African-Americans saw him as much a saviour as poor whites did. His portrait hung in many African-American homes.

In 1936 there were 30 African-American delegates to the Democratic Convention and much to the disgust of Southerners the first African-American congressman, Arthur Mitchell, delivered the opening speech. We need to look beyond the surface of the New Deal to explain this significant shift of allegiance.

Support from Roosevelt's government

Many New Deal administrators, notably Harry Hopkins and Harold Ickes, showed concern for African-Americans and tried to make sure they were included in relief programmes. Eleanor Roosevelt was determined to do all she could to stop racism. She was able to ensure prominent African-Americans met the president to explain the racial problems they faced and she herself made a public statement in 1938 when she sat in the 'coloured' section at the Conference of Human Welfare in Birmingham, Alabama. When the African-American singer Marion Anderson was refused permission to sing before an integrated audience at Constitution Hall in Washington in 1939, Harold Ickes arranged for her to give a concert in front of 75,000 people, including Mrs Roosevelt, at the Lincoln Memorial. These gestures were significant in giving official respectability to the notion that racism was wrong and helped African-American leaders gain confidence in their own struggles. As we will see, when A. Phillip Randolph, head of the African-American trade union, Brotherhood of Sleeping Car Porters, threatened a march on Washington in 1941 to protest against racism in defence factories, Roosevelt set up a Fair Employment Practices Committee to stop such behaviour.

Moreover, the president did employ more African-Americans in government, notably, as we saw on page 148, Mary McLeod Bethune at the NYA. However, while there were more African-Americans in government office, it seems an exaggeration to speak as some did of an 'African-American' cabinet' addressing race issues. The Civil Service tripled the number of African-Americans in its employment between 1932 and 1941 to 150,000. There was also some **positive discrimination**, notably again in the NYA where African-American officials were usually appointed in areas where African-Americans predominated.

It will be seen that if there were few official measures specifically to benefit African-Americans, there were important gestures of support. There were more African-Americans with the ear, if not of the president, then of important figures close to him, and millions of African-Americans benefited from relief measures that, even if still favouring whites, gave them more help than they had ever previously received.

Key term

Positive discrimination Where members of one group are favoured over those of others.

Key question What did the New Deal achieve for women?

Women

Women held more important posts in government during the New Deal era than at any time before or after until the 1990s. Mrs Roosevelt was one of the most politically active first ladies; as Secretary of Labor, Frances Perkins was only one of many women holding government office; and Ruth Bryan Owen became the first female ambassador (to Denmark). Many prominent women had come together through expertise in social work, which was, of course, an asset for designing many New Deal measures. Unfortunately, when government priorities changed with the onset of war, much of their influence was lost.

The New Deal, in fact, did little for women. Unlike African-Americans, they did not tend to vote in as a group. As a result politicians did not set out particularly to win their support. Much New Deal legislation worked against them. In 1933, for example, the Economy Act forbade members of the same family from working for federal government and so many wives lost their jobs. A total of 75 per cent of those losing their jobs through this measure were women. We have seen on page 89 that many measures to curb the Depression took jobs away particularly from married women.

The New Deal did nothing to reverse this process. NRA codes allowed for unequal wages and some agencies such as the CCC barred women entirely. Women suffered particularly in the professions where, even by 1940, about 90 per cent of jobs were still filled by men. There was a strong emphasis that in the job market, men should be the principal wage earners with women's wages only supplementing this. Where women did find employment – which many had to do to balance the family budget – it tended often to be in low-status, poorly paid jobs. On average during the 1930s, at $525 per annum, women earned half the average wage of men.

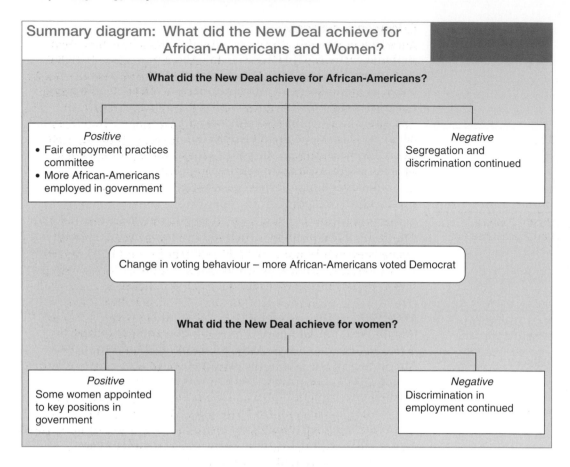

Summary diagram: What did the New Deal achieve for African-Americans and Women?

What did the New Deal achieve for African-Americans?

Positive
• Fair empoyment practices committee
• More African-Americans employed in government

Negative
Segregation and discrimination continued

Change in voting behaviour – more African-Americans voted Democrat

What did the New Deal achieve for women?

Positive
Some women appointed to key positions in government

Negative
Discrimination in employment continued

4 | Impact of the Second World War on the USA

Despite fears of long-distance Nazi superbombers (see page 182), there were only two bombing raids on the USA during the war. Both came in September 1942 when, on two separate occasions, a single Japanese aircraft carrying two bombs was launched from submarines. Their objective was to ignite forest fires and divert essential war resources to fire fighting. Neither mission succeeded. They tended to show how remote the USA itself was from the conflict and how able it was, therefore, to produce the materials necessary for Allied victory.

There is no doubt that involvement in the Second World War rather than the New Deal brought prosperity back to the USA. In this section we will consider the USA during the war in terms of economic and social developments, both of which were to have far-reaching consequences for the subsequent history of the USA. Roosevelt, however, did not live to see these fruits. Having won a fourth term of office in the 1944 presidential election, he died in April 1945. This was one month before the war ended in Europe and four before the Japanese surrendered following the bombing of Hiroshima and Nagasaki with nuclear weapons, research into which had been begun by Roosevelt in 1939.

Key question
What impact did the Second World War have on the US economy and society?

Economic effects

American involvement in war production made the New Deal irrelevant. Between 1941 and 1945, the USA produced 86,000 tanks, 296,000 aircraft and 15,00,000 rifles. Farm income grew by 250%. Unemployment effectively ceased by 1942. In 1944 alone, 6.5 million women joined the labour force. The number of African-Americans working for federal government rose from 50,000 in 1939 to 200,000 by 1944. In the years between 1940 and 1944, five million African-Americans moved to the cities where one million found jobs in defence plants. Gross national product (GNP), meanwhile, rose from $91.3 billion in 1939 to $166.6 billion by 1945.

War production led to huge rises in labour union membership. The National War Labor Board restricted wage rises, however, saying they should not exceed 15 per cent beyond the January 1941 rates, and arbitrated in industrial disputes. There were severe strikes, for example, in the mining industry in early 1943, after which Congress passed the Smith-Connally War Labor Disputes Act. This allowed the president to take over any plant threatened by strike action. Although the right to industrial action became restricted, wages generally rose, and working conditions improved with the introduction of paid holidays and health insurance schemes.

Roosevelt hoped to pay for much of the war production by increased taxes. The highest earners paid 94% tax. This gave a sense of greater equality. The poor did grow more wealthy during the war years and the rich received a smaller proportion of national income as Table 9.3 shows.

Key date

Smith-Connally War Labor Disputes Act: 1943

Table 9.3: Percentage of national income taken by the richest one per cent of the population

Year	% of national income taken by richest 1% of the population
1939	13.4
1944	11.5
1945	6.7

However, while the economy grew significantly during the war years, the most dramatic changes occurred in the lives of ordinary Americans.

Social effects
Movement of people

In addition to the 15 million servicemen and women who were called up, by the end of the war, one in eight civilians had moved to find war work, generally from the south to the north and from east to west. The population of California, where there were large numbers of defence plants, rose by 72 per cent during the war years.

Key question
How did involvement in the war affect the lives of ordinary Americans?

Treatment of Japanese-Americans

Towards the end of 1941, as US–Japanese relations worsened, 2000 Japanese labelled subversives had been rounded up (along with 14,000 Germans and Italians), although there was no official desire for internment. In fact, General John L. Dewitt, Chief of the Army West Coast Command, dismissed any such talk as 'damned nonsense'. However, increasing fears of a Japanese attack on the West Coast led to calls for internment even by respected journalises such as Walter Lippmann. Dewitt, responsible for West Coast security, gave in to this pressure, saying it was impossible to distinguish between loyal and traitorous Japanese and therefore all should be locked up.

Between February and March 1942, 15,000 Japanese-Americans, many of whom had relations fighting in the American forces, voluntarily left Dewitt's area of command. However, other areas of the USA refused to accept them The Attorney-General of Idaho, for example, said his state was for whites only. Dewitt decided on compulsory relocation; 10 'relocation centres' were set up through out the West, where 100,000 Japanese-American were forcibly sent. They had to leave their property unprotected. Much looting went on in their absence. One source estimated the community suffered losses worth $400 million.

The relocation centres, meanwhile, were akin to concentration camps with armed guards and barrack-type accommodation. Riots in the camp at Manzanar left two inmates dead. One of the guards said the only thing that stopped him machine gunning them was what the Japanese might do the American POWs in retaliation.

By 1944, as fear of Japanese attack receded, the internees began to return home. In December 1944, the Supreme Court forbade the internment of loyal Japanese-Americans. Nevertheless, neither their fellow Japanese-American citizens who lived outside Dewitt's command nor German- or Italian-Americans had been interned in this way, and so ill-feeling among many of those involved remained for some time.

African-Americans

African-Americans demanded better treatment during the war. As knowledge of the **Holocaust** in Europe grew, many Americans began to examine their own racial attitudes. However, much prejudice remained and, as we have seen (page 194), African-American leaders called for a march on Washington in 1941 to air their grievances. This worried Roosevelt who was fully aware that the Nazis were accusing the USA of hypocrisy by condemning their attitudes to Jews while openly denying civil rights to African-Americans.

Roosevelt did what he could. He issued Executive Order 8802 to ban discrimination in defence plants and set up the Fair Employment Practices Committee to ensure it was carried out. However, it is impossible to legislate away racist attitudes. There were a series of race riots, culminating in three days' violence in Detroit in 1943 which saw 25 African-Americans and nine whites killed. It was left to the 1960s and 1970s to see real progress in race relations in the USA.

Holocaust
Attempted extermination of Jews and other groups by the Nazis.

Key term

Race riot in Detroit: 1943

Key date

'Rosie the Riveter'. What impression is the government trying to create with this poster?

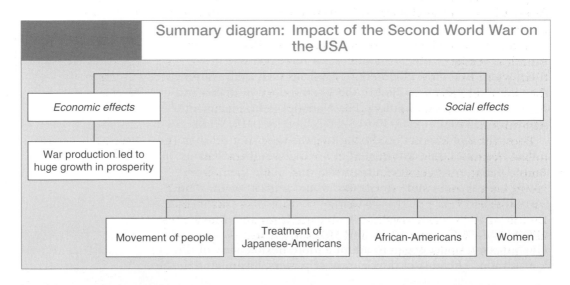

Summary diagram: Impact of the Second World War on the USA

Economic effects

Social effects

War production led to huge growth in prosperity

Movement of people

Treatment of Japanese-Americans

African-Americans

Women

Women

While women found plentiful employment they also found
continuing prejudice and lower pay than their male workmates.
However, because they were not subject to conscription into the
armed forces employers liked them. Despite racial and gender
prejudice African-American women found work in defence plants
because the demand for labour was so acute.

5 | Political Legacy of the New Deal

The political legacy of the New Deal was profound. While it may
not have effected a social, political or economic revolution, many
attitudes in the USA were fundamentally altered as a result of it.

Political realignments

The New Deal created the coalition of African-Americans, urban
blue-collar workers, unions, Southern conservatives and Eastern
liberals that survived largely intact in the Democratic Party. The
Democratic Party became recognised as the party of social reform;
its agenda was the one that contained the programmes to help
the have-nots in society. Inaccurately or otherwise, the
Republicans came increasingly to be seen as the Party of wealth
and big business, the Party that did little for the common man.
These attitudes survive largely today.

> **Key question**
> How did the New
> Deal affect the way
> different groups
> voted?

Changes in the political system

The New Deal saw the growth of the Executive over other
branches of government such as the legislature and Judiciary.
Increasingly, legislation was initiated by the Executive, and state
governments were involved in joint programmes that not only
increased their own activities but also made them more
dependent on federal government for funding and action.
Americans began to look to federal government rather than the
states for action to meet problems.

> **Key question**
> What changes came
> about in the political
> system as a result of
> the New Deal?

However, it was the war years that saw the greatest growth in
American government. Between 1940 and 1945, the federal
government spent double what it had in the preceding 150 years.
The New Deal saw federal government spending grow by 60%
and the war years by 300%. There was a huge increase in
bureaucracy in the development of agencies such as the Supply
Priorities and Allocation Board, the War Production Board and
the Office of War Mobilisation. The National Debt, meanwhile,
rose from $43 billion in 1940 to $296 billion by 1946. While
many of the agencies set up during the war were shut down at the
end of hostilities they had helped to break down the resistance of
many Americans to a large bureaucracy and made them more
willing to accept the new offices that would replace them in the
postwar world.

Supreme Court

The Supreme Court began to adopt a more flexible view of the
constitution. The idea of the division of powers, formulated in the

constitution, began to break down in order to give the Executive more freedom to address what it felt were the needs of the country. This possibly was inevitable and may even have happened without the Depression. President Harding had certainly seen the need to expand the role of federal government and Hoover had believed the government should take a major role for good in the life of the nation.

State and local governments

This development was not just limited to federal government. State and local expenditure had increased from $1 billion in 1902 to $10 billion by 1938. No country could progress successfully in the twentieth century with a nineteenth-century governmental system. In this sense, the Depression and New Deal hastened a process already underway, although as we have seen above it was the war years that really saw an acceleration.

However, there is an alternative argument that together the Depression and New Deal years may actually have stunted the growth of government. Some historians, notably Arthur Schlesinger, Jr writing in the 1950s, have argued that reforms in American government usually take place in times of prosperity. They point to the relative prosperity of the Progressive Era in the first decades of the twentieth century as an example. On the basis of this argument, there would have been pressure for reform in the 1930s if the prosperity had continued. In this sense the Depression may have acted as a break on reform. The New Deal, which was in effect an operation to preserve the existing structure, may have been substituted by something far more radical.

Nevertheless, it is difficult to see how the war ties in with this theory, where the growth of government was a response to national emergency rather than prosperity.

Support for the existing political structure

Key question
How did the New Deal strengthen the existing political structure in the USA?

Perhaps the most important legacy of the New Deal was that it restored hope and confidence in the capitalist and democratic systems of the USA. This was in a large amount due to the personal charisma of Roosevelt himself and the trust people were prepared to bestow on him. However, we have seen that there was comparatively little support for extremist parties even at the height of the Depression. The vast majority of Americans wanted the existing system to provide the solutions to the Depression.

Did the New Deal avert revolution in the USA?

Some historians have argued that the New Deal averted revolution in the USA. This is one of the fascinating 'what ifs?' in history. We shall never know, had Roosevelt not been there in 1932, what a different president may have attempted or how frustrated Americans may have become. We have seen that the ideas behind many of the New Deal measures pre-dated Roosevelt's presidency and that others were initiated in Congress. One historian wrote that Roosevelt 'took his place at the head of the procession only when it was clear where the procession was going'. Whether this was true or not, there can be little doubt that the New Deal was designed to preserve the established structure. Some historians have argued that it was effectively a holding operation until recovery was effected by the onset of war.

Again, we can say with hindsight that this is undoubtedly true. Unfortunately, people at the time do not possess hindsight. It would be absurd to suggest that Roosevelt consciously adopted the New Deal as a holding operation until war came. No one could accurately foresee war until comparatively late in the 1930s. Even then there was a considerable body of opinion that felt the USA should have nothing to do with the conflict, including refusing to sell the belligerents any weapons.

The New Deal needs to stand on its own merits. In this context we have seen that it appeared to have lost direction by 1939, and that Roosevelt's administration was increasingly neutralised by a hostile Congress. Had Roosevelt decided not to stand again in 1940, and had not foreign affairs begun to dominate, the Republican candidate Wendell Willkie may have returned the USA to the *laissez-faire* attitudes of the 1920s. After all, in an election dominated by foreign issues, Willkie did oppose the growing power of the state. However, by this time economic recovery was on its way due to the European war and economic issues did not feature heavily in the campaigns. So we are left with another 'what if?' question that is basically unanswerable.

The New Deal came to the salvation of capitalism and in so doing enhanced the power of the state in a way unprecedented in American history. It did not do enough to address the severity of the problems facing the USA, but there is no doubt that it broke away from existing norms particularly through direct relief and institutional reform. It set important precedents for the future. Perhaps the final verdict may go to the editors of the *Economist* magazine: 'Mr Roosevelt may have given the wrong answers to many of his problems. But he is at least the first president of modern America who has asked the right questions'.

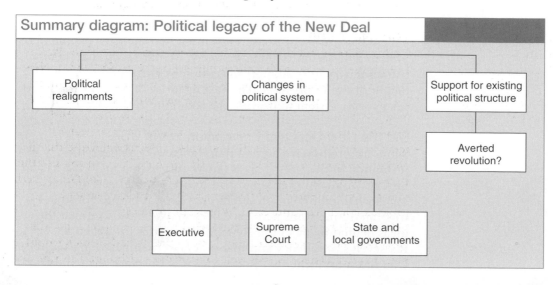

Summary diagram: Political legacy of the New Deal

Key question
How have historians assessed the New Deal?

6 | The Key Debate

There has been heated debate among historians as to what the New Deal achieved. We will in this section analyse some the key elements of these debates.

What did the New Deal Do?

In the years following the New Deal, historians and commentators were generally supportive of it. People involved in the process knew they were making history. Studs Terkel, a broadcaster and oral historian, interviewed various participants in the 1960s. Gardener C. Means, a New Deal employee, felt that it marked a turning point in American government, with the end of nineteenth-century ideas of a limited government role. Raymond Moley agreed that it led to a growth in government power but felt the opportunities for radical change were lost during the second New Deal. Some argued that the enhanced role of the government in responsibility for people's welfare marked the growing maturity of the nation – bringing about what American historian Carl Degler called, 'a third American Revolution'. He meant by this the huge growth in government and break with *laissez-faire*. William Leuchtenburg, a historian of the New Deal, wrote that 'it is hard to think of another period in the whole history of the republic that was so fruitful or a crisis that was met with such imagination'.

Schlesinger and Leuchtenburg

Arthur M. Schlesinger Jr and William Leuchtenburg, writing in the late 1950s and early 1960s, both felt that the New Deal showed a compassionate response to crisis. Leuchtenburg argued that the New Deal created a more just society by recognising previously unrecognised groups such as organised labour. However, it only partially addressed these issues; groups such as slum dwellers, sharecroppers and African-Americans still felt excluded in a society that was still racially segregated.

The 'New Left'

Key term

New Left
School of historians critical of the New Deal for not adopting more radical changes.

In the 1960s historians of the '**New Left**' such as H. Zinn, Paul Conkin and Barton J. Bernstein became more critical of the New Deal. They tended to see the New Deal as a wasted opportunity for radical change. It was felt that the piecemeal solutions of the New Deal enabled capitalism to prevail. In the words of Paul Conkin, 'the story of the New Deal is a sad story, the ever recurring story of what might have been'. Bernstein wrote that it 'failed to solve the problem of the depression, it failed to raise the impoverished and it failed to redistribute income'. Conkin argued that the New Deal should have improved social justice and produced a more contented, fulfilled population.

It was felt by historians of the New Left, for example, that the New Deal never consulted people as to their needs, which would have involved them in the political process – although this was not strictly true, for example where ordinary people were involved in running the Tennessee Valley Authority.

More recent views

In addressing the points raised by the New Left, as we have seen in this chapter, the New Deal was not intended to effect radical change. Historians of this school have therefore tended to criticise it for something it was not rather than to examine it on its own merits. In the 1970s, historians and economists, notably Milton Friedman whose monetarist theories were discussed on page 95 often attacked the New Deal for the opposite reasons: that it had set the USA on the wrong course. Government spending, they argued, fuelled inflation; Governments taking responsibility for people's livelihood fostered **welfare dependency** and stifled entrepreneurial creativity. These historians favoured the working of the free market; they saw the election of President Reagan in 1980 as a turning-point, reversing the movement begun by the New Deal for governments to take responsibility for people's lives.

> **Welfare dependency** Where people come to rely on state benefits.
>
> *Key term*

Leuchtenburg has more recently argued that since the writings of the New Left, it has generally been assumed that the New Deal failed. Historians tended to debate whether it failed because of the deficiencies of Roosevelt or the powerful conservative forces that opposed radical change. Leuchtenburg, on the other hand, feels that the New Deal achieved a lot, not least the dramatic growth in federal government. Ordinary citizens looked increasingly to it to solve many of their problems where previously they had looked to it to solve none of them. The legacy of this increased role was, moreover, permanent. British historian D.K. Adams showed that President Kennedy's speech outlining his New Frontier programme in 1961 was a paraphrase of a 1935 one by Roosevelt.

David Kennedy goes on to acknowledge there was much the New Deal did not do, for example, bring economic recovery, redistribute National Income or end capitalism. However, it achieved much, notably the reform of the economy so that the benefits of a capitalist system could be more evenly distributed. Methods of achieving this included:

- the recognition of organised labour
- greater regulation of abuses in the economic system
- greater financial security through, for example, the introduction of old-age pensions.

It is important to consider not what the New Deal failed to do but what it did achieve in a political system designed originally to prevent the growth of federal government. In so doing the New Deal mended the failings of capitalism through the existing system and therefore possibly averted a far more radical programme.

Some key books and essays in the debate
Barton J. Bernstein, The New Deal: The Conservative Achievement of Liberal Reforms, in *Towards a New Past: Dissenting Essays in American History* (Pantheon, 1967).
Paul Conkin, *The New Deal* (Routledge and Kegan Paul, 1967).
Carl Degler, The Third American Revolution, in *Out of Our Past* (Harper and Row, 1957).
Milton Friedman, *Free to Choose: A Personal Statement* (Harcourt-Brace-Jovanovitch, 1980).
David Kennedy, *Freedom From Fear* (Oxford University Press, 1999).
William E. Leuchtenburg, *Roosevelt and the New Deal* (Harper and Row, 1963).
William E. Leuchtenburg, *The FDR Years: On Roosevelt and his Legacy* (Columbia University Press, 1995).
Arthur M. Schlesinger, *The Age of Roosevelt* (3 volumes, Houghton Miflin 1956, 1958, 1960).
Studs Terkel, *Hard Times* (Penguin, 1970).
Howard Zinn (ed.), *New Deal Thought* (Bobbs-Merrill, 1966).

7 | Conclusion

Key question
What conclusions can be drawn about the impact of the New Deal?

We have seen that the first decades of the twentieth century had seen an unprecedented growth in government (see pages 5–6). Of the three Republican presidents of the 1920s, only Coolidge sought to reverse this trend. Therefore, the New Deal continued a process already underway, although into avenues that would have horrified earlier presidents. There is a story that former President Hoover refused to apply for a social security card. Although he objected to being 'numberfied', the agency sent him one anyway as they did to everyone. The idea that everyone in the country could be affected by any one federal government domestic measure would have been unthinkable in 1920.

Industrial relations had moved into the modern era with more of a partnership between government, employers and unions. The government also recognised the importance of big business. While small self-reliant businessmen may have been heroes in the American dream, as we have seen, American capitalism developed in reality through the power of big business. Although it may not always have been realised at the time, it was largely the interests of big business that the economic measures of the New Deal benefited. The gains of this were clear during the war, when businesses were relatively easily able to adapt to large-scale armaments production.

The people and the states increasingly looked to the government for help with their problems. The USA was becoming urbanised to a noticeable degree, and legislation such as the 1937 National Housing Act recognised this. The tensions we examined in Chapter 2, which resulted particularly from the rural–urban divide, had not gone away and have continued to resurface in American history. Many of Roosevelt's supporters in the South later turned against him because they felt legislation was increasingly favouring northern cities to the detriment of rural areas.

However, even in the countryside things had changed. Agencies such as the TVA and REA had helped rural areas move into a modern era with their provision of facilities such as electrical power. Farmers were now expecting loans and subsidies from the government through the AAA. The tentacles of government, it seemed, were everywhere. The USA had moved from a land of self-reliant individualism with very little government interference to one where the government increasingly took responsibility for people's lives and welfare. The Depression had shown that the economy was not self-righting and that the American Dream was largely impossible to realise unaided, however much initiative and ability to work hard one might possess. In the end, the Depression had eroded much of the American mythology we considered in Chapter 1, particularly the notion of self-reliance. It became necessary in the 1930s to address a harsh reality and the significance of the New Deal was that it did precisely this.

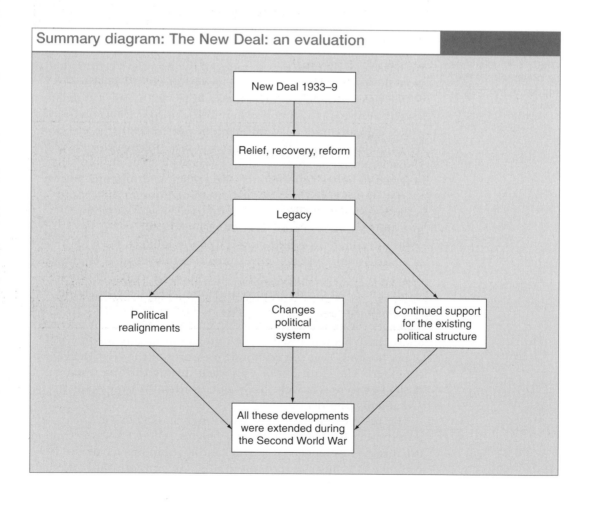

Summary diagram: The New Deal: an evaluation

New Deal 1933–9

Relief, recovery, reform

Legacy

Political realignments

Changes political system

Continued support for the existing political structure

All these developments were extended during the Second World War

Study Guide: AS Questions

In the style of Edexcel

How far did the New Deal improve the lives of the poor and disadvantaged within the United States in the years 1933–1945?

(36 marks)

Source: Edexcel, May 2003

Exam tips

The cross-references are intended to take you straight to the material that will help you answer the question.

Your answer needs look at a wide range of areas and offers a balanced analysis in terms of success and failure. You might consider areas such as

- NRA and WPA (pages 125–8 and 148–9)
- labour relations and the Wagner Act (page 151) and social security (pages 152–4)
- the prosperity of the war years (page197).

In the style of AQA

Explain the most important reasons why prosperity returned to the USA during the years 1939–45.

Study tips

You need to consider a wide range of issues, for example:

- the wartime economy and war production
- wider employment opportunities, for example for African-Americans and women
- improved wages and working conditions for many Americans.

Better answers may consider a hierarchy of factors and show how they were interconnected. You could also show how far the New Deal had been successful and how far prosperity was returning to the USA as a result of the New Deal before the economy was stimulated by war production.

Study Guide: Advanced Level Questions

In the style of OCR
Study Passages A–D and answer the questions that follow.

Passage A

From: a speech by Herbert Hoover, 1936. A former Republican president criticises the New Deal in a speech delivered during the 1936 presidential election campaign.

Through four years of experience, this New Deal attack upon free institutions has emerged as the most important issue in America. All the men who are seeking mastery in the world are using the same weapons. Their philosophy is founded on the coercion and compulsory organisation of men. Their ideas are not new. Most of them had been urged on me. I rejected the notion of 'economic planning' to regiment and coerce the farmer. That was born of a Roman despot 1,400 years ago and grew into the AAA. I refused national plans to put the business of government in competition with its citizens. That was born of Karl Marx. I vetoed the idea of recovery through stupendous spending to rime the pump. That was born of a British professor [Keynes].

Passage B

From: H. Zinn, New Deal Thought, *1966. A New Left historian suggests that the New Deal did not achieve fundamental change.*

When the reform energies of the New Deal began to wane around 1939 and the depression was over, the nation was back to its normal state: a permanent army of unemployed and twenty or thirty million poverty-stricken people effectively blocked from public view by a high, prosperous and fervently consuming middle class.

What the New Deal did was to refurbish middle-class America which had taken a dizzying fall in the Depression, to restore jobs to half the jobless, and to give just enough to the lower classes (a layer of public housing, a minimum of social security) to create an aura of goodwill.

Passage C

From: T.A. Bailey, Probing America's Past, *Volume 11, 1973. An historian surveys the debate about the accomplishments of the New Deal.*

Conservative critics of Roosevelt condemned his radicalism, and during his lifetime and shortly thereafter one frequently read of the 'Roosevelt Revolution'. With the lengthening of perspective, historians began to label him more commonly as a progressive rather than radical. In possibly saving America by a relatively mild injection of socialism, he may have averted a violent overture and thus saved the capitalist system. He may have headed off collectivism by a major dose of reformism.

Writers of the radical New Left have downgraded the extent of Rooseveltian reform. In particular they have stressed the opportunities for socialistic change that were not pushed, and have written off the New Deal as a holding operation for American capitalism. More specifically, critics charge that Roosevelt short-changed the 'forgotten men', especially labourers, unemployed blacks, unskilled workers and slum-dwellers.

Passage D

From: D. Nasaw, The Course of United States History, *Volume 11: From 1865, 1987. Another historian provides a positive assessment of the New Deal.*

Despite its failure to end the Depression, the New Deal stands as one of the most creative periods in American political history. The United States survived the worst extended economic downturn in its history, with the political system intact, indeed strengthened, at a time when democracy was under siege throughout the world. The federal government accepted the responsibility for intervening in economic life when private initiatives faltered and for protecting and promoting key elements of the welfare of its citizens. America's welfare state was born during the Great depression of the 1930s.

The New deal's accomplishments, while substantial, went only so far. Federal programmes remained small, benefits limited and temporary. Not everyone benefited equally from the New Deal programmes but the majority of Americans in the 1930s were simply too grateful for federal aid to complain that it did not go further. Such federal assistance, coming at a time when many citizens had few, if any, personal resources to fall back on to deal with unemployment, illness and old age, was often the difference between survival and going under.

(a) Analyse the differences between the judgements in Passages B and D about what the New Deal achieved.   (15 marks)

(b) Using Passages A to D, explain why the New Deal has continued to be an issue of debate among historians.
          (30 marks)

Source: OCR exemplar materials 2000

Exam tips

(a) In this question, you need to focus on the differences in interpretation and perspective.

- Passage B concentrates on the social and economic aspects of the New Deal while Passage D emphasises the political aspects; the New Deal safeguarded democracy in the USA while it was under threat elsewhere.
- Note too that the sources adopt different criteria; Passage B looks at the long term to suggest that opportunities for major changes were missed while Passage D looks at what the New Deal did for Americans at the time.

(b) You need to consider all the passages and how their differing perspectives show that the New Deal is open to interpretation. This means that historians will still debate its meaning and significance

- Passage A is from a Republican perspective during an election campaign so would attempt to blacken the New Deal
- Passage B is from a Left-wing perspective and sees the New Deal as an opportunity missed for fundamental change. However, other passages, for example C, suggest the purpose of the New Deal was to save capitalism and thereby avoid fundamental change.
- Passage B concentrates mainly on social and economic aspects, while C suggests the New Deal saved the capitalist system and D looks at the political impact at the time.

Glossary

Agricultural businesses Large-scale farms using machinery and techniques of mass production.

Allotment Each Native American family was given a plot of 160 acres to farm. This went against the traditional idea of common land ownership.

Alphabet agencies New government bodies set up to tackle problems. They were so-called because they became known by their initials, e.g. AAA, CCC.

America First Campaign Campaign to keep the USA neutral.

American Federation of Labor (AFL) Organisation representing American labour unions.

American Medical Association US doctors' professional association, governing medical practices.

Anarchists People who believe in no government, no private ownership and the sharing out of wealth.

Arms embargo Government order prohibiting the movement of weapons.

Assimilation Native Americans should adopt American lifestyles and values. Their traditional lifestyle should disappear.

Atlantic Charter Joint declaration by Roosevelt and Churchill for a peaceful postwar world.

Belligerents Those who were fighting a war.

Bootleggers People who made alcohol illegally to sell.

Broker Person who buys and sells stocks and shares.

Bull market Stock market where there is lots of confidence and lots of buying and selling.

Bull pool Method by which unscrupulous brokers bought and sold stock to and from each other to keep prices high.

Bureau of Indian Affairs Government agency dealing with Native Americans.

Cartel Group of companies agreeing to fix output and prices, to reduce competition and maximise their profits.

Chain gangs Groups of convicts chained together while working outside the prison, for example in digging roadside drainage ditches.

Collective bargaining Discussions between employers and employees (usually represented by labour unions) about working conditions and pay.

Consumer durables Goods that can last a long time, e.g. motor cars, electrical appliances.

Contour ploughing Ploughing across hillsides so that the crested grooves retained the soil. Prior to this farmers had often ploughed up and down. In heavy rain the soil could get washed away.

Customs Union Agreement to abolish trade barriers between participating countries and raise those for other countries.

Dawes Plan 1924 Offered Germany scaled-down reparations and provided it with a loan of $250 million to help stabilise its currency.

Disarmament Getting rid of or reducing weapons.

Equalisation fee The fee farmers would pay to join the proposed McNary-Haugen scheme. It was based on the difference between the price the Agricultural Export Corporation paid farmers for their produce and the price they could be sold for on the world markets.

Executive   The branch of government that makes policy.

Executive Office of the President   The president's staff.

Executive order   Right of the president to force through his decision.

Farm lobby   Politicians and interest groups who put forward the farmers' case to the federal government and Congress.

Farmers' Holiday Association   Pressure group set up to increase pay and conditions for farmers.

Federal aid   Help from the federal government for specific issues.

Federal Reserve Board   A centralised system that allowed banks to run their own affairs with only limited government interference.

Federal system of government   Where there is both a central system of government and state governments – each state having its own powers that are not subject to interference from central government.

Federal Trade Commission   Body charged to ensure businesses were operating fairly.

14 Points   President Wilson's blueprint for a peaceful postwar world.

Free market   A system that allows the economy to run itself without government interference.

'Good Neighbour'   Policy of cultivating good relations with Canada and Latin America.

Government deficit spending   When the government spends more than it receives in income.

Greater East-Asia Co-Prosperity Sphere   Economic alliance of countries set up by Japan.

Greenbelt communities   New towns in rural areas based on careful planning with residential, commercial and industrial sectors separated.

Gross national product (GNP)   The amount earned over the country as a whole.

Hoboes   People who wandered around the USA in search of work.

Holding companies   Where one huge company would obtain a controlling interest in smaller companies to control the market.

Holocaust   Attempted extermination of Jews and other groups by the Nazis.

Inauguration   The ceremony that begins the president's term of office.

Inter-state commerce   Trade between different states.

Interventionism   To interfere in the affairs of other states to protect US interests.

Isolationism   The policy by which USA detached itself from the affairs of other states.

Ku Klux Klan   In the 1920s this was a racist group advocating white supremacy and adopted tactics of terror to intimidate other groups such as African-Americans and Jews. It was particularly prevalent in the Southern and Midwestern states.

Labor union   American term for trades unions, set up to look after the interests of their members.

Laissez-faire   An approach where the government deliberately avoids getting involved in economic planning, thus allowing free trade to operate.

Lame duck presidency   The period between one president coming to the end of his term and his successor taking over.

League of Nations   International organisation to encourage co-operation between nations and keep the peace between them.

Legislature   The branch of government that passes laws.

Lend-lease   Scheme whereby the USA loaned goods and weapons to Britain until the war was over.

Management science The application of technological principles to running a company.

Market structure How the capitalist system worked through supply and demand.

Mass production Making large numbers of the same item using machinery and conveyor belts.

Means-tested benefits Where the levels of welfare benefits are based on the recipient's income.

Middle America Phrase used to describe the vast majority of Americans who just want to get on with their lives without government interference. It also implies decent living and high moral standards. There is some implicit suggestion that the phrase refers primarily to Americans who live away from large cities in small semi-rural communities.

Moonshine Illegally manufactured alcoholic drinks.

Moratorium Term given to Hoover's offer to postpone debt repayment for 18 months.

New Left School of historians critical of the New Deal for not adopting more radical changes.

New York Times Index An indicator of how well stocks and shares are doing based on the 25 leading stocks.

'On the margin' Buying stocks and shares on credit.

Open door policy Policy of granting equal trade opportunities to all countries.

Palmer Raids Mass arrests of suspected revolutionaries.

Payroll tax Tax paid by employers for each of their employees.

Per capita income Income per head of the population.

Positive discrimination Where members of one group are favoured over those of others.

Price fixing Where companies agreed to fix prices between them, thereby preventing fair competition.

Progressivism Movement to expand the role of government in dealing with economic and social problems.

Prohibition Banned the transportation, manufacture and sale of alcoholic beverages.

Pump priming Expression used to suggest government spending would lead to economic growth.

Recession Downturn in the economy.

Rediscount rates The interest rates at which banks borrow money from the Federal Reserve banks.

Religious fundamentalism Involved, among other things, a belief in the literal truth of the Bible and a desire to live one's life according to its teachings.

Reparations Under the postwar settlements Germany had been required to pay compensation of $33,000 million to the victorious countries.

Republic Country led by a president rather than a monarch.

Repudiation of war debts Where countries ceased repaying their war debts.

'Return to normalcy' Harding meant by this a return to minimal government with people being dependent on their own efforts and limited US involvement in foreign affairs.

Rome-Berlin-Tokyo axis Friendship agreement between Italy, Germany and Japan.

Roosevelt Recession Downswing in the economy associated with Roosevelt's cutbacks in Government spending in 1937.

Share-croppers Farmers who rented land and were paid by the landowners a percentage of what they produced.

Socialist economic system   An economy run by the state where all large-scale enterprises are managed by the government.

Sovereignty   A nation's control over its own affairs.

'Speakeasies'   Illegal clubs where alcohol was sold.

Still   Place where illegal alcohol is made.

Subsistence   Minimum income necessary for survival.

Suffrage   The right to vote.

The March of Time   Series of documentaries produced to show the Allied cause sympathetically.

Ticker   Ticker-tape on which stocks and shares transactions were recorded.

Time and motion   A system in which production techniques are allocated set times for completion and production targets laid down on this basis.

Trusts   Large companies that got together to control manufacture, supplies and prices to ensure others could not compete, and therefore guarantee maximum profits for themselves.

U-boats   German submarines.

US Chamber of Commerce   Non-governmental organisation responsible for speaking for business in the USA.

Veterans' Administration   Organisation to help ex-servicemen.

Veto   The president's refusal to pass laws he disagrees with.

Voluntarism   The notion that business and state government should solve the Great Depression through their own voluntary efforts.

Wards   Electoral districts in the USA.

Welfare dependency   Where people come to rely on benefits.

White supremacy   The racist belief that white people are superior to those of other ethnic origins.

Work ethic   The feeling that people should work hard and the unemployed should go out and find a job. It derived from the Puritan notion that how well one worked was a sign of one's worth, both personally and socially.

Young Plan 1929   Offered further scaled-down reparations.

Index